SEEING AND KNOWING

SEEING AND KNOWING

Women and Learning in Medieval Europe 1200 – 1550

edited by

Anneke B. Mulder-Bakker

BREPOLS

British Library Cataloguing in Publication Data

Seeing and knowing : women and learning in medieval Europe 1200-1550. -
    (Medieval women : texts and contexts ; 11)
    1.Women intellectuals – Europe – History – To 1500 2.Women scholars –
    Europe – History – To 1500 3.Women mystics – Europe – History – To 1500
    4.Mysticism – History – Middle Ages, 600-1500. 5.Knowledge, Sociology of –
    History – To 1500
    I.Mulder-Bakker, Anneke B.
    305.4'2'094'0902

ISBN 2503514480

© 2004, Brepols Publishers n.v., Turnhout, Belgium

D/2004/0095/8
ISBN 2-503-51448-0

Contents

Abbreviations

AASS   *Acta Sanctorum* (Antwerp, 1643–1770; Brussels, 1780–86, 1845–83, and 1894– ; Tongerloo, 1794; Paris, 1875–87)

CCCM   Corpus Christianorum. Continuatio Mediaeualis (Turnhout: Brepols, 1966–)

CSEL   Corpus Scriptorum Ecclesiasticorum Latinorum (Vienna: Hoelder-Pichler-Tempsky, 1866–)

PL   *Patrologiae Cursus Completus*, Series Latina, ed. by Jacques-Paul Migne, 221 vols (Paris, 1844–1866)

Contributors

Anne Bollmann was Assistant at the Sonderforschungsbereich 231: 'Träger, Felder, Formen pragmatischer Schriftlichkeit im Mittelalter', University of Münster, from 1991–1998. Since 1999 she has been involved in another project in medieval studies at the University of Groningen: 'Cultural-Change: Dynamics and Diagnosis'. Her doctoral thesis is on: 'Frauenleben und Frauenliteratur in der Devotio moderna: Volksprachliche Schwesternbücher in literarhistorischer Perspektive'. Her publications include the book-length study: *Schwesterbuch und Statuten des St.-Agnes-Konvents in Emmerich* (1998).

Kirsten M. Christensen is Assistant Professor of German at the University of Notre Dame. She is completing a book on the mystical theology of Maria van Hout. She has also published several articles on medieval mysticism and devotion, including 'The Poetics of Piety: Late-Medieval German Catechisms as Literature' in *Kulturen des Manuskriptzeitalters*, edited by Arthur Groos and Hans-Jochen Schiewer (2004).

Ruth Mazo Karras is Professor of History at the University of Minnesota, Twin Cities. She has published widely on issues involving gender and sexuality in medieval western Europe. Her most recent book is *From Boys to Men: Formations of Masculinity in the Later Middle Ages* (2003). She is working on a general history of sexuality in the Middle Ages and a study of mixed marriages and quasi-marital relationships.

Lezlie Knox is Assistant Professor of History at Marquette University. She received her PhD from the Medieval Institute at the University of Notre Dame and previously taught at California State University, Long Beach, where she was also Director of Medieval and Renaissance Studies. She has published 'Audacious Nuns: Conflict between the Franciscan Friars and the Order of Saint Clare', in *Church History*, 69 (2000), 41–62, and is completing a monograph entitled *Beyond Clare: Gender and Reform in the Medieval Franciscan Order*.

Thom Mertens is Director of the Ruusbroec Society (Antwerp) and Professor of the History of Dutch Religious Literature at the University of Antwerp. He is one of the editors of the new Dutch-Latin-English edition of Ruusbroec's *Opera omnia* (Jan van Ruusbroec, *Opera omnia*, 10, *Brieven / Letters* (1991). His research is mainly concerned with late medieval Dutch literature. A recent publication is 'Middelnederlandse bijbelvertaling', in *Medioneerlandistiek. Een inleiding tot de Middel-nederlandse letterkunde* ed. by Ria Jansen-Sieben, Jozef Janssens, and Frank Willaert (2000), p. 275–84.

Anneke B. Mulder-Bakker is Senior Lecturer in Medieval History and Medieval Studies at the University of Groningen. Her publications on historiography, hagiography, and gender studies include *Sanctity and Motherhood* (1995), *De kluizenaar in de eik* [The Hermit in the Oak] (1995), *The Invention of Saintliness* (2002). She has completed a book, *Lives of The Anchoresses. The Rise of the Urban Recluse in Medieval Europe* (University of Pennsylvania Press, forthcoming).

Bert Roest studied History and Medieval Studies at the universities of Groningen and Toronto. He now teaches at St Bonaventure University, New York. He has written *Reading the Book of History: Intellectual Contexts and Educational Functions of Franciscan Historiography 1226–ca. 1350* (1998) and *A History of Franciscan Education (c. 1210–1517)* (2000), as well as several articles on Franciscan historiography and the development of a Franciscan school network between the thirteenth and the sixteenth century. At present he is preparing a volume on late medieval literature of religious instruction, and a study on early modern educational discourses.

Wybren Scheepsma studied Dutch and Medieval Studies at the University of Groningen. In 1997 he obtained his doctorate with the thesis *Deemoed en devotie. De koorvrouwen van Windesheim en hun geschriften* from the University of Leiden. An English translation of this book, *Medieval Religious Women in The Low Countries. The 'Modern Devotion', the Canonesses of Windesheim and their Writings*, will be published by Boydell & Brewer in 2004. Until 2002 he worked at the University of Leiden on a project concerning the so-called 'Limburgse sermoenen', the oldest sermon collection in Dutch (Brill, forthcoming).

Werner Williams-Krapp is Professor of German Language and Literature of the Middle Ages at the University of Augsburg . He has published many books and articles on late medieval religious literature, vernacular hagiography, mystics, drama, sermons and theology. He has also edited numerous German prose works. His most prominent publications include: *Die deutschen und niederländischen Legendare des Mittelalters* (1986), *Überlieferung und Gattung. Zur Gattung 'Spiel' im Mittelalter* (1980), and with Ulla Williams, *Die Offenbarungen der Katharina Tucher* (1998). Currently he is working on a history of German literature in the fifteenth century.

Introduction

ANNEKE B. MULDER-BAKKER

Juliana of Cornillon, originator of the popular feast of Corpus Christi and author of the Corpus Christi liturgy, which celebrates Christ's presence in the Eucharist, once fell into an ecstatic vision as she was thinking of the mass and of what happens as people take communion. In this vision she contemplated 'with the eyes of a pure heart' the Trinity in heaven and watched the communion of the saints where she:

> *saw* how Christ shows himself whole, unbroken, and perfect in the bread to everyone who receives him unto salvation. Yet, at the same time, she *saw* that he remains unbroken and perfect in himself.[1]

In other words, by looking around in heaven and observing the Trinity in action she received knowledge of divine truth. Juliana perceived the tenets of the Christian faith in visual form, a knowledge that was understood to be of equal value to what theologians acquired when they studied the Scriptures. Indeed, the author of Juliana's Life comments:

> She understood most of [the visions] with an intelligence so pure and clean that she seemed to have a share in the undiluted truth of our future knowledge. As for all the articles pertaining to the Catholic faith, she had been so fully instructed by the One *that teacheth man knowledge* (Psalms 93. 10) that she had no need to consult masters or books about them. Indeed, because her teacher was the anointing, *unctione magistra*, she had received such an indestructible foundation of the orthodox faith that she once said whatever might happen (that is, whatever heretical from the straight

---

[1] I am much indebted to both Lezlie Knox and Bert Roest, as well as to the Brepols reader, for their criticism and helpful comments on an earlier draft of this Introduction—*Vie de Sainte Julienne de Cornillon*, ed. and trans. by Jean-Pierre Delville in *Fête-Dieu (1246–1996)*, 2 vols (Louvain-la-Neuve–Turnhout: Brepols, 1999), II, pp. 60–62; here quoted from the English translation of Barbara Newman, *The Life of Juliana of Mont-Cornillon* (Toronto: Peregrina, 1988), pp. 53–54; emphases mine.

traps were set before her), she would never be able to deviate path of the faith. Nor did the sage's proverb *that the searchers of majesty shall be oppressed by glory* (Proverbs 25. 27) apply to her. I think the rash searchers are to be understood not as those who are ravished into glory, but as those who force their way in. Juliana, however, did not rush in to scrutinize the secrets of divine majesty through her own rashness, she was snatched up and admitted to them by the condescension of God's Son.[2]

Contemplating therefore 'with the pure eyes of the heart', *mundi cordis oculis*, and 'being instructed by the Holy Spirit', *unctione magistra*, she acquired knowledge that was perceived to be compatible with what the doctors derived from books; knowledge of theological nature that is. Yet, in its modes and its benign acquisition it was also perceived to surpass the 'aggressive' scrutinizing of the scholastics. Following Juliana and Eve, the author claimed it to be the highest possible form of divine knowledge, indeed a share in the undiluted truth of our future knowledge.

This example raises several issues of significance for research into the transmission of knowledge and learning in the Middle Ages and its relation to problems of gender, the theme of this volume. According to the author of Juliana's Life, although some people (in particular women) had no access to formal theology and sacred learning, they nonetheless demonstrated considerable knowledge of the divine. Juliana, in any case, possessed such knowledge. She had not gained it by the usual route—or so modern scholarship considers it to be; for medieval believers the 'usual' route of book learning could as easily be considered a 'detour' in comparison with the more direct path of visual instruction as imparted by the feminine *magistra*, the Holy Spirit. While the doctors of the Church had their knowledge only from 'hearsay', she, as an unschooled woman, was a direct witness, an eyewitness of divine truth. The implications were twofold. Firstly, Juliana had an incontestable authority. She was simply incapable of error or of falling into heterodoxy. Her knowledge was actually even more reliable than that of the learned doctors. Secondly, this divine illumination was thought to be superior to book learning. The hagiographer characterizes the quest for knowledge by the scholastic experts as a rather aggressive activity: the doctors, continually running after veiled truth, were in Juliana's eyes more like intruders who forced their way into the secrets of heavenly majesty.[3] Visionary women like Juliana did not rush in but waited patiently until they were benignly admitted by God's Son himself. In return they received a higher form of knowledge, 'in the sight of the Lord'. This was knowledge of seeing and knowing.

Therefore this example from the Life of Juliana of Cornillon advances a higher form of knowing, seeing and knowing, while, at the same time, recognizing the traditional dichotomy between the two ways a person might acquire sacred

---

[2] *Life of Juliana*, I. 20: trans. by Newman, p. 54.

[3] Juliana is probably referring here to the agonistic structure of theological education at the thirteenth-century university, which Ruth Karras discusses in her contribution to this volume.

knowledge during the later Middle Ages: via a scholastic route or via a visionary one. The former is the method of school-educated doctors, which allows this author to associate it with men and the latter with women. Those who have grown up with gender studies and have learned to use gender as 'a useful category of historical analysis' will immediately recognize this distinction.[4] In examining the roles played by medieval women, scholars have shown how when some women were denied access to higher education and excluded from the ecclesiastical hierarchy, they understandably took refuge in visions and revelations received directly from God. The example alludes, however, to the possibility that still another route was conceivable, higher than the other ones and open to men and women, a third route where the logical and the visionary merged into an illuminative and imparted knowing. This volume will certainly not deny that gender played a role in defining access to the two different types of learning, but it also wants to investigate still other ways of seeing and knowing, considerably more complicated, but also more challenging, as another medieval voice testifies.

The pastoral writer Caesarius of Heisterbach (d. 1240) also acknowledges that God uses two different routes to pass divine knowledge on to humankind. His explanation, however, is not explicitly gendered. Caesarius distinguishes between learning, the *scientia* of the schools written down in books, and God-given knowledge that is not dependent on books but directly transmitted, like Juliana's insights. It is passed down in visions and divine conversations. He explains that God, Lord of all knowledge, determines himself how and to whom he benignly grants his sacred knowledge. He gives it to one person or takes it away from another, just as he chooses. Caesarius gives examples of priests bereft of wisdom and lay brothers endowed with the gift of speech. He speaks of the spirit of prophecy of lay people and their mystic raptures. As if to test and subsequently to legitimize such visions, he tells the story of a priest in his own abbey in his own time—a trustworthy example therefore—who had a dream about Christ's birth. Notwithstanding his initial doubts, the priest, and consequently the common faithful learn to understand that such dreams are highly meritorious, especially when they are preceded by holy meditation, *meditatio*. As real as the Bible itself and Church writings, and of equal historical value, they constitute solid knowledge. The content of these visions is not essentially different from theological or scriptural knowledge; only the format and the route along which it is gained differ.[5] In Caesarius's opinion, priests were to be concerned with learning. Devout lay believers might obtain knowledge of equal value but along a different path, one independent of the Church and the schools.

Cautious now of overhasty conclusions that solely associate the masculine with book learning and the feminine with divine illumination, we should rephrase our

[4] Joan Wallach Scott, 'Gender: A Useful Category of Historical Analysis', *American Historical Review*, 91 (1986), 1053–75.

[5] Caesarius of Heisterbach, *Dialogus miraculorum* VIII. 2, ed. by Joseph Strange, 2 vols (Cologne: Lempertz, 1851; repr. New Jersey: Gregg Press, 1966), II, p. 83.

above observations. In medieval society men and women, *litterati* and *illiterati*, clerics and laity, educated and uneducated, seem capable of acquiring knowledge, even scriptural knowledge and sacred learning. But they often proceed along two distinct routes: the route of schooling and learning as opposed to that of seeing and hearing. These routes seemingly belong to two different worlds and what could be termed two essentially different cultures: the world of written knowledge on the one hand, and the oral world of mainstream medieval culture on the other. This at least becomes clear in the thirteenth century as universities and scholastic learning start flourishing. If we wish to investigate the role of gender, we must first inquire about the characteristics of both of these worlds and the patterns of expectations that applied to men and women in these worlds. It is particularly important to investigate the role women actually played in both oral and written culture. Only then can we enquire into still other ways of knowing and pose the question of whether gender offers an explanation for the patterns we have uncovered.

For our studies it means, firstly, the recognition that both worlds had their own tools for mapping out reality and structuring their thought, their own ways of thinking and writing.[6] Trained in logic and rational discourse, the world of learning structured its thought accordingly. It produced texts that exhibit these characteristics: Latin treatises and learned books, with quotations from the Fathers and a sophisticated interplay of question and answer. Outside the stronghold of the learned people thought along different lines, and envisaged their world in different ways. Texts belonging to this other world, the world of mainstream culture and more traditional forms of monasticism, also show different characteristics. What is needed, then, is an analysis of methods and modes used in both worlds and of the consequences for gender as a category of analysis.

Secondly, divine and sacred knowledge as such was not the privilege of schoolmen only, it was not monopolised by the world of learning—however eagerly scholastics may have pursued such. Other theologians, men such as Eckbert of Schönau, James of Vitry, or Hugh of St Cher, were aware of the limits of bookish learning. Consequently, divine knowledge was not only transmitted in Latin tracts and learned books but in other genres of texts as well, texts (partly) belonging to that other world, such as saints' Lives and legends, visions and revelations, spiritual autobiographies and exempla, liturgical texts and sermons, letters and letter collections, in both Latin and the vernacular. These genres have forms and features of their own. Obvious characteristics such as a scholastic manner of quoting from the Fathers, logical discourse, a clear and precise writing style, a rigid discipline of structuring the text, are lacking here. We have to ponder the implications. No benefit is gained, for example, by using the characteristics of scholastic treatises as criteria for these other types of texts.

---

[6] See, for example, the seminal studies of Walter J. Ong, *Orality and Literacy: The Technologizing of the Word* (London: Routledge, 1982), and Jack Goody, *The Interface Between the Written and the Oral* (Cambridge: Cambridge University Press, 1987).

Thirdly, authors in both worlds rely on different forms of authorization or legitimation. Whereas the texts of the learned are embedded in the authoritative Latin tradition of the Church, and, with their quotations from the *auctoritates*, radiate authority in themselves, texts from the world of seeing and knowing need other and more explicit forms of authorization.

The World of Learning

Higher Education

In modern scholarship the study of schooling and the various ways culture was transmitted is almost automatically limited to the study of the cathedral school and the university. Research into the transmission of knowledge in the Middle Ages has been focussed almost exclusively on higher education and Latin learning. Since the rise of history as an academic discipline in the nineteenth century, scholars have enthusiastically targeted those centres of instruction that were new in the twelfth and thirteenth century, believing they could well be the cradle of modern academic traditions.[7] The classical form of instruction with a teacher and textbooks, the *artes liberales*, a sophisticated curriculum, training in Latin and logic, the privileged institutions of education and scholarship, the *studium generale*, the *universitas* of students and teachers, the *licentia docendi*—these were the objects of study. Theologians and philosophers immersed themselves in the textbooks of Gratian, Peter Lombard, and Peter Comestor, the Latin *Sententiae* and *Summae*, the scholastic treatises of Hugh of St Cher or Henry of Ghent.

Lay people and even religious women had no part in this form of learning. Excluded from the clerical world, they were automatically barred from the cathedral school and university, which offered professional training for the clerical life. They thus remained outside the field of vision of modern researchers.[8] Moreover, our

---

[7] John Van Engen in *Learning Institutionalized. Teaching in the Medieval University*, ed. by John Van Engen (Notre Dame: University of Notre Dame Press, 2000), p. 2 notes: 'they write as insiders'; Ulrike Wiethaus, 'Learning as Experiencing. Hadewijch's Model of Spiritual Growth', in *Faith Seeking Understanding: Learning and the Catholic Tradition*, ed. by George C. Berthold (Manchester, NH: Saint Anselm College Press, 1991), pp. 89–116 (pp. 90–94).

[8] One example: the *Dictionary of the Middle Ages*, ed. by Joseph R. Strayer and others, and published in the 1980s, ignores women completely in its lemma on 'Schools', 'Scholarship', etc. The *Lexikon des Mittelalters*, 9 vols (Munich: Artemis, 1980–1997) based on recent German research discussed later in this Introduction, contains a lemma 'Erziehungs- und Bildungswesen', in which Laetitia Boehm provides illuminating information on the education of men and women, even though she, too, perpetuates the practice of using scholastic scholarship as the criterion also for women, see *Lexikon des Mittelalters*, III, col. 2196–2203. A good introduction to university education can be found in John W. Baldwin, 'Masters of

medieval forebears themselves typically ignored women—even the learned women among them who were well versed in Latin: the cleric was busy creating a niche for himself, his own domain of clerical scholarship. Women had no place there. As Ruth Karras argues in her contribution to this volume, even if clerics started a theological dispute by using a *casus* involving women—using women to think with—'they refused to follow up on the feminine aspects of the questions offered'. By doing so 'the masters were saying that they did not matter'. The difference between men and women did not matter, not because men and women were equal in all things, but because women fundamentally did not matter.[9]

In other words, because modern scholarship focussed mainly on higher education and the university—in which women had no part—the erudite women who did exist and who themselves may have contributed to learning went unnoticed and certainly unstudied. And if one of them did happen to slip into the sights of a research project, she was judged according to the criteria of academic learning.

Learning and its Modes

There is a second reason why the erudition of some women has not been recognized until recently. The same scholars who shaped the academic discipline in the nineteenth century were influenced by the post-medieval educational ideal of the humanists, the *paideia* articulated by the Berlin professor Wilhelm von Humboldt as *Bildung*, the German ideal that has been described as 'an intellectual narrowing of a culture dominated by the skills of reading and writing'.[10] Central to this educational ideal was not only the transmission of the classical cultural heritage but especially the training and discipline—the 'civilizing', in the modern sense—of the pupils. Nineteenth-century schoolboys had to be drilled in reading letter by letter and in faultless spelling. They had to be trained to write neatly between the lines and according to grammatical rules. They had to develop a flowing style of writing, become acquainted with the canon of great authors and learn the proper ways to quote their works. The rote recitation of grammatical permutations flourished in this time, as did a capella singing—in short, what Clanchy has called the training of training.[11]

Paris from 1179 to 1215: A Social Perspective', in *Renaissance and Renewal in the Twelfth Century*, ed. by Robert L. Benson and Giles Constable (Cambridge, MA: Harvard University Press, 1982), pp. 138–72.

[9] See Ruth Mazo Karras's contribution to this volume, 'Women to Think With'.

[10] Boehm, 'Erziehungs- und Bildungswesen', col. 2196: 'eine intellektuelle Verengung auf eine von Lese- und Schreibfähigkeit beherrschte Kultur'.

[11] Michael Clanchy, *From Memory to Written Record. England 1066–1307* (Oxford: Blackwell, 2nd edn, 1993), especially the Introduction.

Historians studying the learning of the Middle Ages from this perspective have had an eye only for the book knowledge of *litterati* and clerics, for rational and logical learning acquired by systematic reading in the schools. Knowledge was seen as synonymous with Latin book learning, scholastic thought, the study of the Church Fathers and the *auctoritates*. It was knowledge derived during disciplined training in schools and classrooms, in disputations and scholastic discussions. And this is actually still true today. In our scholarly practice we still measure 'learning' of the past and the present mainly in terms of academic training. The reading of well-written studies, the acquisition of received wisdom, critical reflection—in short, the gaining of general knowledge and insight—is not perceived as sufficient to make a person a good scholar. For this, the expectation is that one needs to learn 'scientific' methods of research, how to construct a logical argument, and especially all the time-consuming minutiae involved in making good footnotes and in 'editing' a text. These are considered as the skills that distinguish the professional from the autodidact. John of Salisbury indicated as much already in the twelfth century: 'persons who have not learned the Latin quotations properly are unlettered, even though they have been initiated into the world of letters'; *qui istorum* (the Latin *auctoritates* studied in the cathedral schools) *ignari sunt, illiterati dicunt, etsi litteras noverint.*[12] This is part of the anxiously guarded domain of the professionals. Lay people and women who had no academic training lacked these skills. Since they produced no 'scholarship', it was assumed that they also had no academic knowledge. Our aim in this volume is to avoid using, consciously or unconsciously, training in academic skills as the criterion for literacy, erudition, and education. For us academic training is not necessarily the equivalent of higher knowledge and understanding. We wish to distinguish form from content.

There is also a third reason why we tend to attach great value to the learning of men and not to that of women. Ever since Herbert Grundmann opened up the study of women's spirituality female writers are often reduced to aliterary creatures who, in an emotional outburst, committed their inner feelings to paper. Their mystical writings were not viewed as literary products with a literary function—and thus to be analyzed with literary criteria—but as unmediated life experience, as *Erlebnismystik*. These women were driven into the corner of the 'possessed', of the rapt and visionary ecstatic. They were considered incidental and exceptional cases, extraordinary and enigmatic, 'different' and therefore no mates of reasonable men, literary authors and scholars alike.[13]

---

[12] John of Salisbury, *Policraticus or the Frivolities of Courtiers and the Footprints of Philosophers*, VII. 9, ed. and trans. by Cary J. Nederman (Cambridge: Cambridge University Press, 1990).

[13] Herbert Grundmann, *Religiöse Bewegungen im Mittelalter* (first edition in 1935 but only influential after the second edition of 1961): Herbert Grundmann, *Religious Movements in the Middle Ages*, trans. by Steven Rowan (Notre Dame: University of Notre Dame Press, 1995); for admiration of this seminal study but also criticism see Martina Wehrli-Johns,

Thoroughly immersed in and proud of the nineteenth-century educational ideal of a high, rational culture—in Berlin of that time, automatically associated with a Protestant aesthetic—these same scholars created their male medieval forefathers in their own image. Anselm and Thomas, John of Salisbury, and Gilbert of Tournai, were moulded into rational, sober intellectuals, just as rational and sober as the modern researchers themselves hoped to be. Medieval thinkers were divested of everything irrational and illogical that could damage their reputation as 'true' scholars. They were made models of logical and rational argumentation. Women might be susceptible to emotional outbursts, the common people might wallow in irrational delusions and superstitions, but learned men were moderate and rational. In other words, these researchers forgot about the third route of seeing and knowing. As a result, the (auto)biographical outpourings of medieval authors—about their God-given 'insights' and 'illuminations', for example—were ignored as 'irrelevant'. Only now are we reading them again, thanks to work such as that of Mary Carruthers on Anselm's struggle with his *Proslogion*:

> Then suddenly one night during matins the grace of God illuminated his heart, the whole matter became clear to his mind, and a great joy and exultation filled his inmost being. Thinking therefore that others also would be glad to know what he had found, immediately and ungrudgingly he wrote it on writing tablets and gave it to one of the brethren of the monastery for safekeeping.[14]

Is this not strongly reminiscent of the way Juliana received her inspiration about the Eucharist? Or of how Thomas Aquinas spent long hours at night praying for insight? Where we have learned to construct a deep divide between visionary women and learned men, people of the Middle Ages were much more inclined to see them as kindred spirits. Were they not both searching for God's revealed knowledge, a knowledge that came to them through years of study (also by women) and in visions or illuminations (also of men)?

'Voraussetzungen und Perspektiven mittelalterlicher Laienfrömmigkeit seit Innozenz III', *Mitteilungen des Instituts für Österreichische Geschichtsforschung*, 104 (1996), 286–309 and the literature mentioned there. See also Beatrice Acklin Zimmermann, 'Neue Perspektiven für die theologische Erschliessung sogenannter frauenmystischer Literatur', *Freiburger Zeitschrift für Philologie und Theologie*, 38 (1991), 175–91.

[14] *The Life of Saint Anselm by Eadmer*, ed. and trans. by Richard W. Southern (Oxford: Nelson, 1963), pp. 29–30, cited by Mary J. Carruthers in *The Book of Memory: A Study in Medieval Culture* (Cambridge: Cambridge University Press, 1990), pp. 199–200. See also Arjo J. Vanderjagt, 'The Performative Heart of St Anselm's *Proslogion*, in *Anselm: Aosta, Bec and Canterbury*, ed. by David Luscombe and G. R. Evans (Sheffield: Sheffield Academic Press, 1996), pp. 228–37.

The World of Seeing and Knowing

In 1992, Anne Clark showed how wrong modern scholarship was.[15] In her brilliant study of Elisabeth of Schönau's *Book of Visions* written down by her brother Eckbert, she explains that after Elisabeth (d. *c.* 1165) had begun to distribute her visions she encountered considerable misunderstanding and urged her brother to come to her convent to mediate between her and the outside world. Eckbert was a learned priest who had studied under the Parisian doctors. He started to collect all the evidence of his sister's visions and 'worked over these records, translating, polishing, revising, until he had a text that satisfied his judgement about what was appropriate to be published.' But he did more as well. Aware of the limits of his own bookish learning and deeply convinced of his sister's 'access to knowledge beyond that which he had gained in studies in Paris', he questioned Elisabeth about what she saw and presented her with unsolved academic problems. Elisabeth interviewed her angel about them and received answers.[16] The two ways of acquiring knowledge are portrayed as working together harmoniously and complementing each other. A third way here begins to take shape. Clark's study is one of a growing number of fine books on women authors. Evidence is accumulating that some women were highly educated and trained in theology. It is becoming increasingly clear that they wrote work of high quality, even though not exhibiting the characteristics of academic scholarship. We are learning to value their writings on their own terms. More and more they are seen as conveying important devotional or divine knowledge. Scholars like Bernard McGinn and Nicholas Watson have coined the term 'vernacular theology' for this phenomenon.[17] I prefer to term it 'common theology'—analogous to the 'common law' of lived practice versus the 'written' or Roman law of the learned tradition. The realization is growing that besides the 'bookish' theology of scholasticism other forms of theology co-existed. In this connection attention is also being paid to their—at times difficult—collaboration with male scribes and supervisors and to the influence these men exerted on their work. The inspiring volume *Gendered Voices* in particular has pointed the way for further research in this

---

[15] Anne L. Clark, *Elisabeth of Schönau. A Twelfth-Century Visionary* (Philadelphia: University of Pennsylvania Press, 1992).

[16] Clark, *Elisabeth of Schönau*, pp. 54, 18.

[17] Bernard McGinn, *Meister Eckhart and the Beguine Mystics: Hadewijch of Brabant, Mechtild of Magdeburg, and Marguerite Porete* (New York: Continuum, 1994), pp. 4–14; Nicholas Watson, 'Censorship and Cultural Change in Late-Medieval England: Vernacular Theology, The Oxford Translation Debate and Arundel's Constitutions of 1409', *Speculum*, 70 (1995), 822–64. Compare Kurt Ruh, *Geschichte der abendländischen Mystik* (Munich: Beck, 1990–99) and other scholars in Germany who characterized the emergence of a 'Theologia Deutsch' as a male phenomenon (see, for example, Tauler) with women as recipients.

area.[18] There is also great interest in the way women legitimized their writing.

As yet, however, little research has dealt specifically with the dynamics of cultural transmission and the place these works occupied in the culture of seeing and knowing. Also rare are studies and comparisons of the routes along which men and women gained their knowledge and of the consequences this had for the function of their work in the transmission of knowledge. In the case of women in particular attention remains focussed on incidental, exceptional products. This is also true if we broaden our view to society outside the small circle of academic learning.

The World of Seeing and Hearing

Non-academic Education

It is mainly in Dutch and English scholarship that considerable attention has been paid to non-academic forms of education. Elsewhere this interest has yet to gain momentum.[19] But here, too, the participation of women in these forms of education has remained largely outside the scope of research. Thus the impression remains widespread that medieval women, like most non-clerical men, were 'unschooled', deprived of all higher forms of learning and education.

The particular studies of women mentioned above have produced a growing body of evidence contradicting this negative image. Of the fifteen or so *mulieres religiosae* from the Low Countries, of whom we have more or less detailed biographical information, two-thirds were well-educated, sometimes exceptionally so. Beatrice of Nazareth was schooled by teachers in the city and enjoyed advanced training in manuscript writing and calligraphy. She is the supposed author of the oldest mystic tract in any vernacular, *The Seven Manners of Love*.[20] Ida of

---

[18] *Gendered Voices. Medieval Saints and Their Interpreters*, ed. by Catherine M. Mooney (Philadelphia: University of Pennsylvania Press, 1999).

[19] Jean Verger, 'Schule' in *Lexikon des Mittelalters*, VII, col. 1585. See Nicholas Orme, *From Childhood to Chivalry. The Education of the English Kings and Aristocracy 1066–1530* (London: Methuen, 1984); Nicholas Orme, 'Lay Literacy in England, 1100–1300,' in *England and Germany in the High Middle Ages*, ed. by Alfred Haverkamp and Hanna Vollrath (Oxford: Oxford University Press, 1996), pp. 35–56; Caroline M. Barron, 'The Education and Training of Girls in Fifteenth-Century London', in *Courts, Counties and the Capital*, ed. by Diana S. Dunn (New York: Stroud, 1996), pp. 139–154; Veronica O'Mara, 'Female Scribal Ability and Scribal Activity in Late-Medieval England: The Evidence?', *Leeds Studies in English*, n.s. 27 (1996), pp. 87–130; Mary C. Erler, *Women, Reading, and Piety in Late-Medieval England* (Cambridge: Cambridge University Press, 2002); and Regnerus R. Post, *Scholen en onderwijs in Nederland gedurende de Middeleeuwen* (Utrecht: Spectrum, 1954). See also Walter Simons, *Cities of Ladies: Beguine Communities in the Medieval Low Countries, 1200–1565* (Philadelphia: University of Pennsylvania Press, 2001), pp. 6–7.

[20] See Wybren Scheepsma's contribution to this volume.

Gorsleeuw was a learned woman who wrote liturgical works in Latin.[21] Juliana of Cornillon must have received a similar education and authored a complete office with Latin texts and music for the feast of Corpus Christi, a feast she invented herself.[22] Her pupil Eve of St Martin wrote in French, in her own hand, memoirs of her mistress and the new feast. The above-mentioned Ida of Gorsleeuw attended the famous chapter school of Borgloon, where Christina the Astonishing very likely also gained her knowledge of Latin and Holy Scripture. While Christina was living as a recluse in Borgloon, she expounded to visitors the Latin text of the Bible. These life stories indicate that certain chapter schools were occasionally, and perhaps regularly, attended by women. We know that Lutgart of Tongeren also expounded Holy Scripture—which her hagiographer explains as a kind of miracle. Of others, like Maria of Oignies, Odilia of Liège, Margaret of Ypres, and Ida of Nivelles, we know that they possessed at least a psalter or devotional booklets.

These women confirm what we have recently learned from the many studies of Hildegard of Bingen, Elisabeth of Schönau and the *Sister Books* in Germany, Julian of Norwich and Margery Kempe in England, as well as holy women elsewhere in the world.[23] Women were often highly educated. Legends about holy women from the past corroborate this image. The transformation of Gertrud of Nivelles into a learned woman provides a case in point. A late-medieval version of the Merovingian Life relates that when Gertrud lost her father at age fourteen, she continued living with her mother and was then sent to school: 'And she had her go to school and learn the Holy Scripture [...] and she was especially eager to learn the gospels of Christ [...]. And she diligently committed these flowers of Holy Scripture to memory.'[24]

The time has come to abandon the idea of a few learned women living as exceptions on the margin. We have to search for general patterns in the schooling and education of both men and women, and for general patterns in their narratives. But at the same time we have to realize that the large majority of them lived in a different world from that of the textually learned; that they used different ways of acquiring and transmitting culture and knowledge. In brief, we must shift our attention from the schools and universities, from scholars and scholarship—the small sphere that comprised at most a few percent of medieval society—to the world in which most medieval people lived, the world of seeing and hearing. If we place our point of departure here, we arrive at completely different, even contradictory insights regarding the roles of men and women in the transmission of culture and knowledge.

---

[21] *Vita Ide Lewensis*, in AASS, 29 October (3rd edn, Paris–Rome, 1864), LXI, pp. 100–35, (pp. 113–14): 'liber ferialis non minimus, in quo leguntur in Matutinis lectiones'.

[22] For these and the following women see my *Lives of the Anchoresses* (forthcoming).

[23] See also Caesarius of Heisterbach who omits certain exempla, giving the following reason: 'I will refrain from giving further details, as I do not wish to cause embarrassment to the women who will perhaps read what we are discussing here [in Latin]'. See *Dialogus miraculorum*, XI. 57–58, ed. by Strange, II, p. 310.

[24] *Leven van Geertruyden* in The Hague, KB, MS 73 H 13, fol. 92vo.

We also gain very different perceptions of the possible significance of books as conveyors of knowledge alongside oral or aural forms of cultural transmission.

Imitatio morum

A search for patterns in the transmission of culture and knowledge outside the institutional circuit can profit from studies like those by Horst Wenzel, *Hören und Sehen*; by Mary Carruthers, *The Book of Memory*; and of course the seminal study *From Memory to Written Record* by Michael Clanchy.[25] I wish to draw attention here to two elements of importance to this volume, illustrating them with a quotation from the *Nederrijns Moraalboek*, a Middle Dutch version of the *Bestiaire d'Amour* of Richard de Fournival:

> Inde dar ümbe dat Got den minsche also mint, dat hiene vorsiin wille van al des hie bedarf, so hevet hie den minsche gegeven ene manire van starkheit van siele die heit gedinchenis. Diese gedinchenis die hevet twe porten dit is siin inde horen. Inde elkerlik van diesen twe porten hevet enen weg dar man bi gain mag te gedinchenis. Dat is varwe (*image*) inde worde. Varwe dient den ogen. Inde tie worde den oren [...]. Dar ümbe dat gedinchenis is scat inde hüder van den sinne te gevene, dien man gewint bi cragte van behindigheide. Inde die dut dat gelieden is gelik oft vur üns ware. Inde tüt den selven so kümen bi varwe inde bi worden. Want als man siit gevarwet en storie van Troies of en andere, man siit die dait vanden güden luden die hier bevoren waren regte also of si tegenwordig weren. Inde regte also iest van den worden. Want als man hort en bük lesen Walsg is of Dütsg man verstait daventure van den guden die gewest heben gelik of si tegenwordig weren.[26]

> [And because God so loves the human person that he wants to provide him with all that he needs, he gave him a manner of strength of soul known as memory. This memory has two gates, namely seeing and hearing. And each of these gates has a road that one can travel to memory. They are image and word. Image serves the eyes. And the word the ears [...]. For this reason memory has to entrust its treasure, which is gained by virtue of training, to the guardianship of the senses. And this makes past things seem directly in our presence. And this comes about through image and word.

---

[25] Horst Wenzel, *Hören und Sehen, Schrift und Bild: Kultur und Gedächtnis im Mittelalter* (Munich: Beck, 1995) and the books mentioned in notes 10 and 12. See also Constant J. Mews, 'Orality, Literacy, and Authority', *Exemplaria*, 2 (1990), 475–500; Danièle Alexander-Bidon, 'La lettre volée. Apprendre à lire à l' enfant au Moyen Age', *Annales ESC*, 44 (1989), 953–92; Dennis H. Green, 'Die Schriftlichkeit und die Geschichte der deutschen Literatur im Mittelalter', *Literaturwissenschaftliches Jahrbuch im Auftrag der Görres-Gesellschaft*, n.f. 30 (1989), 9–26 and Alfred Wendehorst, 'Who Could Read and Write in the Middle Ages?', in *England and Germany in the High Middle Ages*, ed. by Havercamp and Vollrath, pp. 57–90.

[26] *Nederrijns Moraalboek*, ed. by Maurits Gysseling, *Corpus van Middelnederlandse teksten tot en met het jaar 1300. Reeks II: Literaire handschriften, deel 6: Sinte Lutgart, Sinte Kerstine, Nederrijns Moraalboek.* (Leiden: Nijhoff, 1987), pp. 343–422 (p. 355).

For if one sees a portrayal of the history of Troy, or something similar, one sees the deeds of good people from the past just as if they were present. And the same happens with words. For if one hears a book read in French or German, one understands the adventure of the good people who lived in the past as if they were present.]

People in the Middle Ages lived largely in a culture that privileged oral communication.[27] Both boys and girls acquired most of their knowledge in the personal 'exchange between an older voice of experience and a younger audience'.[28] Most youngsters learned on the job. The young priest was trained by assisting the old one, the squire by bearing the shield of his knight, the maid by serving her lady. By observing their example they saw before them what they should know, and they learnt by imitating. *Imitatio morum* was central to all education, in the monastery as well as in the household and in urban trades. According to Anne Clark Bartlett, 'Imitation—the fashioning and reconstruction of the self in accordance with the multiple models provided by the holy family, male and female saints, aristocratic ideals, and an assortment of textualized personages—was the chief aim of virtually all forms of medieval (and particularly devotional) discourse.'[29] Indeed, a courtly writer like Thomasin von Zerclaere, in his *Der Waelsche Gast* from the early thirteenth century, advised young knights to choose a virtuous knight, a man with *wistuom, tugende unde sin*, and imitate him in all things.[30] The boy was told to identify with his role model and follow his example in minute detail.[31] He had to imprint on his memory the words of the knights and the images of the knightly deeds, the *varwe* (image) of the *Moraalboek*, and at the appropriate moment call them up, make them appear again before his mind's eye. Whenever he had to act himself during the physical absence of his hero, he was supposed to search his memory and evoke before his inner eye how the knight had acted, or might have acted, in similar circumstances. For a knight in training it was important to store up in his memory as many good examples as possible. These were in the first place drawn from people he had seen himself, but they could also be found in stories told about great heroes from the past (the history of Troy, for example) or in texts he had read about predecessors, such as *Der Waelsche Gast*. These books had a mnemonic function similar to that of the *varwes* stored up in the memory. The texts were not in themselves conveyors of knowledge but useful aids for summoning stored collective

---

[27] See my 'The Metamorphosis of Woman: Transmission of Knowledge and the Problems of Gender', in *Gender and History*, 12 (2000), 642–64.

[28] Marina Warner, *From the Beast to the Blonde: On Fairy Tales and Their Tellers* (London: Vintage, 1995).

[29] Anne Clark Bartlett, *Male Authors, Female Readers: Representation and Subjectivity in Middle English Devotional Literature* (Ithaca: Cornell University Press, 1995), p. 32.

[30] Thomasin von Zerclaere, *Der Waelsche Gast*, ed. by Friedrich W. von Kries, 4 vols (Göppingen: Kümmerle, 1984–85), line 6838.

[31] Thomasin von Zerclaere, *Der Waelsche Gast*, lines 647–52.

knowledge before the inner eye of the reader. The fiction of the personal transmission of knowledge and culture remained intact.

Acquiring knowledge in these circles can therefore be characterized as observing the virtuous deeds of good people in the present and listening to stories about good people in the past, and thus appropriating the collective memory of virtuous deeds in the present and the past. Transmission of knowledge amounts to passing on the stories piled up in the house of memory. Schooling is a matter of making the young observe the good examples in their surroundings and having them read (or listen to) virtuous stories from the past. Schooling is training youngsters to ponder and store up these memorabilia in their hearts. Imprinting examples on one's memory and imitating them at the appropriate time is the essence of all acquisition and transmission of knowledge. Women appear to have shared in this *imitatio morum*. They were even attributed a central role. Zerclaere, for example, stylizes his book as a person, calling it a welcome 'guest' who goes to visit a housewife in Germany and tells her stories about great heroes from the past and other things worth knowing.[32] This mode of learning is almost the polar opposite of what persons from the academic world associate with the process of transmitting knowledge. In the predominantly oral culture learned men with their books did not automatically enjoy greater authority than women.

Not only were the roles distributed along different lines; the format of the stories, the typical narrative form in this world differed as well. Here it was mainly the epic and the history, the saint's life and legend, but also the short forms of exemplum and anecdote that transmitted culture and religion. One example: the Dominican friar Henry Suso, trained as a theologian at the University of Cologne but involved in pastoral duties and preaching, used the format of the Life (*Vita*) or legend, as well as the exempla of the Desert Fathers, the *Vitas patrum*, when addressing the highly learned Elsbeth Stagel and other Dominican women. As Williams-Krapp argues in this volume, Suso's *Vita* was not an autobiography in the sense of 'an historical document of substantial historical authenticity'. Nor was it a hagiographical document to initiate a cult or a canonization process. It was a 'new' narrative genre of an unmistakably didactic nature that held 'a sophisticated blueprint for exemplary spirituality, aimed primarily at women, related within a narrative that draws upon the exemplary Lives of the Desert Fathers and Mothers. The reader is encouraged to imitate the Servant's imitation of this model of perfect spirituality within the limits suggested by Suso.' Williams-Krapp then elaborates on the category of Lives of mystic women who were not putative saints and whose Lives did not pursue canonization. The Life had a more didactic aim and was destined to 'trigger a concrete desire for *imitatio* in the reader'. In its function and strategies it resembled Zerclaere's *Der Waelsche Gast*.

The second conspicuous element in this world is the visual character of its culture

---

[32] Thomasin von Zerclaere, *Der Waelsche Gast*, the book also includes a summary of the *artes liberales* (see cover illustration to this volume).

and religion. Like Juliana and Hadewijch, and like Anselm and the scholastics, the *Moraalboek* employs the metaphor of seeing, in this case of colourful images, that fill the memory, *varwe*. Medieval persons experienced knowledge by observing images or reliving before their mind's eye what they had heard or read in books. Specifically in religion they experienced salvation history by opening the 'eyes of faith', or the 'eyes of the heart', and 'seeing' before their inner eye what happened to Christ. When Juliana saw an image of the Veronica, the true face of Christ, she 'fixed her eyes on the image of the Savior' and experienced on the spot what the image represented. Christ was crucified before her eyes and she lamented as if she were an eyewitness.[33] Pictures, sculptures, mental images (metaphors), words, liturgical celebrations, bread and wine—all these could open the spectators' eyes of faith and allow them to experience what they represented. Devout eyes looked through surface appearances to what lay hidden behind them. The faithful became personally involved in the story of salvation as they saw the holy enacted before their eyes. They became eyewitnesses, like Juliana. This held true for the ordinary faithful in church and in an intensified form for mystic women who were allowed to see hidden things. It even held true for scholars who studied the Scriptures and felt illuminated by God's Spirit. In this culture of seeing and envisaging there is no dividing line between the literate and the illiterate, the seeing and the knowing. The only distinctions are those between 'seeing' what one reads, seeing through recollection what one has read and stored in one's memory, 'inventive' meditation, and visionary experience. It is more a matter of gradation. Augustine already viewed the highest form of understanding of divine truth as an inner form of seeing, a natural continuation of outward seeing with the eyes, and distinguished three forms of seeing/understanding: corporeal, spiritual, and purely intellectual, that is, imageless understanding.[34] From their stronghold of intelligence the theologians and the medieval scholastics construed an intellectual ascent with their own putative imageless insights as the highest form of understanding. Even Caesarius of Heisterbach distinguished a similar gradation of three kinds of visions culminating in imageless understanding. This highest form, however, was perceived by them as intuitive rather than logical, and thus stands on a continuum with visionary experience rather than with discursive logic. It was ascribed to grace. Monastics and mystic women retaliated with their two ways of acquiring knowledge, the scholastic way of rashly intruding and the visionary way of benignly witnessing, while claiming undiluted truth for their own way only.

---

[33] *Life of Juliana*, I. 28: trans. by Newman, p. 63.

[34] *De videndo Deo*, in Augustine, *Epistola CCLVII*, ed. by A. Goldbacher, *Aurelii Augustini Epistolae*, CSEL, 44 (Vienna: Tempsky, 1895–1923), III, pp. 274–331 (278–82); quoted by Norman Klassen, *Chaucer on Love, Knowledge and Sight* (Cambridge: Brewer, 1995), p. 7. Mary Carruthers, *The Craft of Thought: Meditation, Rhetoric, and the Making of Images, 400–1200* (Cambridge: Cambridge University Press, 1998), pp. 171–220 (p. 177), also speaks of the 'fixed gaze of his eyes when a person was meditating'.

To return to the question raised at the beginning: if we take as our point of departure the oral and aural world of medieval culture, should we view a claim to direct inspiration as a shrewd strategy to obtain authorization for visionary women who would otherwise enjoy no authority whatsoever? Or was it rather a matter of claiming the highest form of authority for women, who were already recognized as conveyors of wisdom? Or are both true then, but for the two different worlds, one of learning, the other of seeing and hearing?

The Characteristics of the Texts

The common narrative form of transmitting envisaged and experienced knowledge was, besides the saint's Life and the fairy tale, the short form of the exemplum, and the anecdote. The discursive or abstract argument was the prerogative of schooled theologians; the short story and the exemplum, or a collection of exempla, were the popular genres of the *illiterati*. By stringing together seemingly innocuous anecdotes, calling up memories, describing images and visions, these texts conveyed their theological or devotional message. In a simple and vividly concrete style, they tugged at the heartstrings of listeners and readers, instructed them, and urged them to take their lessons to heart. As Aaron Gurevich has argued in his inspiring study, exempla that were used to convey a religious message had a value similar to that of the inner experiences of the faithful in reliving events. An exemplum Gurevich defines as a short story that takes place anew every time it is told. Believers thus saw the message unfolding before their inner eye with each telling.[35] This gave these texts a greater innate value than Latin treatises.

It is therefore important to make an inventory of the short texts or concatenations of short texts from the world of seeing and hearing and to subject them to a thorough analysis. Before we can proceed to analyze the role and significance of gender, we must first investigate in detail the kinds of sources available to us and try to determine what lay people and women contributed to them. Most of the studies included in this volume serve to expand this inventory.

Wybren Scheepsma argues that Beatrice of Nazareth, when studying Holy Scripture and trying to grasp its meaning, developed the habit of writing down her spiritual exercises. She recorded her own thoughts, at times elaborating on generally known images and metaphors taken from tradition, at other moments, he assumes, reporting her own visions and divine revelations. Two centuries later, in the circle of the Modern Devotion, we encounter similar collections of notes and quotations, for which Thom Mertens has coined the term *rapiarium*. And in the sixteenth century the Carthusian Gerhard Kalckbrenner, as Christensen notes in her study of Maria van

---

[35] Aaron J. Gurjewitsch [English: Gurevich], *Himmlisches und irdisches Leben. Bildwelten des schriftlosen Menschen im 13. Jahrhundert. Die Exempel*, translated from the Russian (Amsterdam-Dresden: Verlag der Kunst, 1997).

Hout, collected notes of a similar character. After Beatrice had become prioress she may, according to Scheepsma, have re-worked her notes into a spiritual diary or handbook of sorts, designed for instruction of the novices and the numerous girls who were entrusted to her. After her death, the vernacular notes or the spiritual handbook served as the main source for the hagiographer as he wrote his Latin Life. Because only that Latin re-working has survived, we know virtually nothing about the vernacular base. But we can still infer from the Latin text that Beatrice, in spite of her excellent training, her knowledge of Latin and the Bible, did not flaunt the intensive reading of monastic literature to which she had gained access. Rather she must have produced primarily a loose series of writings on inner experiences of grace. Also her *Seven Manners of Love*—assuming that she was the author—seems to have been written out of her own rich experience. According to Scheepsma, 'the idea of gaining spiritual knowledge from books without any direct relation to personal faith and life experience was incomprehensible'. Whether this is the reason or not, the fact remains that religious women's texts are as a rule shaped around personal anecdotes and exempla.

Two centuries after Beatrice and in much more uncomfortable conditions Alijt Bake, too, recorded the story of her spiritual life for the benefit of her community. In her case her own writings are preserved, though anonymously. As Anne Bollmann shows, Bake consciously used the method she had learned as a novice, 'namely that of successively compiling, contemplating and rewriting a private collection of excerpts as a *rapiarium*'. She later polished this method in her spiritual autobiography but maintained the loose, 'patchwork' structure, interweaving personal revelations and 'lifelike examples [...] with metaphors and images widely used in the literature and art of the Middle Ages'. At the same time Bake, too, appears to have been highly literate and conversant in Latin and theology.

The same holds true for Maria van Hout as presented in this volume by Kirsten Christensen. And Perrine de Baume, who wrote a Life of Colette of Corbie, did not set up her narrative 'according to existing and authoritative models of "official" hagiographic writing', but as the memoirs of an eyewitness, as Bert Roest argues in his contribution.

These women proved to be capable and creative authors, consciously shaping their reading and personal experiences into literary products designed for a specific readership. They were knowledgeable women, well trained in Latin and the Scriptures, but in their writing they did not follow the academic rules of scholastic debate. They did not quote directly from the Bible and the *auctoritates*. They did not produce a series of arguments pro and con, nor did they construct a scholastic *quaestio*. They avoided all this not only because they had not learned it but also because they had great objections to texts of that kind. In their view scholastic learning hindered the more direct experience of seeing and knowing. They relied instead on forms of their own. Bake, for instance, refused to memorize Latin texts as convent protocol prescribed: 'I cannot keep my heart concentrated on them in a way that I would be enlivened by them as I am in these (her own personal introspection)'.

The studies presented here, written out of a thorough knowledge of the sources and the technical problems connected with them, bring to a light a great many new facts. Supplementary information must still be gleaned from other texts. Only then will it be possible to undertake a more general analysis from the perspective of gender. That remains a project for the future.

Authorization

A last point to consider is the legitimation of the female teachers and writers—for both their actions and their writing. While it may be true that powers of persuasion and an impressive example were more important in oral culture than professional schooling and a diploma, yet great importance is to be attached to having a specific framework from which one could operate with authority. A person needs a recognizable setting to show that his or her words deserve attention. Only then will what he/she says or does be properly appreciated. For men this was often no problem. If they acted in public they typically did so by virtue of their function or their membership in a generally valued institution, such as the Church hierarchy. Clerics did not need an explicit legitimation of what they were doing; their words were almost automatically embedded in the learned Church tradition. For women this was much more problematic. Certainly in matters of religion they needed an extra and explicit legitimation.

A second factor plays a role here as well. As Christensen shows, the Jesuit who wanted to visit Maria van Hout was warned that this famous and influential woman would turn silent and submissive as soon as she was confronted with contentious men. This was less a matter of condescension toward these pugnacious types than of her internalized training to listen passively to teachers and preachers. Clerics, in other words, were trained to speak out while the opposite was true of women. What women needed was an environment in which they would feel free to speak, an ambiance in which their words would be heard, as well as an explicit authorization. Without a divine calling and personal revelations they would appear to be trespassing on the territory of authoritative men or authoritative texts.

Much more factual source study is necessary on this issue as well. Theories and interpretations have too often been constructed on what is known from just a handful of sources. Detailed studies are needed.

The remaining studies in this volume expand on this theme. Thom Mertens argues that the sisters of the Modern Devotion were capable authors, but in a different sense from the one we normally assume. He rejects the idea that women would not have been able to take notes while listening to sermons and afterward expand their jottings into full sermon form. The notes the sisters took while their father confessors preached were a 'skeleton' they later filled out, bringing bare bones to life with the 'flesh' of a full sermon. They edited the sermons, 'making not only stylistic improvements but also additions and changes in the content.' Because it was impossible to memorize all the arguments and all the quotations from *auctoritates* (the Bible and the great Christian writers), they filled in the blank sections with authorities of their own finding, probably using the same heuristic handbooks as the preachers' themselves had used. 'Most striking', according to Mertens, is that the sisters 'took up their role as genuine ghostwriters' by writing complete, well-constructed texts in which an authoritative "I" speaks to the beloved sisters.'

Battista Alfani, a Poor Clare of late-medieval Italy, worked on venerable old texts, translating the Latin *Legenda sanctae Clarae* for the sisters in her convent. However, as Lezlie Knox argues, by expanding detail and adding lively anecdotes, she changed the impact of the text considerably. By having Clare explain that academic learning had to yield to divine inspiration and devotion, Battista Alfani 'may have empowered women to speak out about the nature of their vocation including the role of intellectual life, a topic generally gendered masculine in the Middle Ages.'

Bert Roest focuses his contribution to this volume on the literary activities of Colette of Corbie and her sisters, showing how they, too, in writing and collecting both letters and Lives, created a 'kulturelles Gedächtnis' or a 'textual community with a unified outlook'. For this was the underlying aim of these women's literary activities: the creation of a collective identity that could hold its own against the learned community of the clerics. The focus of my own contribution to this volume is neither a special text nor a person but the figure of the Mother of God, *Maria doctrix*, the ultimate legitimator. Women, in particular women recluses, claimed that Mary, the celestial *doctrix* and *magistra*, taught them where earthly teachers failed, and that she gave them the self-confidence to speak up; and also that she, the Queen Mother in heaven, used spiritual mothers in the anchorhold as her maidens on earth.

This volume has resulted from one of the co-operative projects of the Netherlands Research School for Medieval Studies and the Medieval Institute of the University of Notre Dame, the project 'Transmission of Knowledge and the Problems of Gender', co-ordinated by Dr Anneke Mulder-Bakker and Prof. Mark Jordan. The participants thank these institutions and their then directors, Prof. Alasdair MacDonald and Prof. John Van Engen, for providing financial and moral support. The Dutch participants also feel indebted to the medievalist Dr Myra Scholz, who reshaped their Dutch papers into well-phrased English contributions. And the editor thanks Dr Lezlie Knox for her ongoing advice and assistance.

Translated by Myra Scholz

Using Women to Think With in the Medieval University[*]

RUTH MAZO KARRAS

This article, like the others in this volume, questions a view of the Middle Ages in which men transmitted knowledge formally and professionally, in written Latin, while women did so sporadically, orally, and emotionally rather than rationally. Whereas many of the others do so by looking at alternative modes of knowledge and forms of transmission, this one looks from a new angle at the institutions that scholars have traditionally considered the transmitters of knowledge. The university and its scholastic modes of thought become, not the norm against which other forms of knowledge transmission are measured and found wanting, but rather a peculiar and historically contingent phenomenon.

Medieval university education was heavily gendered masculine, and not simply because women were excluded from it. The process not only systematically excluded women, it trained men in specifically masculine cultural practices involving competition and technical skill. The content of learning excluded women as well: theological education did not so much transmit misogynist teaching as it used women as symbols to discuss other issues. Saying that knowledge transmitted in an all-male environment is masculine knowledge is tautological; by examining practices of teaching and learning and the content of teaching on gender-related topics we may be able to move beyond tautology by connecting the two. Theological quodlibets, with their great range of subjects, provide a rich source of material, and this article deals with the age from which these mainly survive from the University of Paris, from about 1210–1320.

[*] Research for this article was supported in part by a Summer Research Fellowship and a Grant in Aid of Research from Temple University. I thank Joel Kaye for his thoughtful comments on an earlier version of this article; any errors that remain are, of course, my own.

The main feature of the quodlibetal questions relating to gender issues, as a group, is the way they use women to think with rather than as the subject of study. To take one example: Gerard d'Abbeville discussed whether a woman who had taken a vow of chastity could legitimately be released from that vow by the pope in order to marry a tyrant who was threatening all of Christendom if she did not. This question raised issues of papal power and of the common good or the *res publica* balanced against the good of keeping a vow. The good of the individual in this case is not considered. The emphasis is on the vow rather than on the state of virginity, and the vow is an abstract good rather than a contribution to the individual woman's salvation: 'It is not her private utility, but public and common.'[1] He did not consider at all the position of the woman who is to be married to the tyrant or to remain a virgin; her wishes or will simply do not come up. Although the question as posed would seem to raise issues of practical decision-making and feminine behaviour (albeit by way of a far-fetched hypothetical case), Gerard uses it as a bridge to more abstract political issues. The question starts out with a woman but is not *about* women.

As we shall see, this approach is typical of theological quodlibets that might seem at first glance to be gender-related. Women, and indeed men too, are simply tools to get at general issues. The scholastic method, that characteristically masculine form of transmission of knowledge, used syllogism and analogy to reason from the particular to the general. The general issues the theologians addressed did not tend explicitly to include women or gender difference, which somehow fell off their mental maps.

The content of scholastic thought must be considered in the context of the sub-culture from which it came. Social factors limited women's access to the rationalistic world of scholasticism, but no such factors limited men's access to a more emotional way of thinking.[2] Indeed, because so much more men's writing than women's writing has survived from the Middle Ages the models of affective piety are mainly male. The fact remains, however, that while we cannot say that most of those whose surviving writings use emotion as a means to knowing (God or anything else) were women, nor that men primarily used logic, we can say that most of those who tried to understand the world through logic were men. This took place primarily at the

---

[1] Gerard d'Abbeville, Quodlibet 6, q. 3, Paris, BnF, MS lat. 16405, fol. 58^r–58^v (quotation at 58^v); compare also Quodlibet 4, q. 13, fols. 51^r–51^v, and Quodlibet 13, q. 4, fols. 93^r–93^v. Gerard does say that it is impossible to break the vow for the sake of a greater good, for there is no greater good than continence; he says this generally, not only about women.

[2] See Carol Gilligan, *In a Different Voice: Psychological Theory and Women's Development* (Cambridge, MA: Harvard University Press, 1982); Mary Field Belenky, Blythe McVicker Clinchy, Nancy Rule Goldberger, and Jill Mattuck Tarule, *Women's Ways of Knowing: The Development of Self, Voice, and Mind* (New York: Basic Books, 1986), for modern differences in women's and men's ways of thinking. Neither these works nor I make the claim that these differences are biological or innate.

university, and I focus here on one aspect of university study, the disputation, and the way it helped shape a particular mode of thought. Disputations were held in other faculties besides theology, but we know most about theology.

In ordinary disputations in theology, a master would put forward propositions to be debated by his students; each would take a position as 'opponent' of the thesis or 'respondent', answering objections. The master would then 'determine' the disputation by summing up and giving his own view of the question. These disputations usually took place weekly at certain times of the university calendar. There were also 'quodlibetal' disputations held at certain times of the year, where participation was not limited to a master's own students. There was no set topic and anyone could put forward a question. A bachelor acting as respondent, and perhaps also the master holding the quodlibet, would defend his views on whatever subjects were raised, and the master would determine.[3] The specific topics could vary widely, sometimes depending on the interests of the individual master—some dealt with natural philosophy, others dealt with the nature of God, others were more practical.[4]

The disputation gave scholasticism its distinctive characteristics; indeed the statutes of medieval universities explicitly stated the importance of the disputation for developing the students' minds.[5] The disputation form had substantial effects on the texts that were used in the universities: commentaries were written mainly in the form of questions, and though some of them were based on lectures, others grew out of discussions originally conducted orally in the context of a disputation.[6] The

---

[3] Bernardo C. Bazan, 'Les Questions disputées, principalement dans les facultés de théologie', and John F. Wippel, 'Quodlibetal Questions, Chiefly in Theology Faculties', in *Les Questions disputées et les questions quodlibétiques dans les facultés de théologie, de droit et de médecine*, Typologie des sources du moyen âge occidental, fasc. 44–45 (Turnhout: Brepols, 1985), pp. 13–149 and 153–222 respectively. P. Glorieux, 'L'Enseignement au moyen âge: Techniques et méthodes en usage à la faculté de théologie de Paris au XIIIe siècle', *Archives d'histoire doctrinale et littéraire du moyen âge*, 35 (1968), 123–47; Jacques LeGoff, *Intellectuals in the Middle Ages*, trans. by Teresa Lavender Fagan (Cambridge, MA: Blackwell, 1992), pp. 89–92.

[4] P. Glorieux, *La Littérature quodlibétique de 1260 à 1320*, Bibliothèque Thomiste, 5 (Kain: Le Saulchoir, 1925) and Glorieux, *La Littérature quodlibétique* II, Bibliothèque Thomiste, 21 (Paris: J. Vrin, 1935), gives lists of the questions in surviving quodlibets.

[5] Alfonso Maierù, *University Training in Medieval Europe*, trans. and ed. by Darleen N. Pryrds (Leiden: Brill, 1994), p. 127 note 52. A handbook of disputational argument, falsely attributed to Albertus Magnus, gives a good sense of the stylized nature of the argument: *Die Mittelalterlichen Traktate de Modo Opponendi et Respondendi*, ed. by Lambert Marie de Rijk, *Beiträge zur Geschichte der Philosophie und Theologie des Mittelalters*, n.f. 17 (Münster: Aschendorff, 1980).

[6] Anthony Kenny and Jan Pinborg, 'Medieval Philosophical Literature', in *The Cambridge History of Later Medieval Philosophy: From the Rediscovery of Aristotle to the Disintegration of Scholasticism, 1100–1600*, ed. by Norman Kretzmann, Anthony Kenny, and Jan Pinborg (Cambridge: Cambridge University Press, 1982), pp. 11–42.

quaestiones disputatae that survive do not reflect the process as it happened; they comprise the master's *determinatio* and are much more systematic than the disputation itself presumably was, and do not convey the active, fluid give-and-take that we may presume went on in the lecture hall.[7] This disputational method is how the theologians of the thirteenth-century universities proposed to understand the universe. This educational method created a masculine mode of thought among the theologians who represented the elite of medieval intellectual life, as well as among arts students who in terms of their numbers would have a greater impact on society. This agonistic structure also provided a forum for the demonstration of masculinity.[8] Some academics used metaphors from sword fighting and warfare to describe the single combat of the disputation.[9]

The disputation form was not, of course, unique to the universities. Debate poems were a staple of many vernacular literatures as well as Latin.[10] Back-and-forth

---

[7] Jody Enders, 'The Theater of Scholastic Erudition', *Comparative Drama*, 27 (1993), 341–63. Enders reads literary accounts to suggest how the actual *disputatio* might have proceeded. University statutes tell us when they were held, and who could respond or determine, but do not give a picture of the disputation itself. There is not even a clear agreement among scholars as to how significant a role the master played in the first part of a quodlibet: the second part, the *determinatio*, was all his, but a bachelor responded in the disputational part, and it is not clear how much the master himself said about the questions raised there. See Glorieux, *La Littérature*, II, pp. 31–36; Wippel, 'Quodlibetal Questions', pp. 183–85.

[8] I take the term from Walter Ong, *Fighting for Life: Contest, Sexuality, and Consciousness* (Ithaca: Cornell University Press, 1981), pp. 118–48. Ong sees the *agon* primarily as student against master; but in the medieval university it was also student against student and master (who might also be a student in another faculty) against master.

[9] William J. Courtenay, *Schools and Scholars in Fourteenth-Century England* (Princeton: Princeton University Press, 1987), pp. 29–30. Compare Martin Grabmann's description in *Die Geschichte der scholastischen Methode* (Freiburg im Breisgau: Herder, 1911; repr. Graz: Akademische Druck- u. Verlagsanstalt, 1957), II, pp. 20–21. Peter Abelard, *Historia calamitatum*, ed. by J. Monfrin (Paris: J. Vrin, 1962), pp. 63–64, is one example, discussed further by Andrew Taylor, 'A Second Ajax: Peter Abelard and the Violence of Dialectic,' in *The Tongue of the Fathers: Gender and Ideology in Twelfth-Century Latin*, ed. by David Townsend and Andrew Taylor (Philadelphia: University of Pennsylvania Press, 1998), pp. 14–24. John of Salisbury, *Metalogicon*, III. 10, ed. by J. B. Hall, CCCM, 98 (Turnhout: Brepols, 1991), pp. 130–39, also uses this kind of language. See also K. S. B. Keats-Rohan, 'John of Salisbury and Education in Twelfth-Century Paris from the Account of his *Metalogicon*', *History of Universities*, 6 (1986–87), 1–45. Helen Solterer, *The Master and Minerva: Disputing Women in French Medieval Culture* (Berkeley: University of California Press, 1995), p. 29, points out that Abelard invoked the goddess Minerva as his patron. But the use of a classical goddess figure as metaphor (giving up Mars for Minerva) is not the same thing as constructing an activity as feminine, which Abelard clearly did not do.

[10] R. Howard Bloch, *Medieval French Literature and Law* (Berkeley: University of

debate as depicted in poems or embodied in texts written in response to another author did not, however, follow the strict format and rules of the academic disputation. It did not take the formal structure of defense of, or objections against, a thesis, although of course something of that nature is implicit in any argument. Helen Solterer has argued that participation in such literary debates, both by actual and fictional women, was a way for women to talk back and speak out. The woman, however, is always positioned as respondent, leaving the man as the initiator of arguments. And women's participation was more often textual than performed: they did not participate in the spectacle of university disputation, although unusually they participated in the pamphlet war of the *querelle de la rose*. In the university, whether the *disputatio* was between equals or unequals, in practice both parties were men, and the process proved their manhood. Students in disputing with their masters could move from a more subordinate and deferential position to claim the full masculine privilege of speech.

There is another crucial difference between debates in which women participated and those in the universities: the language of discussion. Learning Latin was part of the rite of passage for learned men. It was a sign of social position as well as of gender—not only most women, but also most men would not have the necessary degree of fluency in it. The language of the disputation was not just Latin, moreover, but a highly technical, precise and detailed Latin; its written form was highly abbreviated. In effect, one of the functions of the university was to initiate the student into academic discourse, teaching him the vocabulary and ways of speaking and writing appropriate to the form. And to the extent there existed this separate register of language used only at the universities, it was available to men alone.

What characterized the scholastic method, however, was not just a language and form. It was also the use of logic—not just logic generally but particular logical techniques derived from Aristotle and greatly expanded over the course of the thirteenth century. Minute attention was paid to specific words and the precise order of words in order to draw distinctions and clarify categories. Logic, probably the most important of the arts subjects, was a methodology most notably and fruitfully applied in theology, which included many topics that today would be treated as part of other disciplines. For example, human cognition was important in the context of theological questions: how the mind can know God, whether God and the angels know things in the same way human beings know things, whether the workings of the human mind can provide a model for understanding the workings of the Trinity.[11] It was in the study of theology that the scholastic method was most elaborated and has been thought of as the distinctive contribution of the Middle Ages to European culture.

California Press, 1977), pp. 162–214.

[11] John Marenbon, *Later Medieval Philosophy (1150–1350): An Introduction* (New York: Routledge, 1991), p. 94.

Scholasticism represents the method by which knowledge was transmitted. We return now to the content of that transmitted knowledge as it relates to gender. When we think of scholasticism's attitude to women, misogyny may come immediately to mind, but this connection is somewhat misleading. It was not misogyny in the sense of attacks on women as much as misogyny in the sense of ignoring women or making them irrelevant that characterized the theological disputations.

The idea of women's inferiority was not a new invention of the universities. Scholars have charted the history of misogyny over the course of the Middle Ages, and the emphasis from the Church Fathers onwards on feminine weakness and libido does not make a pretty picture.[12] The idea of woman as sinful or weak in the faith, however, was not the same as the idea of woman as weak in the mind. This latter thread in the skein of misogynist thought is often connected with Aristotle, who described women as in one sense deformed men.[13] Yet the impact of Aristotelian logic did not necessarily mean the enthusiastic reception of all of Aristotle's ideas.[14]

The influence of Aristotelian ideas about gender was perhaps most apparent in the medical faculty. The idea of woman as a deformed man was expressed in terms of reproductive biology, and there were also biological reasons why woman's intellect was thought to be inferior to men's. Joan Cadden notes that the influx of Greek and Arabic learning in the twelfth and thirteenth centuries, although on the surface it 'suggest[s] a simple pattern of concepts about sex difference', by no means created a unequivocal view of women's biological nature.[15] Yet, while in their

---

[12] Howard Bloch, *Medieval Misogyny and the Invention of Western Romantic Love* (Chicago: University of Chicago Press, 1991), describes some of the themes. Marie-Thérèse d'Alverny, 'Comment les théologiens et les philosophes voient la femme', *Cahiers de civilisation médiévale*, 20 (1977), 105–29, gives a good account of patristic views and how medieval writers through the twelfth century used them.

[13] Maryanne Cline Horowitz, 'Aristotle and Woman', *Journal of the History of Biology*, 9 (1976), 183–213. As Joan Cadden, *The Meanings of Sex Difference in the Middle Ages: Medicine, Science, and Culture* (Cambridge: Cambridge University Press, 1993), p. 24, points out, however, this does not mean that the female is useless; she is inferior to the male but necessary for reproduction. The idea of woman as weak and passive, therefore incapable of intellectual activity, may seem the direct opposite of the strand in misogynist thought that constructs woman as sexually insatiable. But, as Cadden (p. 178) points out, 'they share the underlying suggestion that women are empty, void, lacking'.

[14] Jacqueline Murray, 'Thinking About Gender: The Diversity of Medieval Perspectives', in *Power of the Weak: Studies on Medieval Women*, ed. by Jennifer Carpenter and Sally-Beth MacLean (Urbana: University of Illinois Press, 1990), pp. 1–26 (pp. 5–7). For the specific impact of Aristotelian ideas on women, see Prudence Allen, *The Concept of Woman: The Aristotelian Revolution 750 BC–AD 1250* (Montreal: Eden Press, 1985), pp. 361–478.

[15] Cadden, *Meanings of Sex Difference*, p. 106. She notes at p. 163 that 'although there was no significant disagreement with the belief that women were cooler, weaker, less intellectually competent, and generally less perfect than men, there were [. . .] various ways in which those differences could be played out and understood [. . .].'

disagreement over such issues as the reproductive contributions of males and females, the causes of sex determination of the fetus, and the nature and function of sexual pleasure, academics might reject Aristotle's one-seed theory, they nevertheless collectively shared his assumptions about woman's physical and mental weakness. [16] The biological understanding of man as stronger and woman as weaker had, for Aristotle, clear implications for society, and the scholastics were not slow to amplify. These ideas are put forward particularly in Aristotle's *Politics*, and it is especially in commentaries on this work that scholastics, including theologians, accepted this aspect of Aristotelian teaching, accepting Aristotle's justification of dominance over women by reference to nature.[17]

Gender Issues in Scholastic Disputations

That scholastic theologians knew and accepted Aristotelian statements on the weakness of women, however, did not mean that such statements came to dominate their treatment of gender issues that came up in disputations. Given the position of Aristotle as arch-misogynist in feminist histories of philosophy and the importance of Aristotle in scholastic thought, I expected to find these ideas permeating quodlibetal discussions of gender issues. In working through as many quodlibetal questions either dealing with gender issues or making reference to women as I could gain access to in printed or manuscript form (based on the list of questions prepared by Glorieux), I found that the theologians did not gratuitously offer a critique of

---

[16] Cadden, pp. 133–34; see Thomas Aquinas, *Summa Theologica*, 1.92.1, in *Opera Omnia* (Rome: S.C.P.F, 1889), V, p. 396, for his famous dictum that although women as a group were necessary to procreation and deliberately created, 'with respect to individual nature woman is something deficient and lacking'. See also Arlene Saxonhouse, *Women in the History of Political Thought, Ancient Greece to Machiavelli* (New York: Praeger, 1985), pp. 147–50; Kari Elisabeth Børresen, *Subordination and Equivalence: The Nature and Role of Woman in Augustine and Thomas Aquinas*, trans. by Charles H. Talbot (Washington: University Press of America, 1981), pp. 157–78.

[17] Aristotle, *Politics*, 1.12, trans. by Trevor J. Saunders (Oxford: Clarendon Press, 1995), p. 18. The Latin version that medieval scholastics would have known is that of William of Moerbeke: Aristotle, *Politica*, trans. by William of Moerbeke, ed. by Pierre Michaud-Quantin, *Aristoteles Latinus*, 29 (Bruges: Desclée de Brouwer, 1961), p. 21. For examples of medieval commentators, see Albertus Magnus, *Commentarii in octos libros politicorum Aristoteles*, 1.9, in *Opera Omnia*, ed. by Auguste Borgnet (Paris: Vives, 1891), VIII, p. 75; Thomas Aquinas, *Summa contra gentiles*, 4.88, in *Opera Omnia* (Rome: Leonine Commission, 1930), XV, p. 278; Thomas Aquinas, *Sententia libri Politicorum*, 1.10, in *Opera Omnia* (Rome; St Sabina, 1971), XIVIII, pp. 115–16; Aquinas, *Summa theologica*, 1.92.1, p. 397; Nicole Oresme, *Le Livre de politiques d'Aristote*, ed. by Albert Douglas Menut, Transactions of the American Philosophical Society, n.s. 60, part 6 (Philadelphia: American Philosophical Society, 1970), p. 73.

women. Rather, women were notable by their absence from the discourse as well as from the disputation's setting. In discussing the quodlibetal questions I am lumping together scholars who wrote at different times spanning a century, were members of different orders, and took different sides in theological debates. However, despite their differences, these disparate theologians share a set of common assumptions about gender.

Most quodlibetal questions, of course, did not deal with gender specifically, or with women: the nature of God, angels, or humans' relations to them, or of human knowledge, could be and was discussed with relation to *homines*, 'men' in the sense of 'human beings.' They discussed the human soul, not the male, and did not question whether women had souls. When they did deal with issues involving women, however, the theologians tended not to expound gratuitously on feminine weakness, but rather as much as possible to ignore the fact that the issue involved women. This was not because they were gender-blind egalitarians, but because women simply were not interesting to them as women: they were not part of their intellectual world. The masculine stood as the norm for all. They used women to think with only when necessary, and they did not really matter *as* women.

Questions that dealt with strictly theological issues were discussed in very abstract terms, and whatever may have been said in the actual discussion the recorded quodlibets are brief and do not use many concrete examples. When they speak of humans they use the neutral 'homo' and, while the authors undoubtedly had men in mind, what they said in general about the human intellect and the soul was not gender-specific. They excluded women not overtly but more subtly. Other questions, however, did refer to women. Questions about marriage were generally in the province of canon law, but this did not prevent their being asked in quodlibetal disputations, in which various fields of study did overlap. Even so, the theologians who discussed these questions often did not consider women *qua* women.

Durandus of St Pourçain in 1312–13, for example, considered the question of whether a woman who was left a legacy on condition of her marriage could receive it if she became a nun. Durandus did not need to explain the superiority of virginity for women, he simply assumed it, and reasoned that someone who chose a better course should be seen as having fulfilled the requirement. The point was not the good of feminine chastity—which one might have expected him to discuss, if the nature of women and their sexuality had been a great concern—but the nature of legal conditions; a vow of continence counted as matrimony for this particular legal purpose.[18] The questioners had posed the issue in terms of women, but that was not what interested the respondent or the master who determined.

---

[18] Durandus of St Pourçain, Quodlibet, q. 6, Paris, BnF, MS lat. 14572, fol. 6[r]. The identification of this and other authors of quodlibets is from Glorieux, *La Littérature*. Compare the treatment of this question by Eustace of Grandcourt (compilation of Nicolas de Bar, Quodlibet, q. 125), BnF, MS lat. 15850, fol. 37[r], who says simply that she cannot have the money because it would be a violation of the intention of her father.

Another question, on whether marriage was valid if performed after a vow of chastity, was answered by 'Master R. of Arras' with reference to papal power to dispense from vows, without reference at all to the nature of marriage or masculine or feminine chastity.[19] The same master used a question about the marriage debt not to discuss the reasons for this doctrine or the nature of human sexuality, but to assert the superiority of theologians over canon lawyers. If a man contracted marriage but took holy orders before consummation, is he obliged to render the debt to his wife? Yes, although he cannot exact it from her: 'for that which concerns the nature of marriage is of Christ's instituting, and is to be considered by theologians; the other issues [about holy orders] are of positive law and pertain to the jurists.'[20] Again the relative position of a husband and wife is irrelevant. Thomas Aquinas considered that the pope could grant a dispensation in a matter of bigamy, as this was positive law and not natural or divine—he did not consider the differential effects on wife and husband if a marriage is considered valid or invalid.[21] A question of Guy of Cluny on whether virginity lost in mind can be restored became a discussion of the technical concepts of material and formal; he did not take the opportunity to refer to masculine or feminine tendencies to sin.[22]

Even when quodlibetal questions discussed women's subordinate position, the masters did not often refer to Aristotelian doctrine on women's weaker nature. Gerard d'Abbeville considered whether a Jew who converted to Christianity could remain married to a spouse who did not. One of the possible answers he discussed was that a male convert could stay married, but a wife could not, because her Jewish husband might cause her to relapse into error. Gerard did not say, however, whether this is because of women's fickleness, weakness of character, or legal and social subjugation to their husbands.[23] In a discussion of whether a wife could make pious donations without her husband's permission, Adenulf of Anagni, nephew of Gregory IX, made clear that the wife was subject to the husband. But he derived this subjection from biblical (I Corinthians 11) rather than from Aristotelian authority, and when he spoke of the husband and wife as the 'superior' and 'inferior' parties he seems to have been referring to status rather than to nature.[24] He did not need to

---

[19] 'R. de Atrebato' (Nicolas de Bar, Quodlibet, q. 56), Paris, BnF, MS lat. 15850 fol. 26^r.

[20] 'R. de Atrebato' (Nicolas de Bar, Quodlibet, q. 57), Paris, BnF, MS lat. 15850, fol. 26^r; compare Henry of Ghent, *Quodlibeta* (Paris: J. Badio Ascensio, 1518), Quodlibet 5, q. 38, fol. 214^r.

[21] Thomas Aquinas, Quodlibet 4, Art. 13, *Opera Omnia* (Parma: P. Fiacciadori, 1859), IX, p. 514.

[22] Guy de Cluny (Nicolas de Bar, Quodlibet, q. 35), Paris, BnF, MS lat. 15850, fol. 20^v.

[23] Gerard d'Abbeville, Quodlibet 6, q. 8, Paris, BnF, MS lat. 16405, fol. 59^v. Gerard in fact rejected this argument, determining that in either case the couple should separate.

[24] Adenulf of Anagni, Quodlibet, q. 13, Paris, BnF, MS lat. 14899, fol. 147^v–148^r. Compare the briefer consideration by 'R. de Atrebato' (Nicolas de Bar, Quodlibet, q. 55),

condemn women as incompetent or deny their spiritual equality in order to deny their right to any control over the property of the household even for pious purposes.[25]

For the most part, women were simply non-actors. The irrelevance of women's will is reflected in an anonymous quodlibet where, in answering the question 'is *scandalum* a moral sin', the theologian gave the following example: 'if someone plays around (*ludat*) with a woman in the presence of others, and in that he embraces her and kisses her in front of them and throws her on the ground and does such things, even if he does not have the will to commit a sin, to him is imputed whatever happens as a result, since perhaps those who are present, nor the woman, did not have the will to sin before they received the will to sin from his deed, and perhaps they will sin with this woman or with others, or she with these men or with others, which otherwise they would not have done.'[26] The man, not the woman, is blamed; he is committing the *scandalum* by what he does to her. She is entirely passive, having no will to sin when the man was playing around with her. [27] That does not mean that she was being assaulted. Neither consent nor lack of consent is implied. Consent is simply irrelevant. This lack of importance placed on feminine consent to intercourse is not a peculiarity of this author or of thirteenth-century theologians in general; it is pervasive in medieval culture.[28] Yet it is another indication of the insignificance of women as actors to scholastic theologians.

In a remarkable example of how women simply fell out of the picture, Gervaise of Mont St Eloi addressed the question of whether a woman who had taken a vow of chastity but then married committed a mortal sin in every act of marital intercourse.[29] Gervaise began by using a gender-neutral term (*homo*): 'a person [who has taken a simple vow] retains power over his/her own body' (the Latin possessive does not distinguish the gender of the possessor). Then as he turned to the specific case, he slipped into the masculine: '[he] did not give the power over his body to his wife

---

Paris, BnF, MS lat. 15850, vols 25[v]–26[r].

[25] Both Adenulf and Gerard d'Abbeville allow a wife to donate those things that are her *propria*, not marital property; Gerard reached this conclusion based explicitly on natural and civil law. Gerard d'Abbeville, Quodlibet 10, q. 6, Paris, BnF, MS lat. 16405, fol. 80[v]. He did not, however, make any comment about the capacities of women.

[26] Glorieux, *La Littérature*, I, 318.

[27] This passivity may be somewhat noteworthy in light of ideas about feminine lustfulness, but not in light of the notion, found in a wide variety of medieval texts, of sex as something someone does to someone else rather than as something two people do together.

[28] See Kathryn Gravdal, *Ravishing Maidens: Writing Rape in Medieval French Literature and Law* (Philadelphia: University of Pennsylvania Press, 1991).

[29] Gervaise of Mont-St-Eloi, Quodlibet, q. 4, Paris, BnF MS lat. 15350, fols 269[v]–270[r]. His conclusion was no, based on a distinction between a simple and a solemn vow. Compare Aquinas on the same issue: Quodlibet 3.18, *Opera Omnia* (Parma, 1859), IX, pp. 499–500.

until after their first carnal intercourse'. Even when the original question had been posed in terms of a woman's moral status, Gervaise preferred to discuss that of a man. The answer would probably not have been different had he considered a woman rather than a man. However, his shifting the question to the masculine side, while it appears a gender-neutral move, is a sign that to him the masculine was the norm and the feminine insignificant.

Even questions about feminine sexuality were turned into questions not about women themselves but about the nature of the divine. When asked whether God could restore lost virginity, Gerard d'Abbeville replied with a discussion of whether God's omnipotence included the power to falsify.[30] While it may be significant for an understanding of medieval gender relations that women's loss of virginity was so permanent that restoring it might be falsification, whereas for example restoring the dead to life was not, Gerard ignored this issue and used this question as a way of discussing God. Another discussion of whether a man or a woman is more meritorious in preserving virginity became a question not of gender comparison but of what constitutes spiritual merit.[31]

The theologians were often simply not interested in the practical ramifications of the cases they considered. Thomas Aquinas wrote of a case where a Christian man promised to marry a Jewish woman if she would become Christian, and she agreed (*matrimonium per verba de futuro*). He then baptized her, and they had sexual intercourse. Are they married? Normally words of future consent (even if conditional), followed by intercourse, constituted a valid marriage. In this case, however, Aquinas points out, by performing the baptism himself he acquires a bond of spiritual kinship with her. Even if they had previously been married by words of present consent followed by consummation, the marriage would become invalid.[32] Aquinas does not take this opportunity to discuss the advisability of converting Jewish women in order to marry them, nor consider what happens to a woman who has converted in order to marry a man she now cannot marry, possibly pregnant and probably rejected by both communities. Similarly, for Henry of Ghent, a question about whether a widow who remarries must go back to her late husband if he is miraculously resurrected becomes a question about the relation of body and soul, and the issue of the real personal relations involved is not relevant.[33] The theologians are not discussing real cases and for the most part are not concerned with the people they talk about, male or female. This is simply a vehicle for considering the

---

[30] Gerard d'Abbeville, Quodlibet 7, q. 17, Paris, BnF, MS lat. 16405, fols 67ᵛ–68ʳ.

[31] Gerard d'Abbeville, Quodlibet 14, q. 3, Paris, BnF, MS lat. 16405, fols 102ᵛ–103ʳ. Even a discussion of prostitution becomes a discussion of the nature of responsibility for actions rather than of prostitution in particular, Quodlibet 5, q. 9, BnF, MS lat. 16405 fols 55ᵛ–56ᵛ, although this is one place where condemnatory language is used of the women involved.

[32] Aquinas, Quodlibet 6.5, *Opera Omnia* (Parma, 1859), IX, p. 544.

[33] Henry of Ghent, Quodlibet 3, q. 27, fols 87ʳ–87ᵛ.

interaction of kinship and marriage, or the permanence of the marriage bond. Yet the very fact that the situations are not real to them is a reflection of the absence of women from their world.[34]

Women's insignificance in Aristotelian biology complemented their insignificance to theology generally. Ranulph d'Homblières considered whether if only Eve had sinned and not Adam, their children would have contracted original sin. The discussion centred on whether the form which the fetus is said (according to Aristotle) to take from the father's seed includes original sin.[35] The purpose of this question was not to determine which gender was more responsible for original sin, nor indeed to determine the scientific issue of whose seed shapes the fetus.[36] Rather, the fundamental issue is the relation between body and soul. The gender implications, however, even if as a side effect, are significant. If original sin does not come to us from Eve, this may be a positive sign for attitudes towards women; on the other hand, the reason it does not is not because Eve was not sinful (she could still be blamed for tempting Adam) but because woman was simply insignificant in the process of generating a child.

Besides Eve, the other woman whom the theologians gave significant mention was of course the Virgin Mary. But she was not considered in the context of other women, either to exalt or to critique the latter. The question of whether her virginity was a higher good than her divine maternity, for example, was answered with a discussion of the relative roles of physical and mental action in the conception of Christ. The question of her immaculate conception was completely independent of her femininity.[37]

It is hardly surprising, in theological disputations, that participants would attempt to turn the discussion as much as possible to theological issues. They did so by largely excluding women from their mental world. The theologians were doing what they were supposed to do: using the specific questions asked to generalize to larger issues. The women referred to in the questions became in effect tools to think with, or stimuli to the larger discussions. And yet the application of reason and logic to theological questions was not ungendered. In refusing to follow up the feminine aspects of the questions offered, the masters were saying that they were irrelevant. The difference between men and women did not matter, not because men and women were equal in all things, but because women fundamentally did not matter.

The exclusion of both real-life women and real-life men from what was

---

[34] There are a few cases where the real-world issues are considered: for example Gervaise of Mt-St-Eloi, Quodlibet, q. 66, Paris, BnF, MS lat. 15350, fols 284^r–284^v; 'John the Minorite' (Nicolas de Bar, Quodlibet, q. 45), Paris, BnF, MS lat. 15850, fol. 23^v.

[35] Ranulph d'Homblières, Quodlibet 9, Paris, Arsenal, MS 379, fol. 223^r.

[36] On this issue see Cadden, pp. 117–30.

[37] Giles of Rome, *Quodlibeta*, ed. by Peter de Coninck (Louvain: Nemphaeus, 1646), Quodlibet 6, q. 18 and 20, pp. 410–15, 418–24.

theologically important also reflects how this masculine thought worked. The typically feminine affective piety tended to humanize the divine, if only metaphorically, in order better to identify with it. Masculine scholastic thought, on the other hand, dehumanized the human: it was not primarily concerned with pastoral issues but with principles and abstractions. It focused on an intellectualized conception of the world, not a personalized one.

It was not only the content of scholastic theology that made the universities a fertile bed for the creation of a masculine identity that considered women hardly worthy of attention. A misogynist attitude created out of the wish to keep students among the clergy and hence unmarried, the male bonds created by the rarefied intellectual atmosphere, and general currents from the wider society outside the university pervaded the ivory tower as well.[38] Yet in scholastic disputation women were largely excluded from content as well as process. The implications for medieval society and culture of this intellectual and religious movement that was so profoundly masculine and masculist both in its structure and in the content of its teaching are many. Historians need to consider what they are doing when they label scholasticism the characteristic creation of the medieval mind, or the Thomist synthesis as the crowning intellectual achievement of the Middle Ages. It has never been a secret that women were not involved, but most scholars have treated and continue to treat that fact merely as an accident of history. If one views the movement as exclusionary in its very nature, however, rather than exclusionary only by historical accident, it begins to look very different.

Modern scholars have treated scholasticism as important, not through arbitrariness or through sexism, but because many of its dominant ideas, regardless of their historical context, are extraordinarily interesting and fruitful, and because it provided the antecedents of modern theological movements.[39] It was also much respected during the Middle Ages. The question we need to ask is not only 'why have modern scholars privileged this masculine intellectual movement', but also 'why did medieval people privilege it?' Intellectuals in medieval Europe were being trained to examine all questions in an adversarial, disputational manner. They were to prove their manhood by besting someone in logical argument and in adducing of authorities, not by working out compromises or by gentle persuasion. Transferred from the battlefield into the lecture hall and the palace, the combat continued, and made women peripheral not only in the process but even as intellectual tools.

---

[38] Ruth Mazo Karras, 'Sharing Wine, Women, and Song: Masculine Identity Formation in Medieval European Universities', in *Becoming Male in the Middle Ages*, ed. by Jeffrey Jerome Cohen and Bonnie Wheeler (New York: Garland Press, 1997), pp. 187–202.

[39] See Mark D. Jordan, 'Medieval Philosophy of the Future!' in *The Past and Future of Medieval Studies*, ed. by John Van Engen (Notre Dame: University of Notre Dame Press, 1994), pp. 155–58.

Henry Suso's *Vita* between Mystagogy and Hagiography

WERNER WILLIAMS-KRAPP

The narrative strategies used in hagiographic writings were devised to leave no doubt in the audience's mind about the protagonist's sanctity. Therefore, the medieval recipient of the Life of a saint or putative saint would have had no difficulty identifying him or her as such; the protagonist's identity was clearly indicated by the literary stylization, conventions, motifs and *topoi* typical of hagiography. With the establishment of papal canonization proceedings, miraculous deeds performed by the candidate for sainthood also became an essential element of a true saint's Life.

It is important to keep these very basic facts in mind when attempting interpretations of the numerous Lives of German mystics, male and female, written from the thirteenth to the fifteenth centuries: for these Lives, while they do resort to a certain extent to the narrative strategies of hagiography, nevertheless diverge from those strategies in decisive ways. In the past, there has been a wealth of controversy—especially in German scholarship—about the specific character of mystical Lives and their value as historical sources. On the one hand, it has been argued that such Lives are based on hagiographic models and are primarily—some would even say exclusively—mystagogy in the form of legends.[1] This opinion is

---

[1] This position is most clearly formulated by Siegfried Ringler, *Viten- und Offenbarungsliteratur in Frauenklöstern des Mittelalters: Quellen und Studien*, Münchener Texte und Untersuchungen zur deutschen Literatur des Mittelalters, 72 (München: Artemis, 1980) and Ringler, 'Die Rezeption mittelalterlicher Frauenmystik als wissenschaftliches Problem, dargestellt am Werk der Christine Ebner', in *Frauenmystik im Mittelalter*, ed. by Peter Dinzelbacher and Dieter R. Bauer (Ostfildern: Schwabenverlag, 1985), pp. 255–70. A similar approach is taken by Ursula Peters, *Religiöse Erfahrung als literarisches Faktum. Zur Vorgeschichte und Genese frauenmystischer Texte des 14. und 15. Jahrhunderts*, Hermea, n.f. 56 (Tübingen: Niemeyer, 1988); and also by Susanne Bürkle, *Literatur im Kloster. Historische Funktion und rhetorische Legitimation frauenmystischer Texte des 14.*

now dominant within German literary scholarship. At the opposite end of the interpretative spectrum, medieval mystics have recently once again become objects of psychological or medical anamnesis, a procedure popular as early as the 1920s. Whereas a view of mystical literature as a purely literary construction, with an exclusively didactic agenda, seriously limits any effort at historical interpretation of the contents, the other extreme ignores both the immense importance of hagiographic traditions in the stylization and self-stylization of mystics and the narrative strategies employed by the authors, who were, in the German-speaking world, primarily members of the learned clergy.[2] An excellent example of the dilemma that mystical Lives pose for scholarship is the *Vita* of Henry Suso, a work which was quite popular with medieval readers.[3]

Like his Dominican brethren Meister Eckhart and John Tauler, Suso (1295/96–1366) was devoted to writing mystagogical literature in the vernacular as part of his efforts within the *cura monialium*, the pastoral care of the nuns in his order. As a student of Eckhart's, Suso defended his teacher's highly controversial tenets in his early works, but later propagated his own *philosophia spiritualis*. Very little can be said about Suso's life beyond what can be considered historically credible in his writings, and here one must be extremely cautious. It is certain that he was born in Constance and given to the local Dominican convent as a young boy; he studied in Cologne and spent the rest of his life in the monasteries in Constance and Ulm. His large body of writings was assembled shortly before his death into a collection called the *Exemplar*, which begins with the *Vita*.

Jahrhunderts, Bibliotheca Germanica, 38 (Tübingen/Basel: Francke, 1999). See my review in *Zeitschrift für deutsches Altertum und deutsche Literatur*, 130 (2001), pp. 464–69.

[2] Strongly opposed to Ringler's approach is Peter Dinzelbacher, 'Zur Interpretation erlebnismystischer Texte des Mittelalters', in Dinzelbacher, *Mittelalterliche Frauenmystik* (Paderborn: Schöningh, 1993), pp. 304–31 (a revised version of the same article first published in 1988). For a recent review of this controversy within American scholarship see Else Marie Wiberg Pedersen, 'Can God Speak in the Vernacular? On Beatrice of Nazareth's Flemish Exposition of the Love for God', in *The Vernacular Spirit. Essays on Medieval Religious Literature*, ed. by Renate Blumenfeld-Kosinski and others, The New Middle Ages series, 28 (New York: Palgrave 2002), pp. 185–208 (185–87).

[3] See *Heinrich Seuse, Deutsche Schriften*, ed. by Karl Bihlmeyer (Stuttgart: Kolhammer, 1907), pp. 1–195. All quotes are taken from here. For an English translation see Henry Suso, *The Exemplar, with two German Sermons*, ed. and trans. by Frank Tobin (New York: Paulist Press, 1989). Suso's German works are transmitted in more than five hundred medieval manuscripts and eight early prints. The Life belonged to the less popular of his writings, as can be assumed by the comparatively 'small' sum of fifty-five extant manuscripts, most of which do not contain the complete text. It is difficult to arrive at exact numbers for the circulation of the Suso manuscripts since excerpts from his works are to be found in innumerable codices. See Rüdiger Blumrich, 'Die Überlieferung der deutschen Schriften Seuses. Ein Forschungsbericht', in *Heinrich Seuses Philosophia spiritualis. Quellen, Konzept, Formen und Rezeption*, ed. by Blumrich and Philipp Kaiser, Wissensliteratur im Mittelalter, 17 (Wiesbaden: Reichert, 1994), pp. 189–201.

This *Vita* was long considered the first German autobiography, and therefore a historical document of substantial historical authenticity. This is, of course, a highly problematic interpretation. That a pious Dominican friar, for whom humility was *the* cardinal virtue, would conceive an autobiography glorifying his own life is quite unthinkable. But it is also highly unlikely that anyone except Suso could have written the *Vita*: Suso's spiritual daughter, Elsbeth Stagel, has been and is still by some considered to be its author.[4]

In a forthcoming article, Martina Wehrli-Johns suggests an even more unlikely interpretation. She proposes that the *Vita* was a legend actually written by Dominican brethren after Suso's death to create support for Suso's canonization.[5] For a canonization process to be initiated, they would have needed not only a legend in Latin, but also a collection of miracles attributed to the candidate. It needs hardly be said that saints' Lives in the vernacular were totally worthless for any kind of canonization process. Furthermore, the *Vita* did not even succeed in convincing its primary audience of Suso's putative sainthood. In no manuscript of the *Vita* is Suso spontaneously referred to as 'Saint' Henry by an enthusiastic scribe; never, over its entire manuscript tradition, is the *Vita* to be found among saints' Lives.[6] It would also be more than astounding that a *Vita* intended to encourage a cult would have had not Suso as its protagonist but an anonymous Dominican Servant of Eternal Wisdom,[7] who—and this adds to the absurdity of the proposition—is obviously still

---

[4] For a brief review of the authorship controversy see Alois M. Haas, 'Stagel, Elisabeth', in *Die deutsche Literatur des Mittelalters. Verfasserlexikon*, ed. by Kurt Ruh and others, (Berlin: de Gruyter, 1995), IX, cols. 220–23. See also the article by Frank Tobin, 'Henry Suso and Elsbeth Stagel: Was the *Vita* a Cooperative Effort?, in *Gendered Voices. Medieval Saints and Their Interpreters*, ed. by Catherine M. Mooney (Philadelphia: University of Pennsylvania Press, 1999), pp. 118–35. An analysis of gender and power relations in the Life is offered by Ulrike Wiethaus, 'Thieves and Carnivals. Gender in German Dominican Literature of the Fourteenth Century', in *The Vernacular Spirit*, pp. 209–38 (216–22).

[5] Martina Wehrli-Johns, 'Das Exemplar einer Reformschrift der Dominikanerobservanz? Untersuchungen zum Johannesmotiv im *Horologium* und in der *Vita* Heinrich Seuses', in *Predigt im Kontext. Internationales Symposium am Fachbereich Germanistik der Freien Universität Berlin vom 5–8. Dezember 1996*, ed. by Volker Mertens, Hans-Jochen Schiewer and Wolfram Schneider-Lastin (in print).

[6] See Werner Williams-Krapp, 'Kultpflege und literarische Überlieferung. Zur deutschen Hagiographie der Dominikaner im 14. und 15. Jahrhundert', in *'Ist mir getroumet mîn leben?'* *Festschrift für Karl-Ernst Geith zum 65. Geburtstag*, ed. by André Schnyder et al., Göppinger Arbeiten zur älteren Germanistik, 632 (Göppingen: Kümmerle, 1998), pp. 147–73 (168–70).

[7] It is imperative to make this distinction, since Suso's name is never used within the Life. Even though the Life is no longer considered an autobiography in the modern sense, in many publications the protagonist of the Life is still assumed to be Suso himself, as does, for instance, most recently Jeffrey F. Hamburger in two articles in his book *The Visual and the Visionary* (New York: Zone Books, 1998): 'The Use of Images in the Pastoral Care of Nuns: The Case of Henry Suso and the Dominicans', pp. 197–232, and 'Medieval Self-fashioning: Authorship, Authority and Autobiography in Suso's *Exemplar*', pp. 233–78.

alive at the end of the text, whereas in legends, saints or putative saints, of course, never are. No serious evidence supports the notion that the construction and content of the *Vita* could have led to immediate associations with a canonized or putative saint's Life among medieval recipients.[8] How then was the *Vita* to be understood?

Very little in the *Vita* can be taken as support for the assumption that it purports to relate the biography of an individual destined for sainthood.[9] Instead, the text is structured in such a way as to demonstrate an exemplary threefold path to inner perfection, clearly charted out in the prologue. In the first twenty-two chapters of the *Vita*, the Servant leads a life of seclusion within the monastery, with hardly a mention of the *vita activa* required of a Dominican friar. This modern anchorite spends more than ten years meditating and practising brutal forms of asceticism in his cell or in a chapel reserved for him. In contrast, the corresponding figure in Suso's only Latin work, the *Horologium sapientiae*,[10] the *discipulus* studies in Cologne, where he is a pupil of Meister Eckhart, lector of his convent, and involved in pastoral duties and preaching.

In the German *Vita*, it is not until the nineteenth chapter, which relates the beginnings of the second stage of his spiritual development, that other persons play a role in the Servant's *Vita*: they primarily subject him to difficult trials or ask for spiritual counsel, especially the aforementioned Dominican nun Elsbeth Stagel, who is, of course, stylized as the ideal figure for identification by Suso's female audience. She applies and misinterprets the advice given to her by the Servant, only to have his

---

[8] The 'halo' of roses around the Servant's head in some of the Life's illustrations is not to be understood as an attribute of sanctity but as an allegory. The number of roses signifies the number of painful trials still awaiting the Servant (*Deutsche Schriften*, p. 64, lines 5–18, and p. 102, lines 23–25). Therefore Suso does not 'represent himself as a saint' in these images, as suggested by Hamburger, 'Medieval Self-fashioning', p. 240, since he undoubtedly expects the Life's recipients to consult the text when interpreting the images.

[9] Jeffrey Hamburger, 'Medieval Self-fashioning', p. 240, speaks of Suso as 'characterizing himself in terms usually reserved for candidates for canonization'. However, he does not explicate this observation. I see only very few aspects of Suso's self-stylization that could possibly suggest he is encouraging his veneration as a saint. It does not become completely clear how Hamburger defines the hagiographic elements of the Life, since he remarks on p. 278, 'that Suso did not intend to glorify his own person', even though he is supposedly 'bolstering our impression of his sanctity'. Richard Kieckhefer, *Unquiet Souls: Fourteenth Century Saints and their Religious Milieu* (Chicago: Chicago University Press, 1984), p. 6, coined the term 'autohagiography' for texts like the Life. It is, however, not applicable to the *Vita*, because the purported 'hagiographic' elements are simply used too unspecifically as to necessarily provoke allusions to a true saint's life in the medieval reader. This interpretation is substantiated by the manuscript data. Similar terminology is used by Kate Greenspan, 'Autohagiography and Women's Spiritual Autobiography', in *Gender and Text in the Later Middle Ages*, ed. by Jane Chance (Gainesville: University Press of Florida, 1996), pp. 216–36.

[10] *Heinrich Seuses Horologium sapientiae. Erste kritische Aufgabe unter Benutzung der Vorarbeiten von Dominikus Pflanzer*, ed. by Pius Künzle, Spicilegium Friburgense, 23 (Fribourg: Universitätsverlag, 1977).

teachings explained to her in extensive theoretical detail in the final part of the *Vita*.

The concluding section of the *Vita* offers a sophisticated speculative philosophical dialogue between the Servant and Elsbeth on the nature of mystical spirituality. These final chapters clearly demonstrate the great intellectual respect with which the learned friar approached his female audience. Suso, as well as Eckhart and Tauler, did not strive to intimidate their readers with rules and prohibitions, as did their brethren in the fifteenth century, but went to great lengths to direct the mystically inclined onto what they considered the proper path to spiritual perfection, confronting them with philosophical argumentation of great sophistication. All in all, the *Vita* is most certainly an *opus sui generis*.

Works in the fourteenth century dealing with mystical spirituality that were written in the vernacular by men of learning were intended either for mystically inclined nuns or for members of the laity who considered themselves part of a spiritual elite (some calling themselves *Gottesfreunde*). This holds true for the works of Suso, John Tauler and, it can be assumed, for most of Meister Eckhart's writings as well. Suso's *Vita* is clearly aimed at a female monastic readership, an audience that especially in the German-speaking southwest was immensely interested and involved in mystical spirituality. Extreme asceticism was common among these women, for a radical *imitatio* of Christ's passion was in this milieu commonly considered an absolute prerequisite for mystical and paramystical experiences. However, Meister Eckhart and other philosophers, who could accept only the possibility of a highly intellectual form of mysticism, clearly rejected such experiences as wild fantasies and delusions, which would most probably even be damaging to the individual's quest for salvation. Suso, as a devoted student and apologist of Eckhart's teachings, was certainly of the same opinion. Eckhart and Suso saw the highest state of spiritual, i.e., mystical perfection in the state of *bildlosigkeit* (imagelessness). Genuine mystical experiences were for Suso the ones with no images.[11] It has often been pointed out that of the three great Dominican mystagogues, Suso was the most effective in confronting and reconciling mystical theory with mystical practice. If we are to read the *Vita* as a work aimed at educating highly pious, intelligent, and uncommonly educated women in spiritual matters, and intent on convincing them to avoid involvement in senseless, physically self-destructive practices, then every analysis of the *Vita* must focus on the didactic strategies used by Suso and, of course, the spiritual model that he constructs as an exemplary alternative.

The most problematic and misunderstood section of the *Vita* comprises the first eighteen chapters, which tell of the Servant's early years (*anvahenden leben*), in which he brutally castigates his body to the point of seriously endangering his health and even his life. One day, Eternal Wisdom commands him to desist, as he has reached the first level on the road to perfection. Were these chapters conceived as an

---

[11] See Suso's clear stand on the matter in *Deutsche Schriften*, pp. 183, 3–30.

incentive for female readers to imitate the Servant's actions? Just the opposite is the case. In the Servant's correspondence with Elsbeth in Chapter 35, he quite clearly demands that she abstain from any forms of such behaviour, on the grounds that women are too frail for such harsh practices. Penitential practices may be necessary in order to free us from earthly comforts and desires, but they must be undertaken with moderation.

Keeping this position in mind, it appears that Suso designed the first part of the *Vita* to counteract strongly the excessive self-castigation which had become fashionable among Dominican nuns in the southwest; this practice had even become the subject of works written by sisters, who to a certain extent propagated monstrous self-affliction as an almost automatic way of attaining mystical and paranormal experiences. The most radical example of such literature is the *Revelations* of Elsbeth of Oye, a nun in the Dominican monastery of Oetenbach near Zurich. In her 'diary'[12] designed for circulation, Elsbeth tells of horrendous attacks of anxiety and describes gruesome self-destructive practices: she drives a nail-studded crucifix into her flesh and ties it to her body with a belt, she sits endlessly in her rotting habit and does nothing to ward off the worms and maggots gnawing at her flesh, she flagellates herself with a nail-studded whip, etc. As she is experiencing this nightmare, Elsbeth is in contact with Christ, Mary, and John the Evangelist, who actually encourage her to continue with her practices, even though the pain and suffering have become almost unbearable. Elsbeth's writings were widely read in nunneries within Suso's sphere of pastoral influence and were most certainly known to him.

It can therefore hardly be interpreted as a coincidence that in the first part of the *Vita* the Servant practices almost identical forms of violent ascesis: the nail-studded cross strapped to his body, the wounds infested with worms, which he does not combat, the self-flagellation with the hook-studded whip, etc. But I repeat—and this is important—Eternal Wisdom does not encourage the Servant to continue his actions but rather commands him to desist from them. How is this to be understood? The lesson imparted here to an intensely pious man by divine authority is that ascesis can be only a preliminary step on the Servant's road to true mystic spirituality; the lesson is then passed on to the *Vita*'s 'fictional' Elsbeth Stagel with the additional, significant specification that such rigorous ascetic practices are not suitable at all for women. The clear implication is that the type of spirituality described in Elsbeth of Oye's *Revelations* and other works is, for males, limited in value and, for females, simply inappropriate. Thus, rather than a call to emulation, the clear associations with the practices described in Elsbeth's *Revelations* are instead an urging for Suso's

---

[12] Peter Ochsenbein, 'Die Offenbarungen Elsbeths von Oye als Dokument leidensfixierter Mystik', in *Abendländische Mystik im Mittelalter*, ed. by Kurt Ruh (Stuttgart: J. B. Metzler, 1986), pp. 423–42 (p. 425), lists twenty-two manuscripts. An edition is being prepared by Wolfram Schneider-Lastin. See his article 'Das Handexemplar einer mittelalterlichen Autorin. Zur Edition der Offenbarungen Elsbeths von Oye', *Editio*, 8 (1994), 53–70.

female readership to practice moderation instead.[13] In the *Vita* Suso clearly distinguishes between male and female ascetic practices; the self-mutilation practiced by Elsbeth of Oye and the Servant is characterized as distinctly male, and thus inappropriate when engaged in by the former.[14]

Therefore, in my opinion, the first part of the *Vita* is to be read as an analogy to suggesting restrictions on the type of spirituality propagated by Elsbeth of Oye and others. The clear associations to Elsbeth's *Revelations* were designed by Suso to be evident to his female readership, who are requested not to follow Elsbeth's example. In other words, in the *Vita* Suso's narrative strategy aims to counteract what he considers popular and influential narrative with deleterious potential.

Another aspect of the *Vita* that proves very important for the work's interpretation is its stylization, particularly in the first sections, of the Servant as a male Dominican almost exclusively leading a *vita contemplativa* typical of a Dominican nun; this peculiarity is not discussed explicitly in the text. In two important articles on the illustrations conceived by Suso for the *Vita*, the art historian Jeffrey Hamburger[15] has pointed out that 'Suso's feminization of the Servant's role goes as far as to cultivate androgyny' in the images he created to illustrate the 'lower, preliminary stages of the mystical itinerary.'[16] There is, according to Hamburger, an obvious 'blurring of the genders'[17] in the images created by Suso, best preserved in early manuscripts of the *Vita*. The Servant is portrayed at one point in the role of the bride of Christ. Suso appears to feminize the role in order to achieve a maximum of possible identification with the figure of the exemplary Servant within his predominately female audience. German scholarship has sometimes referred to Suso's feminization of the role without, as Hamburger has done, considering the narrative strategies which inspired such stylization. The feminization of the role and the reduction of the Servant's *Vita activa* to a bare minimum are further aspects of the narrative that are designed to optimize the possibilities of the female readership's identification with the Servant.

Taking all that has been said into consideration, it remains to be asked just what Suso was actually propagating as an alternative to the spirituality of Elsbeth of Oye

---

[13] See Werner Williams-Krapp, '*Nucleus totius pefectionis*. Die Altväterspiritualität in der *Vita* Heinrich Seuses', in *Festschrift für Walter Haug und Burghart Wachinger*, I (Tübingen: Niemeyer 1992), pp. 405–21 (p. 418).

[14] The Servant writes to Elsbeth: *Sölich strenges leben und dú bild, von den geseit ist, mugen den menschen nüzz sin, die sich selber ze zart habent und ire widerspenigen natur uf ire ewigen schaden ze mutwilleklich bruchent; daz höret aber dir und dinen glichen nit zu* (pp. 108, 18–21). When Elsbeth castigates herself after having received the aphorisms from the *Vitaspatrum* the Servant writes that she should neither imitate the anchorites nor her spiritual mentor, i.e., the Servant (pp. 107, 13–14). In other words, she should embrace a form of spirituality that is appropriate to the *sexus fragilis*.

[15] Hamburger, 'Images' and 'Medieval Self-fashioning'.

[16] Hamburger, 'Images' and 'Medieval Self-fashioning', p. 202.

[17] Hamburger, 'Images' and 'Medieval Self-Fashioning', p. 249.

and others of a similar conviction. In an article published in 1992, I documented the great extent to which Suso in his *Vita* supported the rediscovery of a fundamental work of Christian literature, which he considered to contain the *nucleus totius perfectionis*: the *Vitae patrum* or, as they are more commonly called, *Vitaspatrum*, including their major Western interpretation in the works of Cassian.[18] Suso devotes an entire chapter of the *Horologium* to the *Vitaspatrum* and their importance for the personal road of the *discipulus* to spiritual perfection. The Desert Father Arsenius is praised there as the *summus philosophus*, the most important philosopher of Christendom, who teaches the *discipulus* the decisive lessons for spiritual growth. An intense scrutiny of the *Vitaspatrum* even leads the *discipulus* to sharply criticize the way in which theology was taught in the Dominican *studium generale* in Cologne. Because the *Vitaspatrum* were being neglected, the road to true *sapientia* had been completely obscured for his teachers and fellow students. The *discipulus* leaves the *studium* in order to live according to the tenets of Arsenius, vehemently berating his brethren's concentration on *scientia*.

The *Vita* similarly stresses the spirituality of the *Vitaspatrum* as interpreted by the Servant. Throughout the *Vita*, Suso demonstrates how the teachings of the *Vitaspatrum* can be applied to a modern devout life, especially in the initial stages of spiritual development. Without a doubt the hagiographic model for Suso's *Vita* is to be found in the lives of the Desert Fathers and Mothers, which, by the way, had been translated into German in the first half of the fourteenth century and had circulated in Suso's immediate sphere of influence before he began his work on the *Vita*.[19] The Servant spends his early life as a virtual hermit, practicing asceticism until he reaches a level of spiritual perfection that allows him to become a spiritual mentor for others. This reminds one, for instance, of the life of Saint Anthony the Great, whose *Vita* is also divided into three distinct parts, the last one also consisting of, just as in Suso's *Vita*, an extensive discussion of the prerequisites for spiritual perfection, which Anthony passes on to his questioning students.

In every stage of the Servant's spiritual development, the *Vitaspatrum* play a decisive role. In the first part, the Servant's radical devotion to a Christocentric piety is precipitated by his reading of the *Vitaspatrum*. Suso tells how the Servant once engraved the abbreviation for the name Jesus, IHS, on his chest right above his heart. He then fell asleep with a copy of the *Vitaspatrum* as his only pillow. In a dream he saw a gem-studded crucifix on his chest whose brightness shone through his cowl. The decision for an unconditional *imitatio Christi* is motivated by the exempla provided in the *Vitaspatrum*. After a life of ascesis, a physically impressive young man comes to him in a vision, saying that the Servant had been long enough in the

---

[18] Williams-Krapp, '*Nucleus*'. The influence of the *Vitaspatrum* on Suso's *philosophia spiritualis* and on the Life is extensively documented in that article. Therefore I shall not repeat that documentation as well as my evaluation of previous scholarship here.

[19] Ulla Williams, *Die Alemannischen 'Vitaspatrum'. Untersuchungen und Edition*, Texte und Texgeschichte, 45 (Tübingen: Niemeyer, 1996).

'lower schools' and offering to lead him to a higher spiritual plateau, the 'highest school'. They go to a place where he is taught the way to *gelâzenheit* (complete self-abandonment, surrender of all earthly attachments) by the 'highest master', who in the *Vita* remains unnamed, but in a similar episode in the *Horologium* is identified as the Desert Father Arsenius.

The more difficult, second stage of spiritual development then begins. The Servant becomes a hermit within the monastery, meditating and praying in a chapel reserved for him. He has the chapel walls decorated with images of the Desert Fathers and aphorisms taken from the *Vitaspatrum*. When the artist becomes nearly blind, he is healed by the Servant's first placing his fingers on the images and then touching the artist's eyes. It is clearly not the Servant himself but the sanctity of the Desert Fathers that is responsible for the miraculous cure. Therefore, the miracle is not meant to support 'our impression of Suso's sanctity' and at the same time 'amplify the moral and didactic justification of images', as Jeffrey Hamburger proposes,[20] but is to be read as an exemplum in praise of the truly enlightening teachings of the Desert Fathers, which possess the potential to cure our spiritual blindness, so that we may find the true path to perfection.

In this chapel horrible demons tempt the Servant, just as they did the anchorites. He refuses to bathe, prays incessantly, sleeps in a sitting position, etc., all practices that are characteristic of the ascesis of the Desert Fathers. As in the case of the anchorites, the Servant refuses food and drink for long periods, and like Hilarion, he avoids fruit, especially apples. As is described by Cassian, the Servant despairs, doubts God's grace, and is tortured by *acedia*.

But the analogies to the *Vitaspatrum* go far deeper. Suso even adapts entire episodes from the *Vitaspatrum* in the *Vita* to illustrate aspects of the Servant's spiritual development. Here we can consider two examples. In the first, Suso tells of how the Servant's sister deserts the convent after falling into bad company, whereupon the Servant goes to retrieve her. When he finds her, she falls upon her knees and begs for forgiveness. The emotional scene ends with her return to the monastery, where she then lives a pious life until her death. A similar episode can be found in the *Vitaspatrum*, where a monk searches for his sister who has fallen into sin. She too falls to her knees in front of him and begs God and him to forgive her.[21]

In another episode in the *Vita*, a woman who has become pregnant out of wedlock accuses the Servant publicly of having fathered the child. As a result the Servant is ostracized and reviled by all, causing him immense inner torment. However, the woman suddenly dies, which is, of course, interpreted as a sign from God that the Servant is innocent. He is once again accepted by society. Something similar is reported of the Desert Father Macharius. He also was unjustly accused by a woman, ostracized and even publicly denounced. God, however, came to his aid: The woman

---

[20] Hamburger, 'Images' and 'Medieval Self-Fashioning' p. 207.

[21] Williams-Krapp, '*Nucleus*', p. 415.

could bear her child only after the truth had been established.[22]

In my German article, I cite a number of further episodes in the *Vita* which are obviously based on the *Vitaspatrum* and most likely had no basis in Suso's biography, as has often been assumed. These episodes are, like all episodes of the *Vita*, unmistakably didactic in nature. For example, the false accusations which the Servant and Macharius willingly endure are related in order to teach us to bear our fate patiently, even if society—which, for the sisters whom Suso addresses, would be the other sisters of the nunnery—has falsely condemned us, because we will inevitably be vindicated by God, now or in the future.

Once again we see that the *Vita* teaches lessons that apply to the experiences of men and women alike. Even if the *exempla* are presented within the framework of a male 'biography', the exemplary nature of the Servant's thoughts and deeds allow immediate possibilities of identification for a female audience. Suso reduces the life of the Servant to a generic pattern, a 'true path' that others can follow.[23] In Elsbeth Stagel's misunderstanding of proper female ascesis, mentioned above, it is a misinterpretation of the *Vitaspatrum* that is at the basis of this near catastrophe. Elsbeth had asked the Servant about the guidelines which had been most rewarding for his spiritual development, whereupon he sent her teachings from the *Vitaspatrum*, which she selectively and overzealously adapted to her life. Elsbeth had focused only on the radical asceticism of the anchorites. Drawing on the ideals of Cassian, the Servant distinguishes between the respective ways in which males and females should interpret and imitate the spirituality of the Desert Fathers and Mothers.[24] This interpretation of what is acceptable ascesis for women belongs to the fundamental teachings of the *Vita*.

That the Servant's life is basically stylized as the life of a modern Desert Father is due not only to Suso's great personal devotion to the *Vitaspatrum* but also to the immense importance of the *Vitaspatrum* and Cassian for the entire monastic movement. They are prescribed reading in Benedict's rule, and they were also of great importance to Dominic as he conceived his order. The Dominicans considered the anchorites their spiritual forefathers.[25] Suso is therefore only revitalizing the original concepts of monastic life as set down in this fundamental body of literature, which he considers to have been flagrantly neglected by the monastic orders of his time.

Modern scholarship sometimes misinterprets the *Vitaspatrum* in ways similar to Elsbeth Stagel. The Desert Fathers and Mothers did not propagate bloody ascesis, as

---

[22] Williams-Krapp, '*Nucleus*'. p. 415.

[23] Hamburger, 'Medieval Self-fashioning', p. 278.

[24] There are, of course, other important aspects to the stylization of the Servant; see the excellent article by Walter Blank, 'Heinrich Seuses *Vita*: Literarische Gestaltung und pastorale Funktion', *Zeitschrift für deutsches Altertum und deutsche Literatur*, 122 (1993), 285–311. However, the stylization of the Servant as a modern anchorite clearly dominates.

[25] Williams-Krapp, '*Nucleus*', p. 410.

about female mystics, whose message he definitely considered to be very problematic. He confronts this popular literature with a narrative that, on the one hand, draws upon the extreme religious enthusiasm of his readers but, on the other, presents guidelines for pious behavior that subtly discourage deviance from orthodoxy. That wild hallucinations achieved through rigorous asceticism are not to be understood as the consummation of spiritual perfection, and mystical union is communicated in the *Vita* through Suso's clear analogies to the Desert Fathers and Mothers. When, in the aforementioned vision in Chapter 20, Arsenius meets the Servant, who has mortified his flesh for many years and now wishes to enter the 'highest school', the Supreme Master smiles benignly and points out that he is only at the very beginning of his road to *gelâzenheit*. Suso expected his intellectually sophisticated female readers to understand and embrace this message.

If we are to search for autobiographical elements in Suso's *Vita*, we can be certain that his account of a lifelong preoccupation with the *Vitaspatrum*, a work that was ignored by his learned brethren and often misunderstood by zealous sisters, reveals the authentic Suso. In his construction of a modern-day Desert Father, he also demonstrates how truly edifying literature—and this includes hagiography—can influence life and even change its direction in fundamental ways, naturally in the hope that his *Vita* would lead to similar results for those who were seeking a way to inner perfection, just as he had throughout his life.

Beatrice of Nazareth: The First Woman Author of Mystical Texts[*]

eatrice of Nazareth (1200–68) is considered the first woman who contributed to the vernacular mystical literature of the Middle Ages. She is credited with autobiographical writings, of which only a Latin version has survived, and a beautifully executed treatise on the love for God (*minne*) entitled *The Seven Manners of Love*. Beatrice wrote her works in her native language, Middle Dutch, or more specifically, the Brabant dialect of Middle Dutch. Her role as mystic and author was played out against the background of an outburst of female religiosity in the prince-bishopric of Liège and the duchy of Brabant in the thirteenth century. Both the Cistercian sister orders and the beguines were flourishing at the time. One of the legacies of this period is a considerable corpus of religious literature, to which women themselves contributed in a wide variety of ways.[1]

---

[*] I am grateful to Dini Hogenelst (Leiden) and Geert Warnar (Leiden) for their valuable comments on an earlier version of this article. Only after its completion did the article by Else Marie Wiberg Pedersen become available to me, 'The In-carnation of Beatrice of Nazareth's Theology', in *New Trends in Feminine Spirituality: The Holy Women of Liège and their Impact*, ed. by Juliette Dor, Lesley Johnson and Jocelyn Wogan-Browne, Medieval Women: Texts and Contexts, 2 (Turnhout: Brepols, 1999), pp. 61–79. Pedersen raises a number of questions that I also discuss here. It was not possible to integrate her points completely into my discussion; I do, however, make a few references to this article in the notes. The same goes for the important study by Jos Huls, *Seuen maniren van minnen van Beatrijs van Nazareth: het mystieke proces en mystagogische implicaties*, 2 vols (Leuven: Peeters, 2002).

[1] For more detailed information about the life and work of Beatrice see, among others, Kurt Ruh, *Die Geschichte der abendländischen Mystik*, II: *Frauenmystik und Franziskanische Mystik der Frühzeit* (Munich: Beck, 1993), pp. 138–57; Roger DeGanck, *Beatrice of Nazareth and the Thirteenth-century* mulieres religiosae *of the Low Countries*, II: *Beatrice of Nazareth in her Context*. Cistercian Studies Series, 121 (Kalamazoo: Cistercian Publications, 1991) and III: *Towards Unification with God: Beatrice of Nazareth in her Context*. Part 3, Cistercian

The situation in the southern Netherlands was conducive to women such as Beatrice taking up their pens to write about religious issues. They began, we might say, to record 'sacred knowledge' and, by doing so, the knowledge became available for further dissemination.[2] That this constituted a break with tradition goes almost without saying. Theology, and thus also religious literature, was traditionally the domain of schooled male clerics, and that did not change. Yet in the thirteenth century religious women took their place on the stage of religious literature, a new phenomenon in the cultural history of Europe. This fact gives rise to several questions. What motivated intellectually and mystically gifted nuns to begin writing about their spiritual experiences? Did they have to deal with clerics who wished to control or correct them theologically or who rather attempted to inspire them? And how did the literary works of these women come to be preserved as part of the tradition, a domain that was of course completely in the hands of clerics?

In this article I will take the figure of Beatrice of Nazareth and her mystical oeuvre as the point of departure to further explore these issues. Discussion will first be devoted to the two texts that are directly related to the life and work of Beatrice: the *Vita Beatricis* and *The Seven Manners of Love* are the most important sources for answering our questions. My focus will be primarily on issues of literary history and philology that have moved somewhat to the background in recent Beatrice research.[3] In addition I will use this opportunity to acquaint an English-speaking public with some worthwhile insights that have recently been published in Dutch.

The Vita Beatricis

Almost everything we know about Beatrice of Nazareth we owe to the *Vita Beatricis*, which provides a detailed description of her life.[4] This hagiographical text

---

Studies Series, 122 (Kalamazoo: Cistercian Publications, 1991); Bernard McGinn, *The Presence of God: A History of Western Christian Mysticism*, III: *The Flowering of Mysticism: Men and Women in the New Mysticism 1200–1350* (New York: Herder-Crossroad, 1998), pp. 166–74.

[2] For my purposes here it is not necessary to give a precise definition of 'sacred knowledge'. I use this term as a working concept to designate the totality of theological and religious knowledge and wisdom which women had at their disposal as a result of study, exchanges amongst themselves, their own experience, and revelation.

[3] For an overview see Gertrud Jaron Lewis, *Bibliographie zur deutschen Frauenmystik des Mittelalters*. Mit einem Anhang zur Beatrijs van Nazareth und Hadewijch von Frank Willaert und Marie-José Govers. Bibliographien zur deutschen Literatur des Mittelalters (Berlin: Erich Schmidt, 1989), pp. 325–50. A number of more recent publications will be mentioned in the course of this article.

[4] *Vita Beatricis: De autobiografie van de Z. Beatrijs van Tienen O .Cist. 1200–1268. In de Latijnse bewerking van de anonieme biechtvader der abdij van Nazareth te Lier*, ed. by Léonce Reypens (Antwerp: Ruusbroecgenootschap, 1964). English translation by Roger

must have been written shortly after her death in 1268 and was apparently commissioned by the abbess of Nazareth. The author remains anonymous: he identifies himself modestly as a 'brother and fellow servant' (Chapter 1). Owing to a note in the oldest manuscript, the *Vita Beatricis* was long considered the work of William of Affligem, abbot of the Benedictine abbey at Sint-Truiden. This attribution is no longer considered accurate.[5] A likely guess is that the author of the *Vita Beatricis* had a pastoral function in Nazareth, but he gives too little information about himself for this to be stated with certainty. We do know that his native language was Dutch, as his Latin contains a good many Dutch features.[6]

The author emphasizes that he has no experience with writing saints' Lives (Chapter 5) but considers himself well-read in that genre. He refers directly to the Life of Ida of Nivelles (d. 1231), a friend of Beatrice, whose life story was also recorded by an anonymous hagiographer (Chapter 50). The composition of the *Vita Beatricis* was inspired by the Life of Lutgart of Tongeren authored by Thomas of Cantimpré, the Dominican who wrote no less than four Lives of Brabantine religious women. Like the *Vita Lutgardis*, Beatrice's life story is divided into three books, which describe successively the *status inchoantium*, the *status proficientium*, and the *status perfectionis*.[7] The *Vita Beatricis* owes a great deal to the literary tradition of female Lives that came to flourish in Liège and Brabant.[8]

The first book of the *Vita Beatricis* describes in considerable detail the period in which young Beatrice discovered the ways of the convent and opted for the religious life. During her schooling by the Cistercian nuns of La Ramée, Ida of Nivelles predicted that the grace of God would become active in her. A short time later that prediction was confirmed by an overwhelming vision (Chapters 49–59). After a period of serious doubt, Beatrice finally made a conscious choice to live as a nun in a convent of Cistercian sisters. The second book relates how Beatrice diligently

---

DeGanck, *Beatrice of Nazareth and the thirteenth-century* mulieres religiosae *of the Low Countries*, I: *The Life of Beatrice of Nazareth: A Thirteenth-century Biography*. Cistercian Studies Series, 50 (Kalamazoo: Cistercian Publications, 1991) and in Dutch: *Hoezeer heeft God mij bemind: Beatrijs van Nazareth 1200–1268*, trans. by Herman W. J. Vekeman (Kampen: Kok and Averbode: Altiora, 1995). I refer in my text only to the chapters of the *Vita Beatricis*; the few passages quoted to illustrate important points are included in the notes.

[5] Reypens, *Vita Beatricis*, pp. 26*–31* already maintained that William of Affligem could not possibly be the author of the *Vita Beatricis*; compare DeGanck, *The Life of Beatrice*, I, p. xxii. A detailed treatment of this erroneous attribution can be found in Guido Hendrix, *Ontmoetingen met Lutgart van Tongeren*, IV: *Het Kopenhaagse leven van Lutgart* (Leuven: Bibliotheek van de Faculteit Godgeleerdheid, 1997). Compare also note 48.

[6] On the quality of the Latin see DeGanck, *The Life of Beatrice*, I, pp. xxvi–xxvii.

[7] Compare Ruh, *Die Geschichte der abendländischen Mystik*, II , pp. 138–40.

[8] On this type of literature see, for example, Ruh, pp. 81–110; McGinn, *The Presence of God*, pp. 153–98 and Susanne Bürkle, *Literatur im Kloster: Historische Funktion und rhetorische Legitimation frauenmystischer Texte des 14. Jahrhunderts* (Tübingen-Basel: Francke, 1998), pp. 193–214.

worked at perfecting her pious life. The focus here is mainly on her spiritual exercises. Finally, the third book deals with the state of perfection. With some regret the hagiographer notes that he can report no miracles worked by Beatrice. Her saintliness is evident, however, from a few heavenly visions she was privileged to receive but especially from the deep love she showed to her fellow human beings. In a kind of supplement following the three books the author makes detailed observations on Beatrice and the seven manners of love. This will be discussed in greater detail in the following section.

What is unusual about the *Vita Beatricis* is that the protagonist herself provided the written basis for her life story.[9] The hagiographer refers in the prologue (Chapter 4) to the vernacular material written by Beatrice which he used for his Life. He considers himself no more than a translator and gives Beatrice full credit of authorship.[10] While it is true, he states, that he made a few additions himself and at some points introduced a different formulation, his main task was to give the Middle Dutch text the 'colouring' of Latin.[11] Earlier scholars hardly saw this as a problem. Léonce Reypens, who published the *Vita Beatricis,* simply calls the text 'the Latin version of the autobiography of Beatrice of Nazareth.'[12] The situation is definitely more complicated than this, however.

---

[9] A question still largely unanswered is how the other authors of the Liège–Brabant Lives came by their material, especially when it was a matter of describing visions or other aspects of the sisters' inner spiritual life. I am thinking here of the 'bridge vision' of Ida of Nivelles, for example, which has ties to existing literary traditions, see Peter Dinzelbacher, 'Ida von Nijvel's Brückenvision', *Ons geestelijk erf,* 52 (1978), 179–94. How could a hagiographer know the content of such visions? Were there perhaps more saintly women who, like Beatrice, kept autobiographical notes and/or wrote down their visions? Were there oral traditions in the Cistercian convents relating to visions and other ecstatic experiences? Or was it usually the hagiographers who determined the final literary form in which such visions were recorded? In some instances confession reports probably played an important role, as in the case of Yvette of Huy. Her life story was written by Hugh of Floreffe by order of his abbot, John of Floreffe, who had been Yvette's confessor and consequently could provide a great deal of information about her spiritual life. Compare *The Life of Yvette of Huy by Hugh of Floreffe*, trans. by Jo Ann McNamara (Toronto: Peregrina Publishing, 2000). In the case of Juliana of Cornillon it was a woman friend, probably the anchoress Eve of St Martin, who left notes in French about the prioress. Compare *The Life of Juliana of Mont-Cornillon*, trans. by Barbara Newman (3rd printing, Toronto: Peregrina Publishing, 1999).

[10] A comparison with the Life of Juliana of Cornillon suggests itself here (see note 9). The anonymous author of this work makes use of notes in French made by Juliana's spiritual friend.

[11] *Vita Beatricis*, lines 32–34: '[…] me solum huius operis translatorem existere non auctorem; quippe qui de meo parum addidi vel mutaui; sed, prout in cedulis suscepi oblata verba uulgaria latino "tantum" eloquio coloraui'.

[12] *Vita Beatricis*, title page; compare pp. 40*–42* on the presumed relation between the original and the translation. DeGanck, *The Life of Beatrice*, I, pp. xxv–xxvii is also of the opinion that the hagiographer did not in the last analysis corrupt Beatrice's original work. Compare Wiberg Pedersen, 'The In-carnation', pp. 63–67.

There can be no doubt that the author of the *Vita Beatricis* influenced the text more than the use of the word *translator*[*em*] in the prologue suggests. In the first place he is the one who places Beatrice's life story in hagiographic perspective. It is hardly imaginable that Beatrice herself would have kept notes about her life from that perspective right from the start. The epilogue also makes it clear that the author took considerable liberties with the content. He reveals there that he had to leave out many of Beatrice's deep observations on the love for God and one's fellow human beings. This topic, he believes, is too far above the heads of his public, the sisters of Nazareth. Unlike Beatrice, most of them were not accustomed to dealing with books and therefore would not appreciate deep thoughts of this kind (Chapters 275–76). Here it becomes evident that the *Vita Beatricis* was consciously tailored for a specific target group.

Recently it has also been shown that the author of the *Vita Beatricis* added material that was not part of Beatrice's literary legacy. Roger DeGanck points out that the passages about bodily asceticism in the *Vita Beatricis* were taken from the first book of the *Vita Arnulfi*. The lay brother Arnulf (1180–1228) from the Cistercian abbey Villers-en-Brabant was known, according to his Life at least, for his zeal in physical self-castigation.[13] Apparently the author of the *Vita Beatricis* was of the opinion that this type of extreme mortification of the body should not be lacking in the Life of Beatrice, possibly with an eye to his public. The thirteenth-century clerics who wrote Lives of religious women and lay persons seem to have placed considerable emphasis on physical exercises. From the point of view of the educated, bodily asceticism was an especially effective means to bring about the sanctification of those who were uneducated. They themselves, as *litterati*, could achieve the same goal by an intensive study of the Bible and theology.[14] Another possible reason for the addition of passages from the *Vita Arnulfi* to the *Vita*

---

[13] DeGanck, *The Life of Beatrice*, I, p. x, note 4. The *Vita Arnulfi* originated a few years before 1236; compare. Simone Roisin, *L'hagiographie cistercienne dans le diocèse de Liège au XIIIᵉ siècle*. Université de Louvain: Recueil de Travaux d'Histoire et de Philologie 3ᵉ Série, 27ᵉ Fascicule, 33 (Louvain-Bruxelles: Bibliothèque de l'Université/Editions Universitaires. Les Presses de Belgique, 1947). The Lives of the lay brothers Arnulf and Abundus of Villers (as well as the Life of Ida of Nivelles) are translated by Martinus Cawley in *Send Me God* (Turnhout: Brepols, 2003).

[14] See Amy Hollywood, *The Soul as Virgin Wife: Mechthild of Magdeburg, Marguerite Porete and Meister Eckhardt* (Notre Dame: University of Notre Dame Press, 1995), pp. 29–30, Katrien Heene, 'Ad sanguinem effusionem: Automutilatie en gender in middeleeuwse heiligenlevens', *Queeste*, 6 (1999), 1–22 (two very similar passages are printed on page 1) and Wiberg Pedersen, 'The In-carnation'. It seems that the male authors of Lives did not quite know how to deal with the inner side of the female religiosity they observed and that for this reason they concentrate on visible outer signals such as exceptional ascetic practices. Compare Karin Glente, 'Mystikerinnenviten aus männlicher und weiblicher Sicht: Ein Vergleich zwischen Thomas von Cantimpré und Katherina von Unterlinden', in *Religiöse Frauenbewegung und mystische Frömmigkeit im Mittelalter*, ed. by Peter Dinzelbacher and Dieter R. Bauer (Cologne-Vienna: Böhlau, 1988), pp. 251–64.

Beatricis is that they were intended as a gesture of the author toward his unlettered public.

A scholar interested in the historical Beatrice of Nazareth therefore finds himself in a tantalizing situation: the Latin *Vita Beatricis* offers us a picture of her based on her own writings, but the contours are blurred by the steamed-up window of hagiography. Ursula Peters has even gone so far as to cast doubt on the very existence of autobiographical notes by Beatrice of Nazareth. Her hagiographer, she maintains, only referred to them in order to lend credibility to his story.[15] That, to my mind, goes too far. More than once the hagiographer makes explicit mention of Beatrice's 'book'.[16] If we are to doubt the existence of such a book, we could just as well wonder if there was indeed such a person as Beatrice. It is important to realize, however, that the author of the *Vita Beatricis* brought his influence to bear on various levels (style, composition, content). He is the author of this text, and not Beatrice of Nazareth.

The Seven Manners of Love

Beatrice of Nazareth owes her fame as a mystical author not to her lost writings but to the short Middle Dutch treatise *The Seven Manners of Love*.[17] This text describes

---

[15] Ursula Peters, *Religiöse Erfahrung als literarisches Faktum: Zur Vorgeschichte und Genese frauenmystischer Texte des 13. und 14. Jahrhunderts*, Hermaea. Germanistische Forschungen. n.f. 56 (Tübingen: Max Niemeyer, 1988), pp. 32–33.

[16] *Vita Beatricis*, col. 233: *eius libro*; col. 276: *in libro suo*; he also alludes occasionally to its material state, see col. 4: *in cedulis*. The medieval Latin *schedula* can denote both a loose page or document and a book or codex, compare J. F. Niermeyer, *Mediae Latinitatis Lexicon Minus* (Leiden: Brill, 1976), p. 945. Compare Wiberg Pedersen, 'The In-carnation', p. 64.

[17] I have opted for this neutral translation; compare DeGanck, *The Life of Beatrice*, I, p. 289: *The Seven Manners of Holy Love*. Ritamary Bradley, 'Beatrice of Nazareth (*c*. 1200–1268): A Search for her True Spirituality', in *Vox Mystica: Essays on Medieval Mysticism in Honor of Professor Valerie M. Lagorio*, ed. by Ann Clark Bartlett and others (Cambridge: Brewer, 1995), pp. 57–74 translates *manieren* with *experiences*, which seems to me to be an interpretation. Amy Hollywood, 'Inside out: Beatrice of Nazareth and Her Hagiographer', in: *Gendered Voices: Medieval Saints and Their Interpreters*, ed. by Catherine M. Mooney (Philadelphia: University of Pennsylvania Press, 1999), pp. 78–98 erroneously translates the phrase as *Seven manners of loving (God); minnen*, it should be noted, is a declined substantive and not an infinitive. The most important Middle Dutch editions are: Beatrijs van Nazareth, *Seven manieren van minne*, ed. by Léonce Reypens and Joseph van Mierlo (Leuven: S. V. De Vlaamsche Boekenhalle, 1926) (from manuscript B, with the variants from H and W); Beatrijs van Nazareth, *Van seuen manieren van heileger minnen*, ed. by Herman W. J. Vekeman and Jacques J. Th. M. Tersteeg. Klassiek letterkundig pantheon (Zutphen: Thieme, 1970), (from manuscript B); *De Limburgsche sermoenen*, ed. by J. H. Kern (Leiden: A. W. Sijthoff, 1895), pp. 570–82 (from manuscript H, as *Limburgs sermoen*, 42); Huls, '*Van seuen maniren*', I, 72–119 offers a transcription of manuscript H and cites all three manuscripts when dealing with the seven manners of love separately. English translations in Edmund Colledge, *Medieval*

the seven ways in which *minne* intervenes in the life of the soul that seeks God. The text does not offer a step-by-step scheme for a mystical ascent. Rather, *The Seven Manners of Love* provides an overview of the different manifestations of *minne* as they can appear side by side and in mixed forms. The treatise is still impressive for the clear and pleasing style with which it captures moments not only of spiritual ecstasy but also of physical sensations and the sense of being forsaken by God, moments characteristic of the life of *minne*.[18]

Only three manuscripts containing the entire Middle Dutch text of *The Seven Manners of Love* are known to us:[19]

> H: The Hague, Koninklijke Bibliotheek, 70 E 5, fol. 190^v–197^r
> B: Brussels, Koninklijke Bibliotheek, 3067–3073, fol. 25^r–40^v
> W: Vienna, Österreichische Nationalbibliothek, 15.258, fol. 252^r–271^v.

The Brussels miscellany was long considered to be the oldest textual evidence. *The Seven Manners of Love* is included in the second part, which is dated around 1350. More recently, however, it has become clear that the manuscript in The Hague very likely dates from the late thirteenth century.[20] Moreover, stemma research reveals that H must be based on an older source.[21] This means that the Middle Dutch *Seven Manners of Love* can definitely be traced back to some time in the thirteenth century. The third, Vienna manuscript dates from approximately 1450; it is quite closely related to H, sharing with it a number of variants that do not appear in B.

The Seven Manners of Love is anonymous in all three manuscripts. It was the Flemish Jesuit Léonce Reypens who finally attributed the text to Beatrice of Nazareth. In 1923 he called attention to 'a hidden pearl of mysticism', an anonymous treatise with the caption '*Van seven manieren van heiliger minnen*' (Of Seven Manners of Holy Love).[22] Two years later he named Beatrice as its author. While

---

Netherlands Religious Literature (London: Heinemann, 1965), pp. 19–29; DeGanck, *The Life of Beatrice*, I, pp. 289–331 (from the Latin of the *Vita Beatricis* and from the Latin translation of *The Seven Manners of Love*, by Reypens).

[18] Introductions of a more general nature and additional literature can be found in Ruh, *Die Geschichte der abendländischen Mystik*, II, pp. 145–57; and McGinn, *The Presence of God*, pp. 168–74.

[19] More detailed information, unless otherwise indicated, is found in the editions described in note 17.

[20] J. P. Gumbert, 'De datering van het Haagse handschrift van de *Limburgse sermoenen*', in: *Miscellanea neerlandica: Opstellen voor dr. Jan Deschamps ter gelegenheid van zijn zeventigste verjaardag*, ed. by Elly Cockx-Indestege and Frans Hendrickx, 3 vols (Louvain: Peeters, 1987), I, pp. 167–81.

[21] See Kurt Otto Seidel, *Die St. Georgener Predigten: Untersuchungen zur Überlieferungsgeschichte.* (unpublished *Habilitation* thesis, University of Bielefeld, 1994), pp. 228–41.

[22] Léonce Reypens, 'Een verdoken parel der mystiek: De *Seven manieren van heiliger minnen*', *Dietsche Warande & Belfort*, 23 (1923), 717-30.

reading the *Vita Beatricis*, Reypens was struck by the remarkable similarities between the fourteenth chapter of the third book, *De caritate Dei et VII eius gradibus*, and *The Seven Manners of Love*. Because the author of the Life states in the prologue that he is translating writings of Beatrice, Reypens concluded that the passage about the seven manners of love also had to be from her hand. He was supported in this view by Joseph van Mierlo, one of the greatest authorities in the area of Middle Dutch literature. Thus in 1925 Beatrice took her place alongside Hadewijch and Jan van Ruusbroec as a new author of Brabantine mysticism—a timely move, it should be noted, considering the struggle then underway in Belgium for the equal status of Dutch.[23]

This rapid canonization of Beatrice as author of *The Seven Manners of Love* evoked little discussion, although the argumentation of Reypens rests on a rather narrow base. Ursula Peters is the only scholar who has questioned this attribution. Her doubt about the actual existence of autobiographical notes by Beatrice automatically leads to reservations on this point—understandably, considering that Reypens and Van Mierlo based their attribution on the statement found only in the *Vita Beatricis* that Beatrice left behind work of this kind.[24] To my knowledge only Amy Hollywood has attempted to refute Peters. She believes that the similarities between the chapter *De caritate Dei et VII eius gradibus* from the *Vita Beatricis* and *The Seven Manners of Love* are so great that the Latin has to be a translation, or, better, an adaptation of the Middle Dutch treatise.[25]

This does not in any way prove the authorship of Beatrice. In principle it is also possible that the original text is a Latin treatise (and this would almost certainly rule out Beatrice as author) which the author of the *Vita Beatricis* applied to Beatrice's life. Yet this possibility strikes me as less likely because the Middle Dutch text gives a great deal of attention to the literary form. In the seventh manner, considerable use is made of rhyme, assonance, and other stylistic devices.[26] It is unlikely that such effects were specially added to a translation from Latin. These formal characteristics seem rather to suggest the author's search for appropriate words. But this cautious conclusion does not yet resolve the uncertainty surrounding Beatrice's authorship.[27]

---

[23] Léonce Reypens and Joseph van Mierlo, 'Een nieuwe schrijfster uit de eerste helft der dertiende eeuw: De gelukzalige Beatrijs van Nazareth (1200(?)–1268)', *Dietsche Warande & Belfort*, 25 (1925), 352–67.

[24] Peters, *Religiöse Erfahrung als literarisches Faktum*, pp. 32–33.

[25] Hollywood, *The Soul*, p. 29 note 14 and Hollywood, 'Inside Out', p. 221 note 14.

[26] For example: Vekeman and Tersteeg, *Van seuen manieren*, p. 55 lines 542–46: 'In lief ende in leet / so es si te dogene gereet, / in doet ende in leuen / wilt si der minnen plegen, / ende int gevoelen hars herten / dogetsi meneghe smerte,/ ende om der minnen wille / begertsi dat lantscap te gewinne.'

[27] A possible clue could be the clearly female narrative perspective in *The Seven Manners of Love*. But here, too, caution is advised. The subject of the text—which defies precise definition—shifts from 'the soul' to 'the heart' to 'love', all three of which are (or at least can

For the time being the reference to her writings in the prologue of the *Vita* remains the most important argument. But just how reliable and useful is that reference? The chapter about the seven manners falls to a certain extent outside the structure of the three-part *Vita Beatricis*. It is found in a kind of supplement which follows the hagiographer's remark that his source—Beatrice's book—says nothing about the gifts of grace Beatrice received during her priorate (Chapter 233). *The Seven Manners of Love,* with its application of the seven manners to the life of love lived by Beatrice of Nazareth comes at the very end.[28] The hagiographer makes no mention of any involvement on her part in writing the treatise on love.

There are, broadly speaking, three possible explanations for the presence of the treatise about the seven manners in the *Vita Beatricis*. First, the author of the *Vita Beatricis* discovered *The Seven Manners of Love* among the writings of Beatrice after her death and applied the text to her life story. Second, he discovered among the writings of Beatrice after her death a text in which she applied the text of *The Seven Manners of Love* (known to her from some other source) to her own life and translated it. Third, he was acquainted with *The Seven Manners of Love* from some other source and applied the content of the text to the life of Beatrice. For the present I see no way to determine which of these possibilities is most likely.

The underpinning of Beatrice's authorship of *The Seven Manners of Love* is thus less firm than is generally—in the footsteps of Reypens and Van Mierlo—assumed.

---

be) feminine substantives in Middle Dutch. Moreover, this perspective could very well have been used by a male author with an eye to a female public. Instructive on this point is Catherine M. Mooney, 'Voice, Gender and the Portrayal of Sanctity', in *Gendered voices*, ed. by Catherine M. Mooney, pp. 1–15 (especially pp. 11–12).

[28] There are various studies that chart the differences between the Latin and the Middle Dutch versions of *The Seven Manners of Love*, all of them, it should be noted, from the viewpoint that the vernacular text is the older of the two and that Beatrice is the author. Herman Vekeman, '*Vita Beatricis* en *Seuen manieren van minne:* Een vergelijkende studie', *Ons geestelijk erf*, 46 (1972), 3–54 searches the *Vita Beatricis* for biographical facts which can be related to the seven different manners of love; Vekeman, *Hoezeer heeft God mij bemind*, pp. 26–29 compares the *Vita Beatricis* as a whole with *The Seven Manners of Love* and concludes that while the Life touches on christological, Trinitarian, and eucharistic themes, the treatise deals exclusively with *minne*. Recently various attempts have been made to uncover gender differences between the two texts: Else Marie Wiberg Pedersen, 'Image of God—Image of Mary—Image of Woman: On the Theology and Spirituality of Beatrice of Nazareth', *Cistercian Studies Quarterly*, 29 (1994), 209–20; Bradley, 'Beatrice'; Hollywood, *The Soul*, pp. 29–39; Hollywood, 'Inside Out'; Wiberg Pedersen, 'The In-carnation', pp. 68–76. Rob Faesen, 'Mystiek en hagiografie: Hoe benadert de anonieme auteur van de *Vita Beatricis* het verschijnsel mystiek?' *Ons geestelijk erf*, 73 (1999), 97–110 discusses the differences in attitude between Beatrice and her hagiographer with regard to the mystical experience and concludes that the author of the Life, convinced of the genuineness of Beatrice's experiences, enters into discussion with possible critics who would consider the immediate unity of God and man impossible here on earth; compare Rob Faesen, *Begeerte in het werk van Hadewijch*. Antwerpse Studies over Nederlandse Literatuurgeschiedenis, 4 (Leuven: Peeters, 2000), pp. 154–69.

It seems quite certain that the Middle Dutch text was known and read in the immediate surroundings of Beatrice and the Nazareth convent, but whether she was actually the author remains, in my opinion, unsure. Conspicuously lacking in *The Seven Manners of Love* are the visions and other supernatural phenomena that appear in such abundance in women's mystical writings of the thirteenth and fourteenth centuries. Also striking are the mystagogic intention and the relative detachment of this text: other women mystics such as Hadewijch or Mechthild of Magdeburg wrote to a much greater extent out of individual experience and intense personal involvement.[29] If *The Seven Manners of Love* was indeed written by Beatrice, this fine treatise is an exceptional specimen of female writing—not only because of its early date but also in view of its overall intent and tenor.

Keeping Silent or Writing

Why did Beatrice write? The only source that can help us find an answer to this question is the *Vita Beatricis*, for *The Seven Manners of Love* offers no biographical information. It has by now also become clear that a great deal of caution is advised when dealing with the *Life of Beatrice*, even if she did lay the foundation for that work herself. All statements about her life must take into account that whatever is said about Beatrice in the Life was filtered through her hagiographer, who naturally worked in the Latin tradition.

The *Vita Beatricis* devotes a great deal of attention to Beatrice's special skills in the area of learning and literature. She is characterized as an intelligent and sensitive girl, whose talent was noticed at an early age. Her first education she received from her mother. At the age of five she knew the psalms by heart and could recite them in the correct order (Chapter 19). When Beatrice was seven years old her mother died. Her father took her to the beguines of Zoutleeuw, who were given the task of guiding her on the path to virtue (Chapter 20). During this same period Beatrice enjoyed approximately one year of education in the liberal arts, most likely in the municipal school (Chapter 21). At about ten years of age she was given as an oblate to the Cistercian convent Florival, where she obtained an appropriate convent education. We can conclude that Beatrice was exceptionally educated for a medieval girl. She must have learned a considerable amount of Latin, which enabled her to immerse herself in the diligent study of Holy Scripture (Chapter 69 and 86). She could also ponder the essence of the Trinity, thanks to a copy of a text on that topic (Augustine's *De Trinitate*?) that she always carried with her, a text undoubtedly written in Latin (Chapter 214). But in her personal communication with Christ she used her native language, Brabantine Dutch. This we can infer, at any rate, from the report of a vision where it is expressly stated that the Lord confirmed the covenant

---

[29] Compare McGinn, *The Presence of God*, p. 170.

between himself and Beatrice in Latin (Chapter 165). Because it is mentioned explicitly that Latin was used in this case, it can be assumed that in other visions they communicated in the vernacular.

The young Cistercian was not only lettered in the metaphorical sense but also did a great deal of practical work with books. Shortly after Beatrice had made her profession in Florival (1216), she was sent for one year to the Cistercian nuns of Rameia to receive instruction in the art of writing and illuminating books (Chapter 50). Whether she actually wrote many manuscripts in Florival we do not know. But her skills proved useful when in 1236 the Nazareth convent was ready for habitation by a first small group of nuns. The preceding half-year Beatrice, together with her sisters Sybilla and Christina, spent copying books for the new convent (Chapter 230). Subsequently manuscripts were also produced in the young convent of Nazareth, and it is quite likely that Beatrice was involved in this production.

An antiphonary of Nazareth has been preserved dating from 1244/45, the time of Beatrice's priorate. According to a colophon, it was written by a sister Agnes (*scriptrice Agnes*), with the musical notation added by Christina (*notatrice Christina*).[30] The latter was probably Beatrice's sister, who succeeded her as prioress in 1268. The manuscript is illuminated in a remarkable style, for which few parallels have as yet been found. The colophon does not mention the name of the person responsible for the illuminations, possibly because they were added later. It is a fascinating thought that Beatrice of Nazareth could very well have been the illuminator of this manuscript.[31] With her special training in that art in Rameia, she was probably one of the few sisters in the new Nazareth who were able to take on the task.

Clearly, books played an important role in the life of Beatrice of Nazareth, but this was probably true of more Cistercian nuns of her time. The question now is what led Beatrice to become an author. Two events reported in the *Vita Beatricis* appear to be of crucial significance here. The first is the vision that Beatrice received while in Rameia, when she was allowed to look upon the Trinity and fathom the essence of God (Chapter 54–59). At that point she must have already realized that she was specially chosen and that this would have consequences for the attitude she would

[30] MS Bornem, Sint-Bernardsabdij, 1 (According to the catalogue mentioned below the present owner wishes to remain anonymous). See *Manuscrits datés conservés en Belgique*, I, *819–1400* (Brussels-Ghent: Editions scientifiques E. Story-Scientia, 1968), no. 9, pl. 34–36; *750 Jaar abdij van Nazareth: Tentoonstellingscatalogus 29 maart–20 april 1986*, (Lier: Liers Genootschap voor geschiedenis, [1986]), Bijdragen tot de Geschiedenis van de Stad Lier, no. 16, pp. 133–40 and ill. 21–33; Jan Goossens, 'Zur Sprachkultur der *mulieres religiosae*', *Niederdeutsches Jahrbuch*, 5/6 (1994/95), 1–31 (p. 18); Judith Oliver, 'Worship of Word. Some Gothic *Nonnenbücher* in their Devotional Context', in *Women and the Book. Assessing the Visual Evidence*, ed. by Jane H. M. Taylor and Lesley Smith, The British Library Studies in Medieval Culture (London: British Library and Toronto: University of Toronto Press, 1996), pp. 106–122 (pp. 106–107 and ill. 53).

[31] DeGanck, *The Life of Beatrice*, I, frontispiece.

have to assume towards her less privileged sisters. The author of the *Vita Beatricis* devotes considerable attention to this problem and emphasizes in the prologue that Beatrice for the most part remained silent about her life of grace (Chapter 4). A little later he illustrates her dilemma with two verses from Scripture: 'Take heed that you do not do justice before men, to be seen by them' (Matthew 6. 1) and 'So let your light shine before men, that they may see your good works, and glorify your father who is in heaven' (Matthew 5. 16). In the end Beatrice did not hide her light 'under a bushel' (Matthew 5. 15) but to a modest degree informed her fellow sisters of the secrets of her heart (Chapter 6).[32] Beatrice, in other words, shared some of the 'sacred knowledge' she had acquired with her fellow sisters. No doubt most of this sharing took place orally, but her work as a mystical writer may also have its roots here.

We know for certain that Beatrice gained experience writing about her spiritual life at an early stage in her monastic career. This was the second crucial event that set her on the path to authorship. The second book of the *Vita Beatricis* describes how she tried to intensify her contemplative life by means of study and meditation. She began to immerse herself with even greater zeal in Holy Scripture and attempted to fathom its meaning (Chapter 86). In this period the young nun developed the habit of writing down her spiritual exercises as a way to remember them (presumably in Dutch). She began doing this in order to resume meditation at a certain point later on if she was pressed for time (Chapter 89).[33] This writing had an exclusively private function and served as an aid to meditation. Unfortunately her hagiographer does not tell us whether this was a normal practice in Cistercian convents. In the life of Beatrice, in any case, it seems to have been the breakthrough. The following section of the *Vita Beatricis* consists of a number of meditation sketches, many of them based on an allegorical image (e.g. 'the convent of the soul', Chapters 111–15), which have a direct bearing on Beatrice's spiritual life. Here it seems we can almost look over the shoulder of the hagiographer into her 'book': Beatrice's own hand cannot be far removed from these sketches.[34]

---

[32] *Vita Beatricis*, p. 15 lines 66–72: 'Huius vtriusque dominici precepti superficialem discordantiam sic in vnam obeditionis sententiam concordauit, vt et hostis antiqui versuitias, secretum suum intra se vigilanter occultando, deluderet, et rursus illud in palam opportuno tempore proferendo, proximorum necessitatibus erogaret. Sicque, diuina disponente clementia, factum est vt lucerna, diu latens sub modio, tanto postea, revelata luce, clarius eniteret in publico: quanto studiosus ad lucendum iam diu preparata fuerat in occulto.'

[33] *Vita Beatricis*, p. 69, lines 39–70 (line 46): 'At quoniam, vt prediximus, ad vacandum singulis, impediente temporis dumtaxat indigentia, prout oportunum fuerat intendere non valebat, ex "illarum qualibet" vnum, quem magis sibi proficuum existimabat, articulum eligens, vt a memoria non excideret, in scriptis hunc redigere consuescebat: et post "hoc" a, in adiutorium inuocata diuina clementia, per singulos temporis portionem partita, nunc hos nunc illos oportunis meditationibus exercebat.'

[34] Compare Ruh, *Die Geschichte der abendländischen Mystik*, II, p. 140. G. Epiney-Burgard and E. Zum Brunn, *Femmes Troubadours de Dieu*. Témoins de notre histoire

It nevertheless remains very difficult to obtain a clear picture of the sort of writings that Beatrice left in Nazareth after her death and that served the author of the *Vita Beatricis* as sources. There are basically two possibilities, which soon become obvious if we consider the ideas of various Beatrice scholars.[35] Either Beatrice kept a kind of personal diary solely for her own use, or she wrote a sort of spiritual autobiography with a certain group of readers in mind.[36] It cannot be ruled out, that in one form or another she worked in both genres. That Beatrice took personal notes for the sake of her prayer life need not be doubted; on this point the *Vita Beatricis* is, as we have seen, absolutely clear. It is certainly possible that notes of this kind served as a source for her hagiographer.

Beatrice would gain greater stature as an author if she did indeed write some form of autobiography. My distinct impression is that there are some indications that she did so. In the first place there is an enormous amount of information about Beatrice's inner life included in the *Vita Beatricis*, and what stands out is that much of it is accompanied by fairly exact indications of time. The statement that she made good progress every day for seven years in the area of study (Chapter 69) or that she concentrated intensely for five years on the passion (Chapter 72) could be interpreted as play with significant numbers. But this cannot be true of the conclusion that Beatrice experienced for approximately one year a state of grace that filled her with gladness and jubilation (Chapter 74–75). Beatrice seems to have written this down

---

(Turnhout: Brepols, 1988), p. 102, nevertheless simply state that the allegorical parts of the *Vita Beatricis* are taken from the Cistercian tradition and therefore cannot be credited to Beatrice. As far as 'the convent of the soul' is concerned, this observation seems to be correct. The content of that sketch is related to the widespread monastic tradition of *Claustrum animae*; see Gerhard Bauer, *Claustrum animae: Untersuchungen zur Geschichte der Metapher vom Herzen als Kloster*, I: *Entstehungsgeschichte* (Munich: Wilhelm Fink, 1973): the tradition of *In claustro animae deus debet esse abbas* discussed on pp. 309–35 is reminiscent of the passage in the *Vita Beatricis*. Beatrice probably used familiar images, drawn either from written or other sources, which she then worked out for her own purposes.

[35] Reypens, *Vita Beatricis*, pp. 40*–44* speaks of a *liber vitae* (compare Chapter 274, line 19), which he imagines to be a spiritual diary covering the period 1215–36; Vekeman, '*Vita Beatricis*', pp. 1617 says 'her oldest work was probably a combination diary-exercise book'; De Ganck, *The Life of Beatrice*, I, p. xxi leaves it open: 'diary or autobiography'; Ruh, p. 139, maintains: 'It can be imagined as a kind of spiritual diary'; Hollywood, *The Soul*, p. 29 and Hollywood, 'Inside Out', p. 80 uses the term 'autobiographical writings' and places 'book' in quotation marks; McGinn, *The Presence of God* p. 167, refers to a 'spiritual' or 'mystical journal' and associates Beatrice with the tradition of spiritual autobiography initiated by Rupert of Deutz.

[36] It would be highly atypical of the Middle Ages if Beatrice wrote her notes exclusively for herself. A contemporary example is the chronicle of the Frisian monastery of Wittewierum by Abbot Emo (d. 1237), in which Emo inserts a great deal of confessional material about his own spiritual life. Compare *Kroniek van het klooster Bloemhof te Wittewierum*, ed. by Hubertus P. H. Jansen and Anteun Janse. Middeleeuwse studies en bronnen, 20 (Hilversum: Verloren, 1991), pp. xiii–xx.

herself in retrospect, something that cannot easily be reconciled with the loose method of keeping a diary.

Also remarkable is the sparseness of information the hagiographer has to offer about the period of Beatrice's life as prioress in Nazareth (Chapter 233). About the thirty-year period following her priorate there seems to have been no material available.[37] Evidently Beatrice's text did not extend much further than the years 1236 and 1237, when Nazareth was founded and began its life as a convent. We also learn from the *Vita Beatricis* that Beatrice tutored numerous girls from the area during these years and instructed them in observance (Chapter 230). Would it not be possible that at this time she wrote a handbook for convent life based on her own experience of following the spiritual path? The combination of Beatrice's great personal talent, her task as novice mistress, and a new convent's need for a spiritual guideline could well have motivated her to write a spiritual autobiography.[38] If this was indeed the case, it can be assumed that she wrote in Dutch, because most of her fellow sisters presumably will not have known sufficient Latin. Obviously a work of this kind would have provided valuable material for the author of Beatrice's Life.

If Beatrice is also the author of *The Seven Manners of Love*, the picture of an experienced sister giving written instruction to her fellow sisters about the spiritual life becomes a great deal clearer yet. This text, as we have seen, is a well-thought-out introduction to the life of love for God and appears to be written from rich experience. Unfortunately we can offer no more than hypotheses here, as the information given in the *Vita Beatricis* does not allow for firm conclusions. Evidently Beatrice of Nazareth's hagiographer did not consider her authorial activities a subject that deserved particular attention.

Beatrice in the Tradition

The second question raised in the introduction is whether confessors or other clerics played a role in bringing about the writings of Beatrice. The answer to this is brief: nothing in the *Vita Beatricis* indicates a relationship of this kind. In the absence of other sources we must assume that Beatrice very likely did her writing independently. Her case then, early as it is, would support Ursula Peters's hypothesis that most mystical writing by medieval women came about without the mediation of confessors, even if they were regularly mentioned in the texts for purposes of

---

[37] The author of the *Vita Beatricis* includes a few visions which he places in the time of Beatrice's priorate, but Ruh, *Die Geschichte der abendländischen Mystik*, II, pp. 144–45 doubts that they are authentic.

[38] In the years 1451–52 Alijt Bake (d. 1455), prioress of the Galilea convent in Ghent, wrote a work of this kind with the title *Mijn beghin ende voortganck*. See the article in this volume by Anne Bollmann

legitimization.[39]

This does not mean, however, that clerics brought no influence to bear on the literary work of Beatrice. They undoubtedly did, but their influence made itself felt only at a later point. And this brings us to the third question in the introduction: how did the works of Beatrice come to be part of the tradition? The Latin *Vita Beatricis* is all that remains of the Middle Dutch writings of Beatrice of Nazareth. There we know that her own voice is distorted by the hagiographer who immortalized Beatrice's life story in Beatrice's name as the prioress of the convent of Nazareth but we do not know to what extent. The centrality of this problem in studying female mystics of the Middle Ages was demonstrated recently with several case studies in the volume *Gendered Voices*.[40] Nearly all writings about religious women are authored by male clerics, who inevitably colour the picture they evoke with gender-specific ideas about female religiosity. Needless to say, this has left an indelible mark on the entire Liège-Brabant *vitae* tradition, to which the *Vita Beatricis* also belongs.

Besides the immediate gender-specific differences in conceptions of male and female religiosity, gender also played an influential role in a broader context. Only men had access to the status of cleric and the office of priest, and thus to the theological schooling—in Latin, of course—that these entailed. Their exclusive position in this area led them to consider themselves *litterati* and to label those who knew no Latin as unlettered.[41] This category includes not only the ordinary illiterate parishioners but also nuns with considerable learning such as Beatrice of Nazareth. In the transmission of her works it is primarily this opposition that seems to have worked to her disadvantage.

There is something unusual going on in the *Vita Beatricis*. If my reconstruction is correct, the nuns of Nazareth had at their disposal literary work left by Beatrice in the form of a diary, an autobiography, or both. Apparently commissioned by the prioress, the anonymous hagiographer nevertheless wrote a *Vita* of Beatrice in Latin. There, as he himself states, he leaves out much of Beatrice's high-level speculation, because his audience (which included the sisters of Nazareth) generally were not as inclined to take pleasure in books as Beatrice herself had been. What, then, would these apparently unlettered sisters have wanted with a life story of their former prioress in Latin? Would they not have benefited much more from the Middle Dutch of Beatrice herself? Faesen argues that the author of the *Vita Beatricis* also had in mind another audience which he assumed would consist of critically disposed readers.[42] The author of the *Vita Beatricis*, Faesen maintains, defends Beatrice

---

[39] Peters, *Religiöse Erfahrung als literarisches Faktum*, especially pp. 101–88.

[40] *Gendered Voices*; the case of Beatrice of Nazareth is dealt with in this volume by Amy Hollywood, who concentrates on the difference between the Middle Dutch *The Seven Manners of Love* and the Latin version of that text.

[41] See Mooney, *Gendered Voices*, p. 7.

[42] Faesen, 'Mystiek en hagiografie'.

against critics who might have objections to her mystical life.

At no point does our anonymous author cast doubt on the value of Beatrice's way of life, for which her writings formed his primary source of information. He sketches Beatrice as a woman with a marked preference for the study of Holy Scripture. In view of his own estimate of the educational level of Nazareth, Beatrice must have been an exception in this respect. The hagiographer relies heavily on Beatrice's own writings and even identifies her as the *auctor* of the *Vita Beatricis*. This is of course a modesty topos, yet more seems to be intended here. The only substantial contribution he attributes to himself is that he adapted Beatrice's words to the standard applied to Latin religious literature. With all his respect for her and for her learning, he was evidently most bothered by the vernacular form in which Beatrice had expressed herself. There seems to have been a clash between the well-meant attempts of a nun who was in the final analysis unlettered and the literary norms of the Latin-bred clergy. For Beatrice's mystical writing to be admitted to the world of letters, her words had to be moulded in a form familiar to the *litterati*.

The case of Beatrice of Nazareth is not an isolated one. More examples can be found in the Cistercian movement in Brabant. In 1320 John of Sint-Truiden, monk of the famous Cistercian abbey Villers, commissioned the writing of a manuscript that compiled various texts (among them the *Vita Arnulfi*)[43] produced by the mystical tradition of which his monastery formed the centre point. Several abbots of precisely this monastery were praised for their intense involvement with the mystical women's movement.[44] The compilation from Villers also includes the *Vita Beatricis*, in fact the oldest extant text of this work. In addition this codex contains at least two other texts with a more or less similar background. *Verbum Christi ad beginam tungerensem* is a short text in which a young beguine from Tongeren relates what she learned in a dialogue with Christ. She makes use of allegorical images such as 'the house in the heart' and 'the habit as bridal gown'.[45] And under the title *De virgine ordinis Cisterciensis* ten visions of an anonymous Cistercian nun are described in summary form.[46] In both cases these are very likely Latin translations or adaptations of Middle Dutch texts written by women. Apparently here, too, the

---

[43] Brussels, Koninklijke Bibliotheek (KB), MS 4459–70. On this manuscript see *Manuscrits datés conservés en Belgique* 1968 (note 31), pp. 28–29, no. 34, pl. 101–02 and *Jan van Ruusbroec: Tentoonstellingscatalogus. Met als bijlage een chronologische tabel en drie kaarten* (Brussels: Koninklijke Bibliotheek Albert I, 1981), no. 6. This is far from being a fine specimen of a manuscript: it is not clearly ordered but consists of loose quires in varying formats, and the writing was done by a number of different hands. The status of this manuscript was apparently low.

[44] See Simone Roisin, 'L'Efflorescence cistercienne et le courant féminin de piété au XIIIe siècle', *Revue d'Histoire Ecclésiastique*, 39, (1943), 342–78.

[45] Stephanus Axters, 'De anonieme begijn van Tongeren en haar mystieke dialoog', *Ons geestelijk erf*, 15 (1941), 88–97.

[46] Léonce Reypens, 'Nog een dertiende-eeuwse mystieke cisterciënzernon', *Ons geestelijk erf*, 23 (1949), 225–46.

original form was not considered suitable for transmission to the world of letters. It goes almost without saying that the Middle Dutch originals were not preserved.

A prime example of this attitude can also be found in the *Catalogus virorum illustrium*, a catalogue of authors produced in the southern Netherlands at the beginning of the fourteenth century. Here two works are attributed to a certain William, monk of Affligem. His first work is a translation of the Latin *Vita Lutgardis* by Thomas of Cantimpré into Middle Dutch verse. The second, the one of interest to us here, appears to be a Latin translation of the 'wondrous' writings of a Cistercian nun.[47] The question of whether William would perhaps be the ideal candidate for the authorship of the *Vita Beatricis* does not concern us here.[48] The important thing is that here, too, we have evidence of clerical interest in the visions of religious women. That material—the *Catalogus* speaks of *materia*—did not meet the formal requirements set by the Latin-trained clerics either. The lettered William is praised for having turned this highly interesting material into an elegant text.

Conclusion

Even if Beatrice of Nazareth did not compose *The Seven Manners of Love*, she is still the earliest known woman writer of mysticism in the vernacular. We know that long before 1236 she already had at her disposal a quantity of material that sprang directly from the practice of meditation. These writings had a primarily private function and therefore have no direct bearing on the question of 'transmission of knowledge'. I consider it unlikely that Beatrice wrote a more extensive work about her own life of grace after the foundation of Nazareth in 1236. The intention of this text would have been to instruct the new sisters of Nazareth in particular in the way of life oriented toward mystical experience then in vogue in the Cistercian convents of Brabant. If this hypothetical text did indeed exist, Beatrice took an important step

---

[47] N. Häring, 'Die Literaturkatalog von Affligem', *Revue bénédictine*, 80 (1970), 64–96 (p. 95): 'Frater Willemvs monachus Haffligeniensis et ibidem aliquando prior, uitam domine Lutgardis a fratre Thoma Latine scriptam conuertit in Theutonicum ritmice duobus sibi semper ritmis consonantibus. Dictauit etiam Latine quandam materiam satis eleganter de quadam moniali Cisterciensis ordinis que Theutonice multa satis mirabilia scripserat de se ipsa'.

[48] Since Erwin Mantingh, 'De derde man: Op zoek naar Willem van Affligem, de auteur van het *Leven van Lutgart*', in *Op avontuur: Middeleeuwse epiek in de Lage Landen*, ed. by Jozef D. Janssens and others, Nederlandse literatuur en cultuur in de Middeleeuwen, XVIII (Amsterdam: Prometheus, 1998), pp. 159–78 suggested another Willem, monk from Affligem, with literary qualities as the author of *Lutgart*, the discussion about the authorship of the *Vita Beatricis* by Willem van Affligem has, in my view, also been reopened; compare Erwin Mantingh, *Willem van Affligem, het Kopenhaagse Leven van Lutgart en de fictie van een meerdaagse voorlezing*, Middeleeuwse Studies en Bronnen, 73 (Hilversum: Verloren, 2000), pp. 29–71. See also note 4.

forward in the area of the literary transmission of religious ideas by women.

There are scarcely any indications that these initiatives of Beatrice and her fellow female mystics were thwarted by their confessors or other clerics. In fact we get the impression that there were a good many clerics in Brabant who showed an interest in women's piety, with the abbots of Villers leading the way. The numerous women's Lives from Liège-Brabant, however gender-coloured they may be, constitute the most important evidence for this. There was also a certain interest in the writings produced by various religious women in the thirteenth century. Nothing suggests that women like Beatrice or the beguine from Tongeren were not allowed to go their own way in this respect. Yet their works hardly have a place in the tradition, unless in Latin translations behind which the originals remain irretrievably hidden.

I suspect that the most important explanation for this should be traced, not to the opposition of man and woman but to that between lettered and unlettered. Reading the vernacular writings of women like Beatrice must have been an altogether strange experience for clerics, steeped as they were in Latin. Approximately one century after the death of Beatrice, the Cistercians of Ter Doest (near Bruges) asked William Jordaens (d. 1372) whether he would translate *Die geestelike brulocht* of John of Ruusbroec (d. 1381) into Latin because they had difficulties with his idiom.[49] It is highly improbable that these Flemish monks did not understand Ruusbroec's Brabant dialect. Much more likely is that the confrontation with a theological exposition in the vernacular left them with a sense of incomprehension. Ruusbroec, it should be remembered, was himself a cleric: after years of service as chaplain in St Goedele in Brussels, he spent twelve years of his life as a regular canon in the monastery of Groenendaal. He was therefore well-versed in Latin and theology. Can we not assume that religious writings by considerably less well-educated women like Beatrice of Nazareth would have struck clerics as even more peculiar?

Translated by Myra Scholz

---

[49] Compare Guido de Baere, 'Ruusbroec's *Spiegel* in the Latin translation of Geert Grote' in *Boeken voor de eeuwigheid: Middelnederlands geestelijk proza*, ed. by Thom Mertens and others, Nederlandse literatuur en cultuur in de middeleeuwen, 8 (Amsterdam: Prometheus, 1993), pp. 156–70 and 413–19 (pp. 159–60).

'Being a Woman on my Own': Alijt Bake (1415–1455) as Reformer of the Inner Self

ANNE BOLLMANN

Around 1451 Alijt Bake, prioress of the Augustinian convent Galilea in Ghent, recorded the story of her spiritual life for the benefit of her community. The first part of her autobiographical sketch, in particular, revolves around the conflicts which she, as a newly arrived postulant, experienced with her superiors and her fellow sisters in the convent. Alijt makes unabashed claims, even at the beginning of her monastic career, as to how much more she knew about true inner spirituality, than they did. This teaching of the individual spiritual life, defined with her own characteristic concepts of knowledge and love, *kennise en minne* and acquiescence and suffering, *laten en lijden*, forms the basic theme of all her works.The striking discrepancy between herself, a mere candidate for a place in the convent, and the Windesheim canonesses, supposedly so much more advanced in their spirituality, Alijt illustrates with the following image:

> And I saw the paths that they were following and that they taught me, which were so many levels below me. Then I saw how they showed me the way when I asked them to. And to speak in terms of a metaphor: It was as if I was up in the loft of the church in order to climb up into the tower and had asked from a distance those standing down below, 'How can I get to the tower?' And as if they had answered then, 'Come down here to us, we'll go get some ladders and tie them together and place them here against the outside of the church and climb up that way.'[1]

Because of limitations of space, the notes in this article mention only a selection of the literature relevant to the topic. For the same reason not all translated quotations could be cited in the original as published by Bernhard Spaapen in *Ons Geestelijk Erf* between 1962 and 1969 (see note 4 below). For fuller references, please consult the author's expanded version of this article, '*Een vrauw te sijn op mijn self handt.* Alijt Bake (1415–1455) als geistliche Reformerin des innerliches Lebens', *Ons Geestelijk Erf*, 76 (2002), 64–98.

[1] Bake, 'Autobiografie', p. 225 (see note 4 below): 'Ende ick sach die weeghen die sij

This, she adds by way of explanation, would also be a way to reach the goal, but it would be long and difficult and extremely dangerous. For a person already in the loft only a short ladder would be needed to climb up to the tower. And even if one were to stumble, the fall would be a minor one with no risk of injury. The long route described above, on the other hand, would be much more time-consuming and might even result in serious injuries.[2] She sums up with an exclamation:

> Oh, behold, my dearest ones, the kind of superiors I had and the kind of paths they showed me. Oh, if I had followed them, how I would have missed my paths and gone astray [...]. Oh, dear children, how harmful it would have been for me and the Holy Church and especially for all of you who are here in this house, if I had done that.[3]

These few words crystallize Bake's understanding of her own key role as a leader and authoritative teacher, not only in her own community but also far beyond the walls of her convent. The metaphor is in addition a good example of her highly creative way of elucidating by means of exempla, a method tailored to the specific readership of the Ghent sisters.

Firstly what were the origins of Alijt's self-confidence in spiritual matters, a confidence that was evidently present already at the beginning of her monastic life and later served as the basis for her activities as prioress and author? And secondly, how does Alijt's understanding of her role as 'spiritual reformer' find expression in her texts? These two questions will be investigated here. To arrive at a clear picture it is necessary to understand Alijt Bake in the historical context of the Modern Devotion and to give her the place she deserves in the reform movement of the late Middle Ages alongside her mainly male colleagues. At present the status generally assigned to her in Modern Devotion scholarship is that of an incidental and exceptional figure. In effect this appears to be an obstacle to an adequate appreciation of her religious leadership and writing in terms of literary history.

Scholarly interest in Alijt Bake's life and work is still in its early stages. Although she was noticed as early as the 1930s and the majority of the works attributed to her

---

wandelden ende die sij mij leerden, die wel soo veel graden onder mij waeren. Dan soo sach ick hoe sij mij den wech wijsden, als ick hun daer naer vrachde. Ende recht naer dese ghelijkenisse te spreeken: Of [op] dat ick "op het" verheemsel van der kercken gheweest hadde om boven inden torre te clemmen, ende hadde hun ghewraecht van verren, aen die die hier beneden stonden: "Waer sal ick op den torre comen?" Ende sij dan gheseijdt hadden: "Compt hier beneden bij ons, wij sullen gaen halen leeren, ende binden die leeren d'een aen dandere, ende legghense hier buijten op die kercke, ende clemmen asoo daerin."'

[2] Bake, 'Autobiografie', p. 226.

[3] Bake, 'Autobiografie', p. 226: 'Och, siet, alderliefste, wat meesterst hadde ick en wat weghen toonde sij mij. Och, oft ick hun gevolcht hadde, hoe hadde ick mijn weghen ghemist en verdoolt [...]. Och, lieve kinderen, hoe schaedelijck hadde dit voor mij en de heijlighe kercke en besonderlijck u lieden, die hier sijt in desen huijse, schaedelijck gheweest, hadde ick dat ghedaen.'

became available in text editions towards the end of the 1960s,[4] she has only recently drawn the attention of researchers working in the areas of the Modern Devotion and mysticism.[5] Their studies focus primarily on Bake's debt to other devotional and

---

[4] Alijt Bake was first pointed out in connection with the reception of Tauler in the Netherlands by Gerhard I. Lieftinck, *De Middelnederlandsche Tauler-Handschriften* (Groningen: Wolters, 1936), pp. 17–22, 369–71. Then came Robert Lievens, 'Alijt Bake van Utrecht (1415–1455)', *Nederlandsch Archief voor Kerkgeschiedenis*, 42 (1958), 127–51; the 'mystical author' was also included in the history of Netherlandic piety by Stephanus Axters, *Geschiedenis van de vroomheid in de Nederlanden*, 4 vols (Antwerp 1950–60), III: 'De Moderne Devotie 1380–1550' (1956), pp. 166–68. The successive edition of a large part of her oeuvre under the series title 'Middeleeuwse Passiemystiek' (II–V) we owe to Bernhard Spaapen: II: 'De vier kruiswegen van Alijt Bake', *Ons Geestelijk Erf*, 40 (1966), 5–64 (henceforth referred to as: Bake, 'De vier kruiswegen'); III: 'De autobiografie van Alijt Bake', *Ons Geestelijk Erf*, 41 (1967), 209–301, 321–50 (henceforth referred to as: Bake, 'Autobiografie'); IV: 'De brief uit de ballingschap', *Ons Geestelijk Erf*, 41 (1967), 351–67 (henceforth referred to as: Bake, 'Brief'); V: 'De kloosteronderrichtingen van Alijt Bake', *Ons Geestelijk Erf*, 42 (1968), with subsections 1. 'De weg van de ezel', 5–32; 2. 'De lessen van Palmzondag', 225–61; 3. 'De louteringsnacht van de actie', 374–421; 4. 'De weg der victorie', *Ons Geestelijk Erf*, 43 (1969), 270–304.—With the exception of 'De weg der victorie' all of the instructional treatises (*kloosteronderrichtingen*) are found in the codex Brussels, Koninklijke Bibliotheek (KB), MS 643/44, compare note 101 below. The following works, because they are included in this same manuscript, have also been attributed to Alijt Bake: 'Een merkelijke leeringhe' (= 'Het Boexken vander passien'), [from The Hague, Koninklijke Bibliotheek (KB), MS 135 F 12 ed. by Dominique Bloemkolk (unpublished doctoral thesis, Rijksuniversiteit Utrecht, 1986)]; 'De trechter en de spin' ed. by Wybren Scheepsma, *Ons Geestelijk Erf*, 69 (1995), 222–34; in 1992 Scheepsma had originally attributed two more treatises in the Brussels Codex to Alijt Bake: 'Van drije pointen die toebehooren een volmackt leven' and 'Van drij pointen die behooren tot een beschouwende leuen', ed. by W. Scheepsma, *Ons Geestelijk Erf*, 66 (1992), 145–67, but he had to retract this later, compare Scheepsma, *Ons Geestelijk Erf*, 68 (1998), p. 106f.; (for earlier editions of the treatises see Dirk de Man, 'Uit twee Middelnederlandse handschriften', *Archief voor de Geschiedenis van het Aartsbisdom Utrecht*, 61 (1937), 559–69; because of parallels in content to her 'Autobiografie' Scheepsma also attributes the following text to Alijt Bake: 'Van die memorie der passien ons Heren', *Ons Geestelijk Erf*, 68 (1994), 106–28.—On the still unpublished 'Exempel van de kreupele Margriet', also found in the complex of texts in the Brussels manuscript that Alijt Bake is believed to have authored, compare the edition of Johannes von Magdeburg, *Die Vita der Margareta contracta, einer Magdeburger Rekluse des 13. Jahrhunderts*, ed. by Paul G. Schmidt, Studien zur Katholischen Bistums- und Klostergeschichte, 36, (Leipzig: Benno Verlag, 1992); see also Anneke B. Mulder-Bakker, 'Lame Margaret of Magdeburg: The Social Function of a Medieval Recluse', *Journal of Medieval History*, 22 (1996), 155–69; Mulder-Bakker, 'Monddood maken liet zij zich niet: De kluizenares Kreupele Margriet van Maagdeburg', in *Vrome Vrouwen: Betekenissen van geloof voor vrouwen in de geschiedenis*, ed. by Mirjam Conelis and others (Hilversum: Verloren, 1996), pp. 45–66.

[5] In addition to the articles and editions already mentioned, the following recent studies should also be noted: Kurt Ruh, *Geschichte der Abendländischen Mystik*, 4 vols (München: Beck, 1990–99), IV (1999): 'Die niederländische Mystik des 14–16. Jahrhunderts', pp. 252–67; Wybren Scheepsma, *Deemoed en devotie: De koorvrouwen van Windesheim en hun*

mystical authors who would have served as models. They therefore pay considerable attention to shared ideals of a spiritual life as a striving to intensify the personal meditative experience of Passion devotion.[6] This study will present the 'Bake phenomenon' by placing more emphasis on her self-understanding as a religious reformer. Pivotal to the investigation are her autobiographical writings: her 'spiritual autobiography', which dates from approximately 1451, and the 'letter from exile', written shortly before her death in 1455 as a self-vindication. Like her other works, these two texts highlight Bake's mystical teaching of the imitation of Christ in the passion as well as her understanding of her own role as 'reformer of the inner life'. But these memoirs show more clearly than her other writings that Alijt's spiritual ideas are not in the first place indebted to an intensive reading of edifying monastic literature to which she gained access.[7] Rather it is primarily the historical and social context of this Modern Devotion author, interwoven with intimate experiences of grace, that served as her point of departure and motivated her claim to religious reform.

Before discussing these writings as evidence of the close connection between her life and her literary work, it is important first to place Alijt Bake and her oeuvre in the context of the Modern Devotion, a religious reform movement in which books and writing acquired fundamental significance for the spiritual renewal envisioned for all areas of a Christian's life.

---

geschriften, Nederlandse literatuur en cultuur in de Middeleeuwen, 17 (Amsterdam: Prometheus, 1997), pp. 175–201; Grietje Dresen, *Onschuldfantasieën: Offerzin en heilsverlangen in feminisme en mystiek* (Nijmegen: SUN, 1990).—On Alijt Bake's life and work see my *Staatsarbeit,* which investigates Alijt's autobiographical writings in terms of the interplay of content and style: Anne Bollmann, 'Studien zur Autobiographie der Alijt Bake von Utrecht' (unpub. *Staatsarbeit,* Universität Münster, 1994); [The results of my research relating to the structure of the autobiography as a mirror of the individual stages on the way of the author's spiritual life are summarized in the study which appeared three years later, *Alijt Bake: Tot in de peilloze diepte van God. De Vrouw die moest zwijgen over haar mystieke weg,* ed. by Rudolphus Th. M. van Dijk (introduction and commentary) and Marianus K. A. van den Berg (translation), Mystieke teksten en thema's, 12 (Kampen: Kok, 1997); in his older work, Rudolphus Th. M. van Dijk, 'De mystieke weg van Alijt Bake (1415–1455)', *Ons Geestelijk Erf,* 66 (1992), 115–33, van Dijk still held different opinions about the course of Alijt's life.]

[6] See Kurt Ruh's studies on the two treatises 'De vier kruiswegen' and 'De weg van de ezel', in Ruh, *Geschichte der Abendländischen Mystik,* IV, pp. 256–64.

[7] In a 'cloak-and-dagger' manoeuvre Alijt Bake managed to smuggle Rulman Merswin's *Book of Nine Rocks* into the convent, and in the space of three hours she assimilated enough of the content to use it as a model for her own programme of meditation exercises. Compare Bake, 'Autobiografie', pp. 334–36. On Rulman Merswin see note 22 below.

Religious Author of the Modern Devotion

Alijt Bake's fate is closely intertwined with the Modern Devotion[8] and in particular with the Windesheim congregation, the strict branch of Augustinian monasteries and convents within this religious movement of the late Middle Ages.[9] She was probably born on 13 December, 1415,[10] but little is known about the place of her birth or the social background of her family.[11] She started her monastic career in the Ghent convent of Galilea, which officially belonged to the chapter of Windesheim after 1438. The convent was founded in the year 1430 by the extremely wealthy and influential Jan Eggaert, Lord of Purmerend and Spaarnland.[12] The original intention

---

[8] For a general introduction to the Modern Devotion in English see Regnerus R. Post, *The Modern Devotion: Confrontation with Reformation and Humanism*, Studies in Medieval and Reformation Thought, 3 (Leiden: Brill, 1968); also John Van Engen, *Devotio Moderna: Basic Writings*, trans. and introd. by John Van Engen, preface by Heiko Oberman (New York: Mahwah, 1988), and the literature mentioned there.

[9] On the Windesheim congregation see *Windesheim 1395–1995: Kloosters, teksten, invloeden. Voordrachten gehouden tijdens het internationale congres '600 jaar Kapittel van Windesheim' 27 mei 1995 te Zwolle*, ed. by Anton J. Hendrikman and others, Middeleeuwse Studies, 12 (Nijmegen: Centrum voor Middeleeuwse Studies, 1996), and the literature mentioned there.

[10] In reconstructing the life of this devout woman we are almost completely dependent on her autobiographical writings. The dates of her birth and of her entry into the order are based on two related references in her autobiographical sketch; compare Bake, 'Autobiografie', pp. 245–46 and 249: 'Ende dit is nu ter tijd van kersdach xi. jaer gheleden dat dit gheschiede, ende doen ick 26 jaeren effen out was. Ende nu opdesen selven dach dat ick dit schreef, welck is op sinte Luciendach [=13 December], ben ick nu 36 jaeren out [...] Aldus soo hept ghij nu hoe ende wat tijt dat ick in dese salighen wech vande ghenaede Godts ghestelt was doen men schreef 1440, eer ick in die heijlighe oorden quam, daer ick altoes den Heere om ghebeden hadde.'—Regarding these conclusions compare Bernhard Spaapen in Bake, 'Autobiografie', p. 246, note 19e, and Lievens, 'Alijt Bake', p. 127.

[11] The assumption that Alijt's roots lie in the Utrecht area is based solely on her own references to that city. As a reaction to her disagreements with her superiors in Galilea, for example, she mentions that she would like to 'return to Utrecht', Bake, 'Autobiografie', p. 239. See for example, Lievens, 'Alijt Bake', p. 127; van Dijk, 'De mystieke weg', p. 122; Dresen, pp. 53–57, 268. These remarks of Alijt, however, clearly refer to her spiritual friends and not to possible family ties. In the final analysis the text offers no basis for a more extensive hypothesis about her place of birth. Alijt's description of her behaviour at large-scale festivities can be interpreted as a reference to a distinguished family background. Compare the quotation in note 26 below and Bollmann, 'Studien', p. 19–20.

[12] Compare Yvonne A. M. Y Bos-Rops, 'Willem Eggaert (*c.* 1360–1417): Een Amsterdams koopman in grafelijke dienst', *Hollandse studiën,* 12 (1982), 59–72; Erik van Mingroot, 'Domus Beatae Mariae de Galilea in Gandavo', in *Monasticon Windeshemense*, ed. by W. Kohl and others, 4 vols., (Brussels: Archives et Bibliothèques de Belge, 1976–84), I, pp. 237–67; van Mingroot, 'Prieuré de Galilée, à Gand', in *Monasticon Belge*, ed. by Léon-E. Halkin and others (Liège: Centre National de Recherches d'Histoire Religieuse, 1890–), VII (1984), pp. 768–70.

was that the community would consist of the mother superior, five canonesses and two lay sisters. In the wake of the final incorporation of the convent into the Windesheim congregation, the number of sisters increased to sixteen. The community continued to grow rapidly and by the year 1500 numbered approximately one hundred members.[13] It was during the first flourishing years of Galilea, around 1438/39, that Alijt entered the community. The dates marking her rapid rise to the top of the convent hierarchy suggest a picture-book career. At Christmas in 1440 she began her novitiate and probably in the following year, at the age of about twenty-six, she made her profession. The ensuing probationary phase as a simple nun lasted only about four years, for by 1445 Alijt Bake was already prioress of the convent.[14]

Alijt began her activity as a religious author, we can infer from our present knowledge, at about the same time that she assumed her office as leader of Galilea. She thus clearly stands in the literary tradition of the Modern Devotion, which was famous for its innovative, consistent and pragmatic use of books and the written word for both the reform of the individual and the organization of communal life.[15] All of Alijt Bake's works can be seen as an expression of this 'modern' program of teaching and leadership which, with its implied 'postulate of writing',[16] encompassed every facet of the devout life.

As a mystic Alijt Bake also belongs to the late medieval women's movement with its broad spectrum of religious forms of life and its flood of edifying texts in the vernacular. The beguine Hadewijch and the Cistercian Beatrice of Nazareth, both of the thirteenth century, are early examples of mystics who wrote in the southern Netherlands and incorporated influences from previous centuries in their work.[17] In

---

[13] *Monasticon Windeshemense*, I, pp. 258–60.

[14] The problematic point in this reconstruction is Alijt's age at the time she assumed office. If she was born on 15 December 1415, she could not yet have been thirty years old, the minimum age required for a prioress, when she was elected to that office in the spring of 1445; on the Windesheim statutes for electing prioresses, see Rudolphus Th. M. van Dijk, *De Constituties der Windesheimse Vrouwenkloosters vóór 1559: Bijdrage tot de institutionele geschiedenis van het kapittel van Windesheim*, 2 vols, Middeleeuwse studies, 3 (Nijmegen: Centrum voor Middeleeuwse Studies, 1986), I, pp. 325–33; II, pp. 749–53.

[15] On the theory and practice of this functional orientation of the written word see Nikolaus Staubach, 'Pragmatische Schriftlichkeit im Bereich der Devotio Moderna', *Frühmittelalterliche Studien*, 25 (1991), 418–61; Thom Mertens, 'Lezen met de pen: Ontwikkelingen in het laatmiddeleeuws geestelijk proza', in *De studie van de Middelnederlandse letterkunde: stand en toekomst*, ed. by Frits van Oostrom and others, Middeleeuwse studies en bronnen, 14 (Hilversum: Verloren, 1989), pp. 187–200.

[16] Staubach, 'Pragmatische Schriftlichkeit', p 428–29.

[17] The unconditional nature of *minne* in Beatrice and Hadewijch is also found in Bake, 'Autobiografie', pp. 298–301, and in her treatise 'De lessen van Palmzondag', p. 242–43.— Historically Hadewijch is barely identifiable. Her phase of literary productivity extended from 1220 to approximately 1240; compare for her work in English translation *Hadewych: The complete works*, trans. and ed. by Columba Hart (New York: Paulist Press, 1980). On Beatrice

this area of personal mysticism new forms of 'mystical speech' were developed. Writing didactic texts based on their experience of God, these women writers attempted to portray this intimate experience more generally as an occurrence in a concrete life dedicated to God.[18] Besides Dutch mystical texts Alijt Bake shows that she is familiar with women's mystical writings outside the Netherlands as passed down to us from Catherine of Siena (1347–80),[19] Mechthild of Magdeburg (*c.* 1207–82) and Mechthild of Hackeborn (*c.* 1242–97/98).[20] Via the Groenendaal mysticism of Johannes Ruusbroec (1293–1381) and his pupil John of Leeuwen, the 'cook of Groenendaal' (*c.* 1314–78), she builds a bridge between the literary tradition of Hadewijch's Brabantine *minne* mysticism and the Rhineland mysticism of the Dominican preacher John Tauler (*c.* 1300–1361),[21] the Augustinian Jordanus of Quedlinburg (before 1299–*c.* 1380) and the 'friend of God' Rulman Merswin (1307–82).[22]

A series of sermon adaptations, religious treatises and exempla, now believed to be some of Alijt Bake's early literary products, date from about 1446, in other words just one year after she took office as prioress.[23] These are primarily works of

---

of Nazareth (1200–68) see the article by Wybren Scheepsma in this volume.

[18] See Ruh, *Geschichte der Abendländischen Mystik*, I, pp. 494–508; Kurt Ruh, 'Beginenmystik', *Zeitschrift für deutsches Altertum*, 106 (1977), 265–77; Alois M. Haas, 'Mystik als Aussage: Erfahrungs-, Denk- und Redeformen christlicher Mystik', 2nd edn (Frankfurt/Main: Suhrkamp, 1997), especially pp. 270–81.

[19] Alijt Bake mentions Catherine of Siena together with St Francis in her treatise 'De vier kruiswegen', p. 20.

[20] Alijt lists these authors in her treatise 'Louteringsnacht van de actie', p. 399. There she just mentions these authors in connection with her thoughts about Passion devotion. Unfortunately Alijt doesn't give any hint as to her sources.—For identification compare Ruh, *Geschichte der Abendländischen Mystik*, IV, pp. 264–65; Mulder-Bakker, 'Lame Margaret of Magdeburg'; on the heart mysticism of Mechthild of Hackeborn see Richard L. J. Bromberg, *Het boek der bijzondere genade von Mechthild van Hackeborn*, 2 vols, (Zwolle: Tjeenk Willink, 1967); Alois M. Haas, 'Mechthild von Hackeborn: Eine Form zisterzienischer Frauenfrömmigkeit', in *Die Zisterzienser: Ordensleben zwischen Ideal und Wirklichkeit*, ed. by Kaspar Elm (Cologne: Wienand, 1982), pp. 221–39 (pp. 227–28).

[21] In the treatise 'De memorie van der passien ons Heren' Tauler is singled out for special praise: 'Och, alleen ken ic een meester inder godheit die daer of leert, die deuote Thauler, die gaet hem naere dan ic ye hoerde in scriften', p. 123.

[22] On Rulman Merswin compare Georg Steer's article in *Die deutsche Literatur des Mittelalters: Verfasserlexikon* (Berlin: De Gruyter, 1987), VI, col. 420–42.—Alijt used Merswin's model of the steps toward spiritual perfection with its image of the nine rocks as a programmatic model of a religious life for her own development, compare note 7.

[23] A colophon in the Brussels codex identifies Alijt Bake as the author: 'Bidt voor diet maecte ende heeft ghescreven / Want sij arm door Gode es bleven / Doe men M Vierhondert screef / Na dat Jhesus ant cruce bleef / Ende XLVI ofte daer omtrent / Soe was dit eerst ghemaect te Ghent / Van zuster Alijt der priorinnen / Van Galileen, God wille haer ziele gewinnen'. See Brussels, KB, MS 643–44, fol. 198va.

Jordanus of Quedlinburg and John Tauler that Alijt adapted for didactic purposes. In keeping with the late medieval sense of author and work, Alijt did not merely copy their work. Although she mentions both authors by name, a close reading of the texts reveals that, drawing on texts by Jordanus and Tauler, she set down her own conception of a spiritual life. It shows that she was remarkably well versed in the technical side of writing.[24] Besides the sermon adaptations, this manuscript contains other edifying texts that elaborate on essential points of Alijt Bake's religious teachings, but their attribution is contested.[25] Her 'spiritual biography' dates from the fifth year of her priorate.

The following section will focus on certain aspects of the spiritual path as presented in Alijt's autobiography. In this work the Windesheim prioress does not stylize herself as the ideal nun without inner doubts or failings, but describes her development with both its successes and defeats as an attempt to follow the mystical path of suffering assigned to her by God. Alijt's uncompromising and at times disarming openness lends the text a confessional character and directness that would have heightened the authenticity of her report.

On a second level the text reveals itself to be a spiritual handbook written as a kind of explanatory appendix to Alijt's other works. The treatise of the 'Four Ways of the Cross' especially, but also her other apologies, sermon adaptations, and exempla, are all placed in the context in which they were composed and presented as the written result of inner experiences of grace as well as other personal experiences on her way to becoming a 'true nun'.

Also important, however, is the way Alijt Bake exploits the medium of writing to legitimize her decision, unique in the Modern Devotion up to that point, and presumably on no authority other than her own, to present herself as an exemplary imitator of Christ in his Passion and to recommend that others follow in her footsteps. That this was not her own decision, however, she attempts to show by

---

[24] Ruh, *Geschichte de abendländische Mystik*, IV, p. 265, describes Alijt's use of Jordanus's sermons as follows: 'Zum Verhältnis Alijts zu ihrer Jordanus-Quelle ist festzuhalten, daß sie nur dem Ausgangspunkt und dem Grundschema verpflichtet ist; auch einige Einzelheiten hat sie aufgegriffen. Aber ihre spirituelle Eigenwelt bleibt immer gewahrt, Fremdes wird eingeformt. Vom vierten Punkte an ist die Jordanus-Vorlage vergessen. Es ist anzunehmen, obschon Untersuchungen fehlen, daß Alijt sich andern Quellen gegenüber nicht anders verhalten hat.' [On the matter of Alijt's relation to her sources, it is clear that she borrowed only the point of departure and the basic structure; she also incorporated a few details. But her own spiritual world is maintained throughout, with alien material reshaped to fit her purposes. From the fourth point onwards she has forgotten the Jordanus text. Although no studies have been made, we can assume that Alijt did not treat other sources any differently.]

[25] It has not yet been clarified just how many works in the Brussels codex are referred to by the colophon mentioned above. The texts in the section found on fol. 154ᵛ to 198ᵛ and linked by transitional commentary of the author are definitely writings of Alijt Bake, compare the construction of Scheepsma, *Deemoed en devotie*, p. 254 (Appendix 2).

describing in detail the external and internal events that led her to take on the role of 'reformer of the inner life'. As she presents it, these activities were required of her, and were justified by a divine calling—an argument which deserves closer scrutiny.

Spiritual Companions

When Alijt Bake entered the Galilea convent in 1439, she was far from being a blank page in matters of spirituality. Her readiness to renounce the world as well as her predilection for meditative prayer and Passion devotion had been reinforced already in her childhood by visions and other divine revelations. At that time, she writes, she felt her first longing for the solitude of a hermit's cell where she could continually and without distraction immerse herself in passion devotion:

> Then the Passion of our Lord first became clear to me, which was given me right from the beginning with all the grace I had ever experienced and which had at times afforded me much sweetness and pleasure, and which I also regularly experienced in the world. Even if I was in a large group, I was sometimes inwardly drawn to think of the Passion and death of our dear Lord, even if I had gone to a dance or was occupied with some other vain pleasure. And I sometimes used to think that if I were outside the world I would want to occupy myself with the Passion at all times. And it seemed to me that this was also supposed to be, and because I desired nothing but to lie at his feet with Mary Magdalene, I sought the solitude of an anchorhold.[26]

Considering that Alijt set out on her path of imitation of the Passion even before entering the convent, it is not surprising that in her 'spiritual autobiography' she regularly speaks about experiences from her secular past. The text that has come down to us, however, includes only a few vague remarks about her youth, for this phase of her life had already been recorded in her 'book of tribulations', an earlier work with which she could presume her readers to be familiar.[27]

---

[26] Bake, 'Autobiografie', p. 252: 'Doen soo quam mij die Passie ons Heeren aldereerst [te] vooren d'ooghen, dat mij altoes van beghin ghegeven was van alle mijn gratien die ick oijnt ghehadt hadde ende daer somtijt grooten smaeck ende soetichheijt in ghehadt hadde, ende die ick oock inder weeerelt plach te oeffenen. Al was ick in groot gheselschap, soo wiert ick somtijts ghetrocken van binnen op de Passie ende doodt ons liefs Heeren te dincken, al hadde ick oock aen den dans gheghaen, of met ander idelheijt becommert gheweest. Ende mij placht somtijt te [te] dincken, hadde ick wt de weerelt gheweest, ick hadde wel altoes inde Passie willen becommert sijn. Ende mij dochte dat het oock alsoo sijn soude ende dat mij anders niet en luste dan voor sijn voeten te ligghen met Maria Magdalena, hierom dat ick die eenicheijt vander cluijse sochte.' On Alijt's connections with the reclusive life compare the remarks of Spaapen in Bake, 'Autobiografie', p. 252, note 23b; see van Dijk, 'De mystieke weg', p. 123–24. Her ideas about the imitation of Christ in his Passion seem to be influenced by Suso, compare note 69 below.

[27] In the part of her spiritual autobiography known to us under the title 'the other book of my beginning and progress' (Bake, 'Autobiografie', p. 218) the prioress makes reference to

Two women played a key role in Alijt's spiritual development. In her search for a practicable way of fulfilling her wish for a more contemplative life, Alijt must have made the acquaintance of her two 'spiritual friends' in Utrecht. She refers to them several times in the course of her text without, however, mentioning their names. One of them had devoted her life to caring for the poor and sick in a hospice.[28] The other led a religious life 'in solitude and poverty'. Alijt describes the latter as 'my dear, faithful, spiritual mother, my lady, with whom I used to live'.[29] To judge from the few references, this spiritual confidant appears to have lived as a recluse in Utrecht, and Alijt was probably her disciple and assistant for some indeterminate period of time. In these *mulieres religiosae* Alijt Bake had come to know two women who had opted for a religious life outside the official orders. Life in an inner-city anchorhold offered religious women special possibilities for realizing the ideal of inner renewal as propagated by adherents of the Modern Devotion in their sermons and writings.[30]

Although the loss of the first part of her memoirs means that the name of Alijt's companion as well as the details of how she devoted her life to God remain obscure, we can infer from the writings of another fifteenth-century Utrecht recluse that passion devotion occupied a central place in her program of exercises. The writings of Bertha Jacobs (1426/7–1514), better known as 'Suster Bertken', who lived for fifty-seven years as a recluse at the Buur Church in the Utrecht city centre,[31] include

---

the 'book of tribulations'. There she described her spiritual apprenticeship in Utrecht prior to her entry into the convent. This part of her memoirs has not survived.

[28] She may have worked in the St Barbara and St Laurentius's hospital (1372/1435). This hospice grew out of a complex that had formerly served as a poor house for needy women (1359) and a beguine convent (1392). Compare Albertus van Hulzen, *Utrechtse kloosters en gasthuizen* (Baarn: Bosch & Keuning, 1986), pp. 47, 106–10.

[29] Bake, 'Autobiografie', pp. 239 and 246.

[30] Anneke B. Mulder-Bakker, 'The Reclusorium as an Informal Centre of Learning', in *Centres of Learning: Learning and Location in Pre-modern Europe and the Near East*, ed. by Jan W. Drijvers and others (Leiden: Brill, 1995), pp. 245–54. On the attitude of the Devout towards the reclusive life see for example Grote's letter to a recluse: Geert Grote, *Gerardi Magni Epistolae*, ed. by Willem J. M. Mulder, *Ons Geestelijk Erf*, 3 (1933), pp. 265–68 (no. 68).

[31] On the life of Suster Bertken see José van Aelst, 'Het leven van Suster Bertken: Kanttekeningen bij de recente beeldvorming', *Ons Geestelijk Erf*, 72 (1998), 262–72; Llewellyn Bogaers, 'Kluizenares midden in de wereld: Suster Bertkens antwoord op haar beladen familiegeschiedenis', *Trajecta*, 7 (1998), 296–318. On Bertha's writings see *Een boecxken gemaket van Suster Bertken die lvii iaren besloten heeft gheseten to Utrecht in dye Buerkercke* ed. by Cornelia C. van de Graft (Zwolle: Tjeenk Willink, 1955); José van Aelst, 'Geordineert na dye getijden: Suster Bertkens passieboekje', *Ons Geestelijk Erf*, 69 (1995), 133–56; and Van Aelst, 'Suffering with the Bridegroom: The "Innighe Sprake" of the Utrecht recluse Suster Bertken', *Ons Geestelijk Erf*, 71 (1997), 228–49; Fons van Buuren, 'Ja zuster, nee zuster. De overlevering van "Die werelt hielt my in haer gewout"', in *Hoort wonder! Opstellen voor W.P. Gerritsen bij zijn emeritaat*, ed. by Bart Besamusca and others,

descriptions of the religious motifs and goals that defined her spiritual life: renunciation of the world and concentration on meditative prayer, supported by intensive personal exercises of penitence and passion. These core teachings coincided with the ideas of Alijt Bake as a young adherent of the Modern Devotion. She, too, felt greatly drawn to the 'vita contemplativa' as practised by her recluse friend. The special blessings bestowed on this woman as well as her prophetic abilities seemed to underscore her true closeness to God and the rightness of the model she had chosen.[32] Alijt eventually followed the advice of her friend and opted for life in a convent.

Various motives may have led the prioress to cite these two women from her Utrecht past as examples of a successful spiritual life. They were obviously the ones who had made Alijt realize that a variety of ideas about religious life styles could be meaningful and effective, and that a decision for one or the other model had to be made in accordance with a person's individual character and social background. They were also the ones from whom Alijt learned to focus completely on the Passion devotion in her striving for oneness with God. Her early training in the methods of meditative inwardness led her to the first steps of 'knowledge and love'. This corresponded to the beginner's stage on the way to a mystical encounter with God and formed the basis for her further spiritual development.

Yet the main reason for their appearance at decisive points in Alijt's life seems be of a more fundamental nature. In the eyes of the prioress, her Utrecht companions were spiritual examples for others because they embodied the ideals of a life devoted to the 'vita activa' and to the 'vita contemplativa' respectively. Their prophetic capabilities were evidence of special grace and closeness to God, which made it possible for them to aid their former protégée with advice and prophecy that reached beyond the bounds of time and space, even beyond the grave.[33]

In view of these inner experiences and inspirations, Alijt must have found the idea of gaining spiritual knowledge from books without any direct relation to personal

---

Middeleeuwse studies en bronnen, 70 (Hilversum: Verloren, 2000), pp. 43–50; Alphonsus M. J. van Buuren, '"Die werelt hielt my in haer gewout". Suster Bertken, haar biografie en haar vijfde lied', *Nederlandse Letterkunde*, 6 (2001), 124–37.

[32] This recluse had foretold the trials and temptations that her protégée would have to endure from the world and the devil, but together with this prophecy she offered the solace that God would never forsake her in all her 'tribulations', compare Bake, 'Autobiografie', p. 238: 'Mijn herte dat track mij seer tuijtrecht te trecken tot twee devote persoonen, dat mijn sonderlinghe vrindinnen waeren ende die seer heylich en verlicht waren, dat sij veel heijmelijckheden van Godt wisten. Ende de eene was die persoone, daer vooren, in dat eerste boeck, af gheseijdt is, die mij al mijn tribulatien vercondichde ende voorseijde, ende mij seijde dat mij Godt niet verlaten en saude, nemmermeer, ende die mij herwaert wijsde met blijschap [...].'

[33] The telepathic, dreamlike visions mentioned in the text remain vague. Compare the scenario containing a revelation of the hospice sister: Alijt's initiative to contact her by letter is declared superfluous when a visionary dream anticipates the written reply.

faith and life experience incomprehensible. In her writing she therefore concentrates on the theme of personal introspection, which she presents to her audience in a lively edifying style. This also explains why Alijt refused, during her novitiate, to memorize texts in Latin as convent protocol prescribed. Instead she continued with her inner meditation on the Passion: 'I don't understand those writings and for that reason cannot keep my heart concentrated on them in a way that I would be enlivened by them as I am in these.'[34] The independent way in which Alijt used Latin writings in her own works shows that this was not from lack of knowledge: it is clear that a few years later she could at least read Latin well.

Moreover, in keeping with her self-understanding as a reformer, the Windesheim sister does not hesitate to criticize other well-respected authors when she finds that their theological and spiritual writings lack relevance to life.[35] Indirectly she is here also encouraging her sisters, as her followers on the path towards inner experience of the passion of Christ, to read with a critical mind the edifying literature presented to them. The encounter with God represents for the Windesheim prioress the highest and only acceptable aim of a devout life, with the reading of devotional texts serving as a preparation for this goal. Consequently Alijt's 'spiritual biography', in which she makes her own mystical—and therefore in the deepest sense of the word private—experiences of grace permanently accessible to others, is constructed completely around her mystical ascents and descents, her experiences of 'knowledge and love' and of 'acquiescence and suffering'.

---

[34]Bake, 'Autobiografie', p. 278–79. See also Alijt's remark about the 'sweet verses', the repeated recitation of which many considered the best way to find the right devotion; in: 'De vier kruiswegen', p. 62.

[35] Bake, 'Autobiografie', p. 326f.: 'Ende hierin soo was den goeden cock van Groenendaele, daer hij soo seer over de minne claechde. Maer in alle sijne [boecken] tot 10 noch in heer Jan Rijsbrock boecken, en can ick niet vinden dat sij lieden soo verre van alder eijghender werckelycheijt gheset waeren in versmaetheijt van dien dat sijt selve versteken en versmaden ende verdriven moesten van hun. Ick hoore wel dat sij lieden den rechten wech onder de ghelaetenheijt onder dat werck en ghestaden Godts hadden, als hun niet beters ghebueren en mocht. Maer dat sijt selve "moeste" versteken en versmaden en verspijen als dese moeste, dat en verneme ick niet in haer boecken. Maer waerom sijt lieten en weet ick niet […].'

A Hundred or a Thousand Levels Above Them'

It was with great expectations that Alijt, already twenty-five years old,[36] entered Galilea with its outstanding reputation. For in view of the spiritual atmosphere in this convent, she would certainly make good progress along her path.

And the signs were promising. When Alijt arrived in Galilea in 1439, Hille Sonderlants (d. 25 January 1445) was prioress, a woman who in the course of her long term of service had lived various forms of the devout life as a beguine and had held leading positions in houses ranging from a semi-religious sister community to a strictly monastic Windesheim convent of canonesses.[37] It is not surprising, then, that Alijt hoped to benefit greatly from a mother superior like Hille Sonderlants,[38] whose experience and reputation in Modern Devotion circles were beyond question.[39] As it

---

[36] Although it was not impossible for adults to enter a convent, it was less common; on the minimum age of twelve years as laid down in the Windesheim statutes, see van Dijk, *De constituties*, II, p. 777. Yet an eighteen-year-old candidate is already referred to as a 'spinster'; see Ernest Persoons, 'Lebensverhältnisse in den Frauenklöstern der Windesheimer Kongregation in Belgien und in den Niederlanden', in *Klösterliche Sachkultur des Spätmittelalters*, Österreichische Akademie der Wissenschaften, Sitzungsberichte, Philosophisch-Historische Klasse, 367 (Vienna, 1980), pp. 73–111 (pp. 81–85). A late entry was considered problematic because it is as a rule easier for young people to adapt to a strict regime such as demanded by the Windesheim communities; see on this issue as a reason for Alijt's adjustment difficulties van Dijk, 'De mystieke weg', p. 125.

[37] The religious career of this woman illustrates the historical development of the women's branch of the Modern Devotion, but in reverse. Hille had started out as a beguine in Cleves before entering the Meester Geert House, the first sister house of the movement founded in Deventer by Geert Grote himself. From there she helped set up the canonesses' convent Diepenveen, where she eventually served as rectrix. Hille was subsequently dispatched three different times to reform women's convents in the northern Netherlands before she was called to be prioress of the Ghent community. See note 39 below on her Lives.

[38] Alijt Bake's motives for requesting a place in a convent far from Utrecht are not mentioned in the writings that have been preserved. One possibility is that she opted for the community in Ghent after hearing about the founding of the convent and the promising appointment of Hille Sonderlants to the position of prioress through the founder Jan Eggaert, whom she refers to as her 'friend' and whose advice she also valued later during her difficulties as a postulant. Compare. Bake, 'Autobiografie', p. 236: 'Ende alle die pointen die mij behaget hadden, die voor "in" dat ander boeck gheschreven staen, daerom dat ick eerst tot dese stede dat herte ghecreech, ende bat daerom hier "te" sijne [...]'; 'Autobiographie', p. 243: '[...] doen ick eerst om dese stede bat'; p. 221: 'Ick meijnde, omdat sij langhe gheestelijcke ghweest hadden, dat sij alle dinck gheweten hadden, ende hilt het seer groot in hunlieden ende sonderlinghe in Mater Hildegont ende in suster Ijde.'

[39] In the accounts of Hille Sonderlants's life written in her former communities, both the Meester Geert House and the convent Diepenveen, she is expressly praised for her reforming activities in Galilea; compare her Life in the edition of the Diepenveen 'Handschrift *D*', under the title *Van den doechden der vuriger ende stichtiger susteren van diepen veen*, ed. by Dirk A. Brinckerinck (Groningen: Wolters, 1904), p. 244: 'een guet reyement'; compare the wording at the end of her biography in the second, still unedited '*Handschrift DV*' containing

turned out, however, Alijt's striving for inner meditative experience was at odds with the ideas of her prioress and the regimen of everyday convent life. Alijt's superiors and fellow sisters reacted with annoyance to her consistent withdrawal from affairs in the house. Interpreting it as a criticism of communal life with its hierarchic structure and strictly prescribed daily routine, they energetically admonished and criticized the postulant[40] and imposed exercises in asceticism, humility, and penitence as a way of persuading her to abide by the rules.

> And they spoke out strongly and did their best to dissuade me from this, saying how I should turn my attention to my failings, in order to know them and overcome them, and to useful outward activities: this is what was proper for a young and inexperienced person and not high things. And they spoke often to me and scorned me and my words and works and were offended by them. And because I could hardly turn to those things which they had set before me, they developed ill feelings towards me because I was so withdrawn into the things my God was teaching me inwardly, and they judged me to be very conceited and opinionated about myself and my own feelings, believing myself better than others, and for that reason keeping to myself and living for myself and nothing else, being a woman on my own […].[41]

For Alijt these urgings to devote herself to 'useful outward activities' were only expressions of distance from God and of religious superficiality. She was confused

---

biographies of the convent, fol. 48[r]: 'Niet langhe hier na waert sie [Hille Sonderlants] priorinne ghekaren toe Ghent ghenoemt toe sancta Marien in Galileen, daer sie [oec] grote vrocht dede ende een goet reyment makede ende een zeer goet beghin gheworden was. Doe voer sie vol goeder warken tot horen ghemynden brudegom dien sie trowellick ghesocht hadde ende purlick ghedient. Int jaer ons Heeren M cccc xlv. Op sunte Pauwels dach dat hie bekiert wart' [25 January]. On the Sister Book from the Diepenveen convent see Scheepsma. *Deemoed en devotie*, p. 319, note 16 (on the contradictory dates given for Hille's death); on collections of sister Lives from Devout women's communities in general see Anne Bollmann, 'Weibliche Diskurse: Die Schwesternbücher der *Devotio Moderna* zwischen Biographie und geistlicher Konversation', in *Kultur, Geschlecht, Körper*, ed. by the Münster Workgroup for Gender Studies (Münster: Agenda, 1999), pp. 241–85.

[40] On the criteria and the rituals that played a role in admitting a candidate into a Windesheim convent see van Dijk, *De constituties*, I, p. 368–70.

[41] Bake, 'Autobiografie', p. 219–20: 'Ende "sij" ontraeden mij seer ende [ende] setten mij daeraf soo sij alderbest mochten, seggende hoe dat ick mij tot mijn ghebreken keeren soude om die te leeren kennen ende te verwinnen, ende tot wtwendegher bedienstelijcker werckelycheijdt: Dit behoorde den jonghen ende onbesochte toe ende niet die hooghe dinghen. Ende "sij" spraecken mij dijckels veel ende versmaeden mij ende mijn worden ende wercken ende veronweerdigh"d" en hun daer af. Ende omdat ick mij tot dien dingen qualijck keeren cost die sij voor[t] setten, soo ghecreghen sij mishaghen ende misnoeghen hier op mij, om dat "ick" soo inghetrocken was in die dinghen die mij Godt van binnen leerde, ende veroordeelden mij seer eijghenwijs "sijnde" ende goetdunckelijck in mij selven, ende mijns selfs ghevoelen ende mij selven beter gheloovende dan imant anders, ende aldus in mijn selven blijvende ende mij selven levende ende niet anders, een vrauwe te sijn op mijn selfs handt […].' (see note 1 above).

and disillusioned by her superiors, who not only fell short of her expectations but, much worse, seemed unable even to comprehend her needs.[42] It consequently seemed pointless for Alijt to seek advice and help from the sisters. Instead she concentrated all the more on her prayers and presented to God her inner doubt and fear of error. Even the threat of being expelled from the convent on the grounds that she was not suited to life there[43] could not dissuade her from trusting solely to God's direct inspiration.

And this, the prioress declares in retrospect, was the correct decision, for whenever it all became too much for her God came to her aid with illuminations and revelations that brought solace and instruction.[44] Alijt's crisis therefore seemed necessary for her to progress further on her mystical path. In a kind of parable God finally revealed the truth to her and showed her how far she, as a newly entered postulant, already stood above those who were supposed to be guiding and teaching her: 'Then I saw where I was standing, a hundred or a thousand levels above them.'[45] Alijt realized that her superiors and fellow sisters could not understand her striving for inner spirituality because they had not had experiences of grace comparable to hers. She tried to find a compromise between her way of mystically experiencing God and the exercises of penitence and humility prescribed by the rules of her community.[46] The mood in the house had also undergone some change, and Alijt apparently no longer stood completely alone in criticizing the worldly tendencies of the community.[47] Mother Hille, however, and other members of the convent were

---

[42] Bake, 'Autobiografie', p. 221–23. goes into great detail about Alijt's contradictory feelings that grew out of her conflict with the 'other teaching' of her community; compare also p. 223: 'Maer dat ick nu soo groot onghelijck vinde in uwer beijde leeringhe, soo verwondert mij dit al te seer, ende en weet niet wien ick ghelooven of volghen sal.'

[43] Compare Bake, 'Autobiografie', p. 224: '[...] ende het schijnt dat mij dese lieden weder wech willen iaghen ende segghen dat ick gheen ghemeijn mensche en ben [...].'

[44] Bake, 'Autobiografie', p. 227–28.

[45] Bake, 'Autobiografie', p. 225: 'Doen sach ick dan waer dat ick stondt, hondert ofte dusent graeden boven hunlieden.' Following this is the parable cited at the beginning of this study, which compares various ways of climbing to the top of a church in order to illustrate Alijt's advanced stage of nearness to God; see note 1 above. A second, supplementary image was tailor-made for the sisters of Galilea who knew their way well around the city: for a trip to Bruges, the sisters direct Alijt on a long, complicated detour through villages in the opposite direction from her destination, while she is already standing at the city gate which leads directly to Bruges; Bake, 'Autobiografie', p. 225–26.

[46] Alijt did go through the official form of confession, which entailed kneeling before her superiors and speaking the formula: 'Het was mijn schult, ick wilde mij gheerren beteren,' Bake, 'Autobiografie', p. 229. On the Windesheim confessions of guilt and disciplinary measures see van Dijk, *De constitutes*, I, p. 406–27.

[47] Bake, 'Autobiografie', p. 236: 'Het begon hier seer wtwendich te worden en sonder discipline [...] ende inden oversten alder meest [...] En men track *ons lieden* oock dicwijle daertoe ende *wij* en mochtens niet vermaenen, noch wedersprecken, om tot becoringhen te

not satisfied with behaviour that was correct in a purely external sense and noted the postulant's lack of honest enthusiasm and thankfulness. Nor could Alijt always keep her resolve to allow her fellow sisters to go their own way and not be bothered by what she considered misguided behaviour. At times her honesty and her love for her fellow sisters compelled her to contradict or correct them, but they would then accuse her of arrogance and obstinacy.[48]

Alijt gave more and more thought to the possibility of leaving Galilea and seeking a different path, outside the convent. She considered asking the prior general of Windesheim to transfer her to a different community.[49] But as she had not yet taken her final vows, the possibility of returning to her spiritual friends in Utrecht also remained open to her. Another option she considered was to transfer to the Franciscan Bethlehem convent in Ghent, founded by Colette of Corbie (d. 1447), who was famous at the time for her reforming activities.[50] The situation escalated when Alijt informed her prioress of her intentions and used the occasion to confront her about her shortcomings as a leader. Owing to her laxness, Alijt maintained, a progressive worldliness contrary to their statutes had crept into convent life.[51] Hille Sonderlants indignantly refused to tolerate such presumptuous and rebellious behaviour, but this only fuelled Alijt's anger, and she shouted: 'Look around to see whether people are practising this or that. I think they are not. It would greatly surprise the father of Windesheim and it would be very grievous to him that you are so deaf and blind.'[52] This threat had some effect and the mother superior, Alijt tells

---

commen' [italics mine].

[48] Bake, 'Autobiografie', p. 228: 'Ende als mij die waerheijt ende die susterlijcke minne somtijts dwanck dat te wedersprecken of te ontschuldighen in mij, om hun daerin te onderwijsen, soo nament sijt noch qualicker ende seijden dat ik hooveerdich, seer [ende] eijghen wijs "ende" onghes "t"orven was [...].'

[49] The prior of Windesheim represented the highest court of appeal within the congregation. During Alijt Bake's career in the convent Willem Vornken served as head of the general chapter (1425–54); see Johannes G. R. Acquoy, *Het klooster Windesheim en zijn invloed* (reprinted Leeuwarden: Dykstra, 1984), II, pp. 106–107, 127.

[50] This Franciscan reformer founded the community in 1442, then worked for a few years in France before returning to Ghent in 1446; she died in the Bethlehem convent the following year. See on this convent its own surviving chronicle, *Een kroniek van het voormalige monasterium Bethlehem der Klarissen-Koletinnen te Gent, geschreven tussen 1509 en 1530*, ed. by Benjamin de Troeyer, *Franciscana*, 47 (1992), 5–157; on Colette of Corbie and her reforming activities see also *Vita sanctae Coletae (1381–1447)*, ed. by Charles van Corstanje and others (Tielt: Lannoo, 1982) and the contribution by Bert Roest to this volume.

[51] Bake, 'Autobiografie', p. 236–37.

[52] Bake, 'Autobiografie', p. 238: 'Besiet dese ende dese sake, of men dit ofte "dat" pleght. Ick meijne wel neen. Het saude den pater van Windecim groot wonder gheven ende het saude hem seer derren dat ghij aldus doof ende blent sijt'. Notice also Alijt's moralizing tactic: she reports the conflict for her readers as a dialogue and thus as 'true to life', but at the same speaks in general terms instead of mentioning specific negative points.

us, attempted to improve her own behaviour as well as certain things in the community. Yet Alijt held to her resolve to leave the convent. Her plan was to return to her spiritual friends in Utrecht and seek their advice before making a final decision about how to proceed with her religious life.[53] The sisters, however, did not want to let her go and wrote to experienced and influential persons in Modern Devotion circles, hoping that they could change her mind. But Alijt no longer trusted anyone and waited for a sign from God that would show her the path she should take.

Divine Calling to be a 'Reformer of the Inner Life'

A key passage in Alijt's 'spiritual autobiography' comes at a point following her decision to leave the convent, while she was waiting only for the written consent of her Utrecht friends.[54] She reports there how her tie with Utrecht was restored in a supernatural way. The hospice sister appeared to her in her sleep and informed her that the recluse had died and that it was God's will that she remain in the convent to carry out her predestined tasks.[55] This dream was only the first in a series of mystical experiences that took place around Christmas 1440, when God revealed to her the path she should follow.

> Ah, then this new way of blessedness which I preach and teach was revealed to me for the first time, when I was transported from myself into God, with knowledge and love, but after that he had to be established in me through acquiescence and suffering, the path I have been walking since that time [...]. For just as Sister Colette was a mother of our order in the reformation of the holy religion, I should also be a mother of our order in the reformation of the inner life [...]. And just as she had the outer life, I would make that same life much more noble from the inside [...] and teach the same way to other people over whom I would rule.[56]

---

[53] Bake, 'Autobiografie', p. 238–39.

[54] Evidently the founder Jan Eggaert intervened in this difficult situation, see Bake, 'Autobiografie', p. 240–41: 'Sij hadden mij nu gheeren gehauden ende stonden seer wel in mij ende hadden nu mij alle lief. Ende hierom soo seijdent sij ende schrevent sommighe devote ende beleefde mannen dat sij mij daer af setten souden of sij mochten. Maer ick en wilde niemants raet hier in leven. Alsoo verre als ick eenich teecken van Godt mocht ghecrijghen [...]. Maer Godt versach mij eenen vrient ende dat was Jan Eggaert, onsen fondator [...].' The involvement of Jan Eggaert in the domestic conflict and the appreciation Alijt shows for him and his advice indicate a longstanding acquaintance between the two. It may have been her relationship with the founder of the house that led her to enter the Ghent convent; see notes 12 and 38 above.

[55] Bake, 'Autobiografie', pp. 242–44.

[56] Bake, 'Autobiografie', p. 244–46: 'Och, daer soo openbaerde mij eerst desen nieuwen wech der salicheijt die ick predicken ende leeren, daer ick doen in overghesedt was van mij selven in Godt, met kennissen ende met minnen, maer daernaer soo moeste "hij" in mij

It was therefore on the highest authority that Alijt was told to become a 'reformer of the inner life' and to impart her teachings on Passion mysticism to others.[57] At this time she was also led into higher spiritual mysteries. This meant that she left the stage of 'knowledge and love' to prepare herself for the most difficult phase of her mystical ascent–descent model, namely that of 'acquiescence and suffering'. The Christmas vision of 1440 legitimized, in her view, her religious mission to instruct others and laid the basis for her spiritual teaching of the ways of the cross.

Her doubts no longer had anything to do with the situation in Galilea. With the sisters showing her increasing love and respect, all external hindrances seemed to have disappeared, and it even became more and more likely that she would assume a leading role in the convent. Alijt's recent revelations, however, also gave her insight into her own errors, and this self-knowledge, she writes, brought doubts as to whether she was suited for a monastic career. From her earliest days as a postulant she had been thinking of possible chances for promotion, but she now realized that these wishes were the expression of a weakness in her character. She feared not only that the burdens of an office would keep her from her inward spirituality but also that her tendency to act without modesty would gain the upper hand and impede her spiritual progress.[58] Looking back, the prioress remarks critically: 'I knew who I was.'[59]

Alijt Bake describes how she prepared herself for her final entry into the order. In order to become a 'true nun' not just outwardly and formally but also inwardly she had to overcome the weaknesses in her character.[60] But Alijt went much further yet. In her advanced stage of spiritual union with God, the level of 'acquiescence and

---

ghevest worden met laeten ende met lijden, daer ick sient dien tijt in ghewandelt hebbe [...]. Want alsoo Suster Colette een moeder was van haren oorder in die reformatie der heijligher religien, alsoo soude ick oock sijn een moeder van onser oorder in reformatien des inwendighen levens [...]. Ende alsoo sij dat leven van buten hadde, alsoo soude ick dat selve leven van binnen noch veel edelder ghecrijghen [...] ende ander menschen dien selven wech leeren, die ick te regeren soude hebben.'

[57] Bake, 'Autobiografie', pp. 245–50. Alijt emphasizes the authenticity of her revelation by noting the date and her age. This type of documentation is infrequent in her autobiography.

[58] Bake, 'Autobiografie', p. 242–43: 'Ende dat dat was dit, dat mij dochte, waert dat ick hier bleve, dat ick procuraterse ende daernae Prioirinne werden saude [...] ick hadde ancxt dat ick alle mijn inwendich goet hiermede verliesen soude, dat ick in simpelheden ende in onder[t] te sijne vercreghen hadde [...]. Dat ander point was, dat mij dochte dat ick niet alsoo puerlijck Godt ghesocht en hadde doen ick eerst om dese stede bat, ende [...] dat hadde ick mij selven ghesaket met die onpuerheijt welcke ick doen niet en achte, [...] maer nu soo vroeech het mij seer swaerlijck.'

[59] Bake, 'Autobiografie', p. 247: 'Ick wist wel wie ick was.'

[60] Bake, 'Autobiografie', p. 248: 'Voirt soo plach ick onsen Heere te bidden altoos dat Hij mij Nonne maken wilde van binnen, eer ick Nonne worde van buijten. Want Nonne dat is niet, ende en waer ick niet wel te niete ghedaen eer ick dat heijlich abijt ende den naeme ontfinghe, soo soude ick den naem en dat abijt te vergheefs ontfanghen.'

suffering', what mattered was to achieve not only outward but—and this was much more difficult—inner poverty as well. Only then would she be safe from all temptation. The shedding of all attachment to earthly things necessary for this Alijt describes as a process of combating one's own nature. The image she invokes is that of 'taking off fourteen items of clothing'.[61]

Could it really be God's will that she become a nun? Once again a voice from Alijt's Utrecht past showed her the way for the future. This time it was her deceased companion who spoke to Alijt in a dream, informing her that she was indeed destined to enter the convent: 'Then she said to me: "You must soon enter the order, it is time."'[62] A further sign from God[63] finally led Alijt to request official admission into the convent. She began her novitiate in that same year, 1440.[64]

Teaching Mystical Passion

The vision of Ascension Day 1441 brought the breakthrough, opening the way to the highest stage of 'acquiescence and suffering'.[65] On the eve of this feast day Alijt was

---

[61] Bake, 'Autobiografie', p. 250–51: 'Ende en hadde gheen eijghenschap in mij gheweest, "ick" en hadde dese temptatie niet gheleden [...]. Och, lieve kinderen, ist niet wel eenen salighen wech sonder eijghenschap te leven, opdat een mensche van allen stricken der booser gheesten der temptacien, der tribulacen in desen tijt ende der hellen ende des vagheviers tenemael mede ontgaet [...].' See also Bake, 'Autobiografie', p. 248, where Alijt first introduces the term 'attachments' ['*eijghenschappen*'] which from then on assume a central place in her account. She differentiates seven outer and seven inner attachments.

[62] While Alijt was present in spirit at the memorial mass offered in honour of her friend in Utrecht, the friend appeared and spoke to her: 'Doen seijde sij mij: "Dat ghij haest in die oorden sult commen, het is tijt"', Bake, 'Autobiografie', p. 246; she goes on to say: 'Welck ick dede naerdat mij dit gheopenbaert was', Bake, 'Autobiografie', p. 247; see note 19q on the same page by Spaapen, who interprets the revelation as a reference to an earlier vision in which her divine mission as 'reformer of the inner life' was made known to her.

[63] This time, the prioress writes, God gave her his sign of permission in the form of a nose-bleed in each of the three successive Christmas masses of 1440; Bake, 'Autobiografie', p. 248–50.

[64] For dates I follow the conclusions of my *Staatsarbeit*; compare note 4 above. Alijt would have preferred to have been invited by one of the sisters to request entry, as was customary in the convent at the time, also for the sake of exercising humility. But she overcame her inner scruples. Compare Spaapen's remarks on this matter, Bake, 'Autobiografie', p. 246, note 19k; on the Windesheimers' procedure for taking the veil see van Dijk, *De constituties*, pp. 368–90.

[65] Compare Bake, 'Autobiografie', p. 249, note 21b by Spaapen, also Bake, 'Autobiografie', p. 250. Before elaborating further on these highest stages, Alijt goes back one last time to the stage of 'knowledge and love'. She reports in detail about the 'mystical-heart' experience in which God showed her his friendly, loving heart and about the comprehensive six-month preparation for her seven-hour general confession that preceded her initiation into 'the four ways of the cross'. On these events see Bake, 'Autobiografie', pp. 262–75, also

engaged in one of her frequent inner dialogues with God. It was then, she tells us, that her calling to be a spiritual leader was confirmed,[66] and she was told that her repeated request for spiritual transformation in the imitation of Jesus's Passion was about to be granted. At this decisive moment, however, the convent bell rang, summoning the sisters to sleep, and again she felt torn between monastic obedience and her inner experience of grace. But God comforted her, saying: 'I shall go with you to your bedside.'[67] Once there, she wanted to 'stay with him' rather than go to sleep. So she called on him again for help: 'Oh, dear Lord, what do you wish me to do? Whom shall I obey? I would like to stay awake with you and have more of you, and the rules of the order force me to be obedient. What shall I do?'[68] God's reply, Alijt tells us, seemed to be that she could have of him what she wished. She therefore stayed with him, true to her conviction that personal obedience to God took precedence over community rules. The subsequent inner dialogue between Alijt and God forms one of the most direct and pithy scenes in her autobiography.[69] When she asked to be instructed in the most difficult stage in imitating the Passion, God replied with an almost teasing smile: 'What are you saying now? Do you want to follow that path, too? That's something for strong men.' Looking back, Alijt tells us, it was as if he wanted to say, 'Admit that you are a weak woman'.[70] And he said this, she adds, in such a friendly and warm-hearted way that he seemed to be testing her. Alijt warded off his objection with characteristic boldness. In the following monologue she argues that it was God himself who had given men their strength. This meant that it was also in his power to give her the necessary strength. And what would help her most to achieve the spiritual greatness necessary to follow him on this difficult path of 'acquiescence and suffering' was not so much manly strength as the power of love.

Spaapen's comment, p. 272, note 37d. Bake's heart mysticism is strongly reminiscent of Mechthild von Hackeborn, see note 20 above.

[66] Bake, 'Autobiografie', p. 296–97.

[67] Bake, 'Autobiografie', p. 298: 'Ick sal met u gaen voor u bedde'.

[68] Bake, 'Autobiografie', p. 298: 'O lieven Heere, wat ghelieft U dat ick nu doen sal? Wien sal ick nu ghehoorsaem sijn? Ick saude gheeren met U waken ende wat meer van U hebben, ende d'ordinantie der oorden dwinct mij ghehoorsaem te sijne. Wat sal ick doen?'

[69] The dialogue form as an expression of the immediate presence of God is also used by Henry Suso; compare Heinrich Stirnimann, 'Mystik und Metaphorik: Zu Seuses Dialog', in *Das 'einig Ein': Studien zu Theorie und Sprache der deutschen Mystik*, ed. by Alois M. Haas and others, Neue Schriftenreihe zur Freiburger Zeitschrift für Philosophie und Theologie, 6 (Freiburg/Schweiz: Universitätsverlag, 1980), pp. 209–80. See also Werner Williams Krapp's contribution to this volume.

[70] Bake, 'Autobiografie', p. 298. The contrast between strong men and weak women is a pervasive topos in the spiritual literature, but Alijt's way of representing this subject as a dialogue in a kind of daily life atmosphere is special.

Although you made them [males] by nature stronger than you made me, you are able to bless me and make me a hundred times stronger in spirit than they are. For what good is the strength of nature to those who lack the strength of spirit? Oh Lord, the power of love is very great and surpasses the strong nature of men. Therefore if you give me this, I shall lack nothing.' And God replied as if he had been defeated: 'Oh woman, great is your faith, your knowledge, and your love. These three compel me to fulfill your desire. I cannot keep it from you. Pray, ask and demand what you will, I shall give it to you and make it clear.'[71]

God then initiated her into the highest and most secret mysteries of the imitation of Jesus's Passion.

The vision of the Ascension of 1441 forms the climax of Alijt Bake's mystical experiences. It was then that she gained access to the last hidden truths about the most difficult level of self-surrender in 'acquiescence and suffering' as found in her model of the 'four ways of the cross'. In the treatise containing her mystical teachings of the cross she describes the last stage of the Passion devotion as a walk in the dark, involving the loss of all inner certainty that had been part and parcel of her sense of nearness to God.[72]

It was very likely towards the end of that year that Alijt took her final vows. We can assume that her persistence in contemplative imitation of Christ's Passion as well as the accompanying spiritual ecstasies and visionary experiences finally convinced her fellow sisters in Galilea that she was genuinely favoured by God and therefore also the best candidate for the office of prioress. But Alijt must also have won the support of those higher up in the official hierarchy to be appointed Hille Sonderlants's (d. 25 January 1445)[73] successor when she had barely reached the age of thirty and was lacking long years of experience as a fully-fledged canoness.

---

[71] Bake, 'Autobiografie', p. 299: 'Al hebt ghijse stercker van naturen ghemaekt dan ghij mij doet, ghij mocht mij van gracien oock doen, en hondert werf stercker maken in den gheest dan sij sijn. "Want" wat baet de sterckheijt der naturen als sij die sterckheijt des gheest niet en hebben. Och Heere, de cracht der minnen die is soo groot en gaet boven die stercke nature der mannen. Hierom, soo sult ghij mij dese gheven ende mij en sal niet on[t]breken. Doen sprack den Heere, recht als verwonnen: "O vrauwe, groot is u gheloove, uwe kennisse en u minne. Dese drije dwinghen mij uwe begheerte te volcommen. Ick en mach niet verberghen. Bidt, vracht en eysscht al dat ghij wilt, ick salt u gheven ende verclaren."'

[72] On 'De vier kruiswegen' note 4 above; see also Robrecht Lievens, 'Een vijfde handschrift van Alijt Bake's vier kruiswegen', in *Ons Geestelijk Erf*, 40 (1966), 419–28.

[73] Jacobus C. van Slee, 'Het necrologium en cartularium van het convent der Reguliere kanunnikessen te Diepenveen', *Archief voor de Geschiedenis van het Aartsbisdom Utrecht*, 33 (1908), 317–485 (p. 326); Wilhelmus J. Kühler, *Johannes Brinckerinck en zijn klooster te Diepenveen* (Rotterdam: Neevens, 1908), p. 244; van Mingroot, 'Prieuré de Galilée à Gand', p. 769–70; see also the quotation from the Sisters' Book of Diepenveen, 'MS DV', fol. 48ʳ, (note 39).

The Rapiarian Structure of the 'Autobiography'

In general Alijt Bake evidently had a preference for short literary forms. Small treatises, concise apologies, and exempla form the bulk of her work. The one exception to this is seemingly her lengthy 'spiritual autobiography' known under the title 'My Beginning and Progress', which has survived only in the codex of the Galilea convent.[74] But this work, too, had a loose, 'patchwork' structure. In view of the emphasis this work places on the inner experience of Passion devotion, the typological term 'autobiography', first applied to the text by Robrecht Lievens,[75] is accurate only if prefixed by the specification 'religious' or 'spiritual'.[76] The text does not offer a clearly structured life story in chronological or thematic order, in keeping with the genre models of her day.[77] It lacks a clear line of organization, and reconstructing her life in terms of dates and individual stages on the mystical path is like piecing together a difficult puzzle. Yet the apparent laxness in composition can be attributed only in part to carelessness and in no way to a lack of technical literary know-how.[78] Rather, Alijt's autobiography reflects the method she learned as a

---

[74] Bernhard Spaapen selected a quotation from the introduction to the text for the programmatic title. On the Ghent codex with its approximately one hundred and eleven pages of text which have come down to us in the form of a late seventeenth- or eighteenth-century copy see Bake, 'Autobiografie', pp. 210–17 (Spaapen's Introduction); Ernest Persoons, 'Enkele nota's over de drie handschriften van Ruusbroec en Alijt Bake', *Ons Geestelijk Erf*, 40 (1966), p. 433–34; Bollmann, 'Studien', p. 52–54. Immediately following this text in the manuscript is a Middle Dutch version of the 'Book of Nine Rocks' by Rulman Merswin, whose model of steps or stages Alijt adopted as the basis for her private programme of spiritual exercises, compare note 7 above.

[75] Lievens, 'Alijt Bake', pp. 127, 139. He was followed by Stephanus Axters, *Geschiedenis van de vroomheid*, III, p. 166 and finally Bernhard Spaapen, who published the text in 1956 under the title 'De Autobiografie van Alijt Bake'. Reflection on the genre typology of the text only comes up in discussions about the various stages of editing, see Spaapen's remarks in Bake, 'Autobiografie', p. 210, note 9; p. 260, note 28–29; p. 272, note 37e; Gaston J. Peeters, 'Vervoort (d. 1555), Roecx (d. 1527) and the "Exercitia Tauleriana,"' *Verslagen en mededelingen van de Koninklijke Vlaamse Academie voor Taal- en Letterkunde*, 5–8 (1966), p. 152.

[76] The description of the text in terms of genre type as well as the sketch of structural literary features is taken largely from my *Staatsarbeit*, see Bollmann, 'Studien', especially pp. 58–60. To my knowledge no other literary analysis of this kind has yet been published.

[77] Compare U. Schulze, 'Autobiographie', in *Lexikon des Mittlealters* (Munich: Artemis, 1980), I, col. 1262; on genre problems in general compare Hans R. Jauss, 'Theorie der Gattung und Literatur des Mittelalters', in *Grundriss der romanischen Literaturen des Mittelalters* (Heidelberg: Winter, 1972), I, pp. 107–38; Walter Haug, 'Entwurf zu einer Theorie der mittelalterlichen Kurzerzählung', in *Kleinere Erzählformen des 15. und 16. Jahrhunderts*, ed. by Walter Haug and others, Fortuna Vitrea, 8 (Tübingen: Niemeyer, 1993), pp. 1–36; *Mittelalterliche Literatur und Kunst im Spannungsfeld von Hof und Kloster*, ed. by Nigel F. Palmer and others (Tübingen: Niemeyer, 1999).

novice and later polished, namely that of successively compiling, contemplating and rewriting a private collection of excerpts as a *rapiarium*. The making of this kind of loosely organized manuscript with private exercises and treasured quotations was valued and promoted in Modern Devotion circles as a proven method for nuturing self-control and spiritual growth. These 'rapiaria' or scrapbooks, which are necessarily heterogeneous in form, owing to frequent additions after irregular intervals and their close connection with the spiritual development of the writer in the context of everyday community life, are a typical example of Modern Devotion reform literature.[79] Alijt Bake had learned this writing as a spiritual exercise in concentration and meditation in early youth. She mentions this herself in her autobiographical sketch:

> And whatever I learned in this way I wrote down, so that I would not forget it. And thus in speaking and pondering and learning and writing and erasing and again rewriting I spent all my time, so that I forgot other chance thoughts.[80]

Later, her positive experience with a rapiarium and with a regular use of books and writing to support a program of spiritual exercises stood her in good stead when she looked for a didactically effective way to record her own religious experiences for the sisters of Galilea. Only from this perspective does the internal logic of her autobiographical text become visible.[81] The most disparate narrative details, from

---

[78] Alijt maintains at times that her knowledge owes little, and at other times nothing at all, to books, compare e.g., Bake, 'Autobiografie', p. 235: 'Ghij sult weten voorwaer dat "ick" noijnt in boecken en studerde dan dat minnende open herte ons liefs Heeren Jesu Christi ofte sijne lieve moeder Maria.' Yet her scepticism about books is aimed primarily at texts that lack a direct relevance to life. Remarks such as these have a topos quality in Modern Devotion writers and should not be taken literally. Alijt, in fact, shows in her writings that she is extremely well-read in the practical and mystical literature of the Modern Devotion, compare also note 34.

[79] For the definition and genre description of the term 'rapiarium' see Nikolaus Staubach, '"Diversa raptim undique collecta": Das Rapiarium im geistlichen Reformprogramm der Devotio Moderna', in *Literarische Formen des Mittelalters: Florilegien, Kompilationen, Kollektionen*, ed. by Kaspar Elm, Wolfenbütteler Mittelalter-Studien, 15 (Wiesbaden: Harrassowitz, 2000), pp. 115–47; Thom Mertens, 'Rapiarium', *Dictionnaire de spiritualité ascétique et mystique* (Paris, 1988), XIII, cols. 114–19; Mertens, 'Het rapiarium', in 'Moderne Devotie: Figuren en facetten', pp. 153–57.

[80] Bake, 'Autobiografie', p. 259: 'Ende wat ick aldus leerde dat schreef ick al op, dat ick niet vergheten en soude. Ende aldus al segghende ende al peijsende ende al leerende ende al schrijvende ende werderwtplanerende ende noch weder schrijvende brocht ick emmer mijnen tijt over, dat ick die ander sonderlinghe ghepeijsen vergat.' This method for aiding one's own *conversio* is already mentioned by Geert Grote in his 'Conclusa et proposita, non vota', compare Staubach, 'Pragmatische Schriftlichkeit', p. 429.

[81] Since the text is no longer available as an autograph, we can only speculate about its original form. One possibility is to subject the text to a close reading without the later additions of chapter markings, headings, etc., in other words to treat it as an 'unstable' totality in which implicit connections and contours can be discovered; see Bollmann, 'Studien'. On

spiritual ideas to visionary revelations of grace to everyday experiences in the convent, all have a place in a diary-like corpus where everything revolves thematically around the mystical transformation of the young sister on her way to spiritual union with God.

A devout rapiarium was originally a collection compiled by an individual for his or her own spiritual development. Only after the writer's death could these intimate writings pass into the common fund of spiritual convent literature and thus become available for collective use.[82] To judge from its constellation of content, structure, and style, Alijt Bake's 'spiritual autobiography' seems to represent a form midway in this transformational process; and as such it seems to have fulfilled several functions.[83] On the one hand the text is apparently a reworking of some of Alijt's earlier notes supplemented with memories,[84] thus a rapiarium in the classical sense. It was made by its owner in order to recollect and reflect on existing texts by going through a new process of writing.[85] On the other hand, the prioress wrote not only for herself but clearly with her sisters in mind. It was for her 'dear children' that she recorded her spiritual experiences. In doing so she hoped to be giving to those entrusted to her a guideline that would help them not only to understand her own mystical participation in the Passion but also to experience it themselves. To achieve this it was necessary to rewrite her collected memoirs as an edifying religious manual. In keeping with this didactic aim, Alijt employed a variety of literary devices: alliteration, numerous repetitions of words and concepts, as well as the direct address of her readers. Also, as in her other works, the author made an effort to link the many separate scenes by adding references to earlier or later passages as well as transitions between paragraphs that had little to do with each other in terms of chronology or content.[86]

---

the later division of the text into sections see note 88.

[82] On this transition from individual to collective possession and use see Nikolaus Staubach, 'Von der persönlichen Erfahrung zur Gemeinschaftsliteratur: Entstehungs- und Rezeptionsbedingungen geistlicher Reformtexte im Spätmittelalter', *Ons Geestelijk Erf*, 68 (1994), 200–28.

[83] The advantage of approaching supposedly difficult texts by way of their 'Sitz im Leben' is also emphasized by Staubach, 'Pragmatische Schriftlichkeit', p. 424.

[84] Alijt's technique of augmenting her written notes with material from her memory is evident from her remarks, for example Bake, 'Autobiografie', p. 241: […] 'as I remember'; p. 285: […] 'as I recall'; compare note 87 below.

[85] John Van Engen has recently shown that a rapiarium must also have been pivotal to the writings of the Modern Devotion mystic Gerlach Peters, see Van Engen, 'The work of Gerlach Peters (d. 1411), Spiritual Diarist and Letter-Writer: a Mystic among the Devout', *Ons Geestelijk Erf*, 73 (1999), 150–77; see also Robrecht Lievens, 'Een Rapiarium uit Jan van Leeuwen', *Handelingen*, 13 (1959), 73–84. A comparison of Alijt's work with that of other mystical writers in the late medieval reform movement, such as Gerlach Peters or Hendrik Mande, is long overdue.

[86] Bake, 'Autobiografie', compare e.g., pp. 232, 251, 262, 276 and 285: 'Nu soo wil ick

For longer expository passages she typically began with one or two sentences that summarized the content in terms of a unifying idea. She took care to subdivide longer sections and thus to present them to her circle of addressees in manageable portions. Conjunctions and repeated stereotypical interjections such as 'ooch' (oh) clearly serve a structural purpose.[87] Also, the shifts in narrative perspective, when the first-person narrator is unexpectedly interrupted by short messages from an authorial narrator, as well as the insertion of dramatic dialogues, breathe life into the work as a whole in a way that would have captured the attention of her audience.[88] Because the mystical experience is embedded in the historical and social world that the author shared with her readers—at least during her stay in the convent—the narrative as a whole would for them have had a heightened claim to authenticity and importance.[89]

Especially impressive are the many images and instances of alliteration that draw attention to key points in the text and make them more comprehensible for the sisters. Her own idiosyncratic views or complicated subject matter Alijt clarifies and supports with exempla drawn from the world familiar to the Ghent nuns. These lifelike examples are often skilfully interwoven with metaphors and images widely used in the literature and art of the Middle Ages.[90] In the parable cited at the beginning of this study, for example, where the climbing of a church tower is compared to the striving for closeness to God, Alijt makes use of the common

---

[het] wort verclaren die ander vier weghen, die haer Godt leerde [...] die hier vooren wat gheroert sij "n" maer niet verclaert. Daerom soo wil ick hier weder verhaelen alst gheschiede ende beter verclaren [...] naer mijn onthauwen [...].'

[87] Bernhard Spaapen made use of the structuring function of these elements when he subdivided the text into short numbered paragraphs. In his edition the literary devices mentioned above actually form the beginning of each section of text. Compare this and a second structuring of the work, very likely not found in the original manuscript either: Spaapen, 'Autobiografie', p. 216–17.

[88] Scholars are still speculating about the shift in perspective between the first-person narrator and the authorial third person. Most of them interpret these irregular jumps in narrative viewpoint as interventions of the copyists. But they could just as well have been part of the original presentation. Through successive stages in a long process of writing Alijt Bake could herself have opted for the more distanced authorial style. A more thorough investigation of these narrative shifts still needs to be undertaken. In her book, *Flowing Light of the Divinity*, Mechthild of Magedeburg (1210–1297) used similar shifts in perspective of the narrator. Perhaps Alijt found a model for her own writings here, but unfortunately we do not have any evidence that she knew this text at all.

[89] The turbulent events described by Alijt in the text, especially the conflicts in the convent with the mother superior Hille Sonderlants in the early 1440s and the change of mood within the sisterhood that eventually led to Alijt being elected prioress, must have been experienced by a majority of the sisters, considering that the text dates from around 1451.

[90] Susanne Bürkle, *Literatur im Kloster. Historische Funktion und rhetorische Legitimation frauenmystischer Texte des 14. Jahrhunderts*, Bibliotheca Germanica, 38 (Tübingen/Basel: Francke, 1998).

medieval motif of the ladder.[91] But the house of God, with its tower reaching towards heaven, also becomes an image of the successive stages of the mystical ascent;[92] and the church represents in a thoroughly classical way the official ecclesiastical power structure.[93] These polished didactic methods and linguistic finesses place Alijt Bake as a spiritual leader firmly within the tradition of written religious culture and in the proximity of other mystical authors such as Gerlach Peters, Hendrik Mande, and the author she quoted repeatedly, Johannes Ruusbroec, all of whom made use of the vernacular for purposes of transmitting knowledge.

Yet Bake sets herself off from these male models, in whom she misses her own conviction that the quest for union with God inevitably and necessarily entails a struggle with the external world and with the self. For Alijt Bake the 'vita activa' and the 'vita contemplativa' belonged together. One could not be complete without the other. For this reason she wanted to record the obstacles she encountered on the way to 'true piety' as much as her throroughly personal encounter with God in the intimacy of her own soul. As a mystic she did not consider herself an 'exception' living on the fringe of society but—specially blessed by God, to be sure, and called to teach—the embodiment of an integrative life of faith. In contrast to her predecessor, Hille Sonderlants, Alijt Bake placed higher priority on the personal experience of God than on the Windesheim convent rule with its traditional and authoritative ideas of a literal transmission of knowledge by means of a special, preselected canon of religious writings for women. This classic form of religious training Bake dared to criticize, going so far as to call it a hindrance in her 'spiritual biography'. As an alternative, and also as a way of substantiating her viewpoint, she described the immense personal benefit she had derived for her own spiritual development from Rulman Merswin's 'Book of Nine Rocks', a work acquired on her own initiative and in an unconventional way. It was this declaration of female independence in thought and action that would eventually prove fateful for the Ghent prioress.

---

[91] Compare Jacob's ladder, Genesis 28. 12; compare also the 'ladder of virtues' in Herrad of Hohenbourg, *Hortus deliciarum*, ed. by Rosalie Green, Studies of the Warburg Institute, 36, 2 vols (London: Warburg Institute, 1979), p. 352; on the image of the ladder and its various meanings see also *Lexikon der Christlichen Ikonographie*, ed. by Engelbert Kirschbaum (Rome: Herder, 1994), II, col. 283–84.

[92] See Friedrich Ohly, 'Die Kathedrale als Zeitenraum: Zum Dom von Siena', in *Schriften zur mittelalterlichen Bedeutungsforschung*, ed. by F. Ohly (Darmstadt: Wissenschaftliche Buchgesellschaft, 1977), pp. 171–274.

[93] Compare also Alijt's 'Conclusio' in which she supplies the interpretation of her image. Bake, 'Autobiografie', p. 226–27.

Deposition and Exile

In her spiritual autobiography Alijt does not go into her election as prioress. When she composed her text in 1451, she had been holding office for approximately six years. The account of her personal experiences breaks off for no obvious reason in the period when she made her profession. Under her leadership the community enjoyed a period of growth and material prosperity, which also led to its involvement in the reformation of three devout convents, starting in 1454. The prophecy that she would become a 'spiritual reformer of the inner life' beyond the walls of her convent for the entire Modern Devotion movement now seemed to be fulfilled.

In 1455, however, the governing body of the Windesheim General Chapter put an abrupt end to the career of the Ghent prioress by forcing her to leave office.[94] Her deposition was followed by exile from the convent and thus separation from her 'dear children'.[95] The sources are silent about what actually happened. Only in one letter, written from exile in 1455 to the rector of the convent[96] do we hear from Alijt herself about the impending proceedings in which she hoped to be vindicated.[97] (Along with a large group of the sisters, he had taken her side.) Essentially this letter is a new apology for her mystical teaching of the imitation of the Passion, presented here in terms of its individual aspects.[98] Alijt writes comforting words for her followers, inside and outside the Galilea convent, who because of her were evidently

---

[94] On a procedure of this kind see van Dijk, *De constituties*, I, pp. 297–308; 2, p. 735; van Dijk, 'De mystieke weg', pp. 130–32.

[95] Spaapen assumes that the Facons convent in Antwerp, the only other convent in the southern Netherlands belonging to the Windesheim congregation, served as her place of exile. See Spaapen's introduction to his edition of Alijt's letter, Bake, 'Brief', p. 351. This view has been generally accepted although no proof has been presented. On the Facons convent see R. de Keyser, 'Domus beatae Mariae in Facons in Antwerpen', in *Monasticon Windeshemense*, I, pp. 223–35; Ernest Persoons, 'Prieuré de Mariendaal, à Anvers', in *Monasticon Belge*, VIII.2 (1993), pp. 563–79.

[96] This may have been Nicolaus van Dunendijc, see van Mingroot, 'Domus Beatae Mariae de Galilea', p. 266; at the time the letter was written a new mother superior had already been instated in Galilea, compare Bake, 'Brief', p. 354.

[97] On the edition of the letter see note 4 above. Alijt was writing a defence that she wanted to send to the Windesheim priors and apparently enclosed a draft with her letter for the rector to read, Bake, 'Brief', p. 354–55. In its apologetic stance Alijt's letter stands in the literary tradition of correspondence with father confessors, a means used by many thirteenth and fourteenth-century women mystics to break out of the isolation of their convents.

[98] As in her autobiography, Alijt employs the stylistic technique of a didactic dialogue when recounting her Ascension Day vision of 1441. Significantly, she here selects the passage on the difference in strength between men and women. Compare note 70 above, and Bake, 'Brief', p. 362.

criticized by the Windesheim authorities. She also explains anew her 'teaching of spiritual inwardness' and emphasizes the authenticity of her reforming task, assigned to her as it was on the highest authority. The defamation and disdain she experienced from secular and clerical powers was in her view one more trial and thus the logical continuation of her path of 'acquiescence and suffering'.

Even after her removal from office, Alijt continued to present herself as a reformer called by God who held firmly to her convictions in the face of adversity. Her earlier realization that there could be great discrepancies between the high rank of a convent superior, as embodied by Hille Sonderlants in the Windesheim hierarchy, and the level of that person's knowledge about the experience of God now seemed to transfer itself to the Windesheim fathers:

> And unless our fathers and brothers, whoever they may be, take heed and genuinely return to this teaching, our order will soon die out, for there is nothing but a little outward form. But of the inward, supernatural life of virtue, on which everything depends, none of them know anything. They continue in their sensual ways, but about the inward, spiritual life they know nothing.[99]

At the same time Alijt's letter suggests how disappointed and hurt she must have been by the actions of her Windesheim superiors. Her physical health seems to have suffered from the stress.[100] Before her 'case' could be officially dealt with, she died in exile on 18 October 1455, barely forty years old.

The great agitation that Alijt Bake must have caused in the Windesheim congregation, even though the conflict did not come to a head in a formal hearing,[101] is evident from the chapter resolution of the same year forbidding all female members of monastic communities, on pain of ecclesiatical punishment, to write on doctrine or visions.[102] In its blunt harshness, this ban on writing sounds like a

---

[99] Bake, 'Brief', p. 366: 'Ende ten sij dat onse vaders en broeders, wie sij oock sijn, haer hooren hiertoe voeghen, ende eenen waerachtichghen wederkeer hiertoe doen, onse oorden sal in corten tijt vergaen, want daer en is niet dan een weynich wtwendichs. Maer van dat inwendighe, overnaturelijck leven der duechden, daert al op staet, daer en weten sij niet met allen af. Sij loopen al in sinnelijcker wijse voirt, maer van het inwendich, gheestelijck leven en weten sij niet.'

[100] Bake, 'Brief', p. 359: 'torturing my body'.

[101] Neither in the Windesheim archives nor in the sources from Galilea or other convents has any material survived on the case of Alijt Bake. Nor does the chapter resolution of 1455 contain any direct reference to the Ghent prioress. Only the concurrence of her deposition and the Windesheim writing ban, the elimination of her name from the colophon of the Brussels manuscript KB, MS 643/44, and the otherwise anonymous transmission of her writings point to a causal relationship between the Windesheim ordinance and her activities as a spiritual teacher and writer.

[102] *Acta Capituli Windeshemense: Acta van de kapittelvergaderingen der Congregatie van Windesheim*, ed. by Sape van der Woude, Kerkhistorische studiën, 4 ('s-Gravenhage, 1953), p. 53: 'Nulla monialis aut soror cuiuscunque status fuerit conscribat aliquos libros, doctrinas philosophicas aut revelationes continentes per se interpositamve personam ex sua propria

helpless attempt to silence people like Alijt Bake on the matter of her inner spiritual experiences, for she certainly did not stand alone. Her inner strength threatened to unleash an almost charismatic self-sufficiency and independence of the female Devout as they pursued their spiritual path, an attitude for which Alijt Bake had fought her uncompromising battle: 'being a woman on my own'.

Looking Ahead

Because Alijt's 'spiritual autobiography' and 'letter from exile' were handed down only within the secluded walls of her own convent, it was long believed that she had failed not only as prioress but also as Modern Devotion author. It appears that the chapter resolution had a decisive effect and that Alijt's works fell prey to the general ban on writing. There would have been very little chance for her confessional and mystical writings to survive in any form whatsoever.[103]

More recently, however, it has become clear that this assumption was too pessimistic. Despite all prohibitions, Alijt Bake's teaching of the 'reformation of the inner life' did enter the canon of late medieval and early modern edifying literature —by detours, under new titles, and in anonymously transmitted adaptations. The Brussels codex mentioned above, which contains the largest known collection of Alijt's texts, no longer stands alone. In other sources more and more works are being discovered with clear traces of Alijt's mystical teaching, both in terms of content and stylistic features. Here, too, the author's preference for short literary forms proved advantageous for the dissemination of her teaching.

Future research may uncover more about the personality of the author and her conviction that in her thought and actions she stood above all secular and ecclesiastical authorities. We can be sure that Alijt's spiritual teaching, with its concepts of 'acquiescence, suffering, and love', did not simply 'come out of the blue'. First investigations of her work have clearly shown how much was conditioned by the time and personal circumstances in which she lived. The

---

mente vel aliarum sororum compositas sub poena carceris si qui inposterum reperti fuerint praecipitur omnibus quod statim illi ad quorum conspectum vel aures pervenerit eos igni tradere curent, similiter nec aliquem transferre praesumant de latino in theutonicum.'

[103] On Alijt Bake's crossed out name in the colophon of the Brussels codex, KB, MS 643/44, see notes 23 and 101 above. The total absence of mystical writings by other women authors in the Modern Devotion movement who might have followed in Alijt's footsteps also seems to indicate the all-pervasive effect of the chapter ordinance. The writings of Jacomijne Costers (1462/63–1503) from the Antwerp Facons convent, quite possibly Alijt Bake's place of exile, contain a note by the copyist saying the author intentionally recounted her eschatological vision of 1489, experienced after her bout with the plague, from the perspective of an authorial 'he'. Compare the text edition of Wybren Scheepsma, 'De helletocht van Jacomijne Costers', *Ons Geestelijk Erf*, 70 (1996), 157–85 (p. 161). The copyist of the codex repeats this remark after finishing the text.

Windesheim sister reveals herself to be a woman on the brink of modernity, well-read in classical and patristic texts as well as in the mystical literature of her time. Her pragmatic use of books and writing shows her to be an author standing firmly in the tradition of the Modern Devotion who wishes to make public her own remarkable understanding of religious issues. In her 'spiritual autobiography' everything comes together in a kind of symbiosis: mystical experiences, the function of a living example, and legitimation as 'reformer of the inner life'.

Alijt's life story in a way is a familiar tale: a precocious, spiritually gifted young nun encounters hostility from her congregation that deeply resents her superior airs and general non-conformity. We all recognize this pattern from earlier centuries. Perhaps Alijt's tragedy was that she thought that in the late medieval reform movement of the Modern Devotion it would be possible for religious women to follow their own path of faith. However, within the hierarchical monastic world of the Windesheim congregation women still were predestined to obedience and subservience.

In any case, the reaction of the Windesheim fathers to her reformist activities through the spoken and written word creates the impression that in the mid-fifteenth century female Devout were allowed less spiritual latitude in their convents than within the confining walls of an anchoress's cell.

Translated by Myra Scholz

The Gender of Epistemology in Confessional Europe: The Reception of Maria van Hout's Ways of Knowing*

KIRSTEN M. CHRISTENSEN

In his *Sacrarium Agrippinae* of 1607 Erhard of Winheim mentions the existence of a manuscript, likely in Latin, by the prolific Carthusian author and translator Laurence Surius about the spiritual life of the beguine mystic and visionary Maria van Hout (d. 1547 and also known as Maria van Oisterwijk).[1] Unfortunately, this Life is apparently no longer extant, but the fact that it was written says much more about Maria van Hout's significance to the Cologne Carthusian community and to other male religious of her day than any scholarly mention of it has acknowledged. Although she enjoyed a reputation of sanctity, there is no evidence that an official canonization process was ever initiated for Maria. Thus the Life more likely served to retain the memory of her spiritual formation and virtue as a model

---

* I wish to thank Valerie Hotchkiss for her thoughtful comments on this article, and David Price for his insight and help in my early considerations of the material for this study. I am also indebted to the Brepols reviewer for her many helpful suggestions.

[1] Erhard of Winheim, *Sacrarium Agrippinae* (Cologne, n.p., 1607), p. 210. This section of Winheim's work describes paintings and inscriptions in the Chapel of Saint Mary at the Cologne Charterhouse, and, in this particular passage, the gravesite of Maria van Hout: 'At the top of the chapel, near the choir, [...] was buried in 1547 the remarkable virgin Maria of Oisterwijk, who was great in accomplishments and hidden sanctity, and of whom the venerable Father Laurence Surius wrote a manuscript that still exists, which contains, among other things, her praises [Insuper in sacello choro vicino [...] Maria de Osterwick virgo admirabilis, magna meritis et occultae sanctitatis 1547 sepulta fuit, de qua ms. Codex venerabilis P. Laur. Surii adhuc superest, in quo inter alias eius commendationes]. See also Johannes Kettenmeyer, 'Maria von Oisterwijk (d. 1547) und die Kölner Kartause', *Annalen des historischen Vereins für den Niederrhein*, 144 (1929), 1–33 (pp. 1–2).

for succeeding generations. Anneke Mulder-Bakker explains that even the Lives of many actual saints 'should not in the first place be viewed as instruments in the canonization procedure but as a means of storing good examples'.[2] Surius was apparently concerned with exactly such memorial Lives. His *Anthology of Saints' Lives, Ordered by Months and Days According to the Roman Calendar* (*Sammlung der Leben der Heiligen geordent nach Monaten und Tagen gemäß dem römischen Kalendar,* first published 1570–1575 and in an expanded second printing in 1618) was *the* recognized collection of saints' Lives until the advent of that of the Bollandists. Adam Wienand argues that while 'the Bollandists create[d] a selection of critical sources [...] Surius, on the other hand, want[ed] merely to create a book of devotion.'[3] This is not to say, though, that Surius wrote for an unlearned audience. On the contrary, Paul Holt argues that Surius made changes in the source material for his collection of saints' Lives primarily when the language or style of the original required him to take the sensibilities of a humanist readership into account.[4] Surius's Life of Maria van Hout might thus also have had both the same devotional purpose and learned audience as his other hagiographical endeavours.

That Maria's life and work inspired devotion is further substantiated by other writings about and by her. Most significantly, Gerhard Kalckbrenner, procurator and later prior (1536–1566) of the Cologne Carthusian monastery of St Barbara, published Maria's devotional treatises and letters in 1531 under the title *Der rechte wech zo der evangelischer volkomenheit* [*The Right Way to Evangelical Perfection*].[5] In his foreword to this edition of her works and in a separate Latin translation and publication of one of her treatises, Kalckbrenner wrote two Lives of sorts, both of which—the second much more elaborately than the first—portray Maria as a woman whose spiritual trials had sanctified her.[6] Knowledge of Maria's piety grew when Kalckbrenner and his Carthusian brethren brought her to live amid the confessional

---

[2] Anneke B. Mulder-Bakker, 'The Metamorphosis of Woman: Transmission of Knowledge and the Problems of Gender', *Gender and History*, 12 (2000), 642–64 (p. 648).

[3] 'Die Bollandisten schaffen [...] eine kritische Quellensammlung [...]. Surius dagegen will nur ein Erbauungsbuch schaffen'. Adam Wienand, 'Laurentius Surius', in *Die Kartäuser: Der Orden der schweigenden Mönche,* ed. by Marijan Zadnikar and Adam Wienand (Cologne: Wienand, 1983), pp. 276–82 (p. 276).

[4] 'Vor allem mußte er Rücksicht nehmen auf das Sprachgefühl der humanistisch gebildeten Kreise.' Paul Holt, 'Die Sammlung von Heiligenleben des Laurentius Surius', *Neues Archiv der Gesellschaft für ältere deutsche Geschichtskunde,* 44 (1922), 341–64 (p. 356).

[5] *Der rechte wech zo der evangelischer volkomenheit* (Cologne: Johann von Kempen, 1531), hereafter as *Der rechte wech.*

[6] This second Life appears in a preface to a letter from Maria to Kalckbrenner that he published in 1532. *Frater Gerardus ab Hamont procurator Carthusiensium in Colonia, pio lectori gratiam et pacem a domino nostro Jesu Christo* (Cologne: n.p., 1532), cited hereafter as *Frater.* The manuscript original is most likely no longer extant. References are to a printed copy of the letter housed in the Basel Universitätsbibliothek, D.A. VI 19, Nr. B13.

turmoil of Cologne in 1545. From the time of her move until she died on 30 September 1547, she associated with and influenced some of the most prominent religious leaders of the day, including Peter Canisius, founder of the first Jesuit community in Germany. The impact of her associations with these men is preserved in a diverse array of mostly brief, yet revealing references to her in various documents and correspondence. Pieced carefully together, these fragments make visible a life characterized by visionary gifts and spiritual leadership of both women and men. Although early scholars describe Maria as obscure, and her works as simple, she appears to have enjoyed a rather profound reputation as a holy woman, both in her native Brabant and later in Cologne. Arnoldus Janssen, for example, in his biography of the influential Cologne cleric, Nicholas Esch, writes that Maria inspired both religious and non-religious, including, he emphasizes, married men and women. He claims that Maria's influence was so profound that it made people of the world seem more like people of orders.[7]

Maria van Hout's special impact on the male religious with whom she associated seems to have centred on her epistemologies of the divine. Male reception of Maria's life and writings suggests that 'feminine' ways of knowing and accessing God took on new, even urgent appeal to clerics in the wake of the Reformation. These ways of knowing included direct spiritual manifestations (such as auditions, visions, and revelations), and the use of the body as a receptacle and transmitter of spiritual knowledge. This is not to say that male mystics did not also sometimes partake of such experiences. Rather, it is clear that such direct access to God had become feminized, and thus generally marginalized, in the worst cases denigrated or punished, over the course of the Middle Ages, especially after the flowering of women's mysticism in the twelfth and thirteenth centuries. Carthusian and Jesuit interest in Maria van Hout seems to represent an attempt at dismantling such epistemological boundaries in the Church, a dismantling that was directly linked to the crisis of the Reformation. In more positive terms, Maria's life and works were apparently in timely confluence with new—or newly pressing—devotional needs in the Church. Indeed, the Cologne Carthusians had long been publishing mystical texts, which they continued with renewed fervor as confessional debates increased. And they 'published' Maria van Hout as a living mystical text, an utterly orthodox woman who embodied multiple ways of knowing, which I will separate, for the purposes of this study, into three broad (and sometimes overlapping) categories: the spiritual, the physical, and the intellectual.

---

[7] Arnold Jans, '*Vita Domini Nicolai Eschii Pastoris Beginagii Sanctae Catharinae in Diest*', (n.p., before 1580), Brussels, Bibliothèque Royale, MS 653, fol. 29ᵛ–30ʳ; see also Kettenmeyer's discussion of and excerpt from Esch's *Vita* in 'Maria van Oisterwijk', pp. 6–8.

Spiritual Ways of Knowing

Maria's spiritual ways of knowing are the subject of a letter of 9 November 1546 from Cornelius Wischaven, the first Flemish Jesuit, to fellow Jesuit Leonhard Kessel in Cologne. This letter shows that Maria's male associates desired not only to understand, but indeed to acquire and imitate her ways of knowing God. Wischaven writes to Kessel with counsel for the latter's spiritual life. In a curious passage, Wischaven instructs Kessel on interacting with Maria, who by that time had been living in Cologne for about a year. Wischaven's claim that he knows Maria well implies that she was a frequent part of the spiritual life of the Jesuits in Cologne and in the Low Countries, and that they considered her an awesome, even intimidating spiritual figure who commanded their deference:

> I would like to ask you for one thing in love: whenever you visit Maria, comply with the following precaution (I believe, namely, that I know her to some degree): if you want to make progress in spiritual matters, you should not contend with her by emphasizing your opinion or your own judgment or by contradicting her. For when mystics (*spirituales*) encounter such a person, they are immediately silent and become submissive, and they consider such things [i.e. contentious discussions] with which they [i.e. persons who engage in such discussions] occupy themselves to be deceptive.[8]

Ulrike Wiethaus interprets Maria's silence as a refusal of the male 'mode of discourse'.[9] If that mode of discourse was scholarly disputations, then such a refusal was undoubtedly essential, since Maria almost certainly did not have the requisite education. In addition, one might argue that Maria had no choice but to refuse to dispute, since doing otherwise, especially in the wake of fifteenth-century guidelines for the discernment of spirits, would arguably have destroyed her credibility as a mystic.[10] Maria appears, though, to have found a way to exercise rhetorical power

---

[8] 'Preterea unum oratum ex charitate velim, quod si contingat, te vel ipsum ad Mariam ire, servetis hanc cautelam (quandoquidem puto me eam aliqualiter cognoscere), si vultis in spiritualibus proficere, nunquam debetis cum ipsa arguere, ostentando ingenium vestrum vel proprium iudicium seu replicando. Nam cum talem spirituales inveniunt, statim tacent et submittunt se ipsis dantque sese victos, et accipiunt sibi huiusmodi pro brixio, qui eos exercent.' *Rheinische Akten zur Geschichte des Jesuitenordens 1542–1582,* ed. by Joseph Hansen (Bonn: Hermann Behrendt, 1896), pp. 67–68.

[9] Ulrike Wiethaus, '"If I Had an Iron Body": Femininity and Religion in the Letters of Maria de Hout', in *Dear Sister: Medieval Women and the Epistolary Genre,* ed. by Karen Cherewatuk and Ulrike Wiethaus (Philadelphia: University of Pennsylvania Press, 1993), pp. 171–91 (p. 176).

[10] For a thorough and useful look at the development of the Church's teachings on *discretio spirituum,* see Rosalynn Voaden's excellent study: *God's Words, Women's Voices: The Discernment of Spirits in the Writing of Late-Medieval Women Visionaries.* (York: York Medieval Press, 1999), especially Chapter 2.

within such constraints. Wiethaus points, for example, to Maria's own admission that she often 'yielded' to her interlocutors 'as if to flatter them',[11] and thus convincingly portrays Maria's silence as actually 'an adroit manoeuvre to control the situation'.[12] Significantly, Wischaven himself seems quite aware of Maria's manoeuvring. Joseph Hansen suggests that Wischaven's word choice implies an understanding that '[mystics] appear to be submissive, but, in reality, they place no value on persuasion.'[13] Wischaven is thus arguably offering more than a knowing wink to his colleague and a defensive strategy for 'dealing' with Maria. His advice is not a criticism of Maria's appropriately submissive behaviour, but rather apparently of Kessel's own predisposition to dispute. Indeed, Wischaven's statement that deference toward Maria is necessary in order to 'make progress in spiritual matters' is a de facto and willing admission that Maria's way is the right way, even if it was still unfamiliar terrain for the learned Kessel. That Kessel was not compelled to interact with Maria but was apparently seeking her out underscores the genuineness of his desire to learn from her.

The Jesuits energetically proselytized in response to the Protestant threat, and maintained close ties to the Carthusians, who combated Protestantism predominantly through the publication of devotional and mystical texts. These facts make it clear that Wischaven's advice to Kessel is also not a call to reject learnedness.[14] Rather, his counsel on interacting with Maria points to a realization that spirituality need not be learned to be profound, and that the way of knowing of *spirituales* like Maria could offer an important enhancement to their bookish learning and to their efforts to defend and promote the faith. In other words, the confessional times seemed to have elicited for these Jesuits a fundamental reassessment of affective spirituality and of knowledge beyond books. Indeed, Wischaven's note to Kessel is partly about Maria personally, but predominantly about her spiritual ways of knowing. It is less a denigration of some quirk or stubborn streak in Maria's nature, or even in female nature, than a genuine assessment of how mystics act and interact. Importantly, the

---

[11] Wiethaus, 'If I Had an Iron Body', p. 176. The entire passage from Maria's letter is as follows: '[...] dan ich gewan altzyt meer mit bidden dan mit sprechen, und ich gienge yn ouch mit exempelen vur, und ich buegede mich under sie recht off ich mit yn gesmeicht hedde.' All references to the letters are taken from: *De Brieven uit 'Der rechte wech' van de Oisterwijkse Begijn en Mystica Maria van Hout (d. Keulen, 1547)*, ed. by J. M. Willeumier-Schalij (Leuven: Peeters, 1993), here p. 94. The letters are the only portion of the text that have been edited to date.

[12] Wiethaus, 'If I Had an Iron Body', p. 176.

[13] 'Sie unterwerfen sich scheinbar, erachten aber in Wirklichkeit das Zureden für nichts'. *Rheinische Akten*, p. 68, note 1.

[14] See Sigrun Haude's discussion of Carthusian efforts to oppose the Protestant Reformation in 'The Silent Monks Speak Up: The Changing Identity of the Carthusians in the Fifteenth and Sixteenth Centuries', *Archiv für Reformationsgeschichte*, 86 (1995), 124–40 (especially p. 130).

term Wischaven uses—*spirituales*—is not female-specific. Further, it is worth noting that Wischaven passes on this advice to Kessel 'in love'. He genuinely wants to help Kessel progress spiritually, and he presents conforming to 'the mystics'' way of knowing and conversing as a crucial first step.

Such an interpretation of genuine deference to Maria's spirituality by male religious is substantiated by a rather remarkable, and as yet unpublished document, now located in the Hessische Landes- und Hochschulbibliothek in Darmstadt. The distinctive and elegant hand of Georg Garnefeld, librarian at St Barbara from 1618–1633, identifies the little volume as 'Collectanea V. P. Gerardi Hamontani', i.e. Gerhard Kalckbrenner.[15] This attribution is not unassailable, however. For one thing, a comparison to letters signed by Kalckbrenner show that Kalckbrenner himself did not act as scribe for the book, even if he authored it. Kettenmeyer considers it unlikely that Kalckbrenner would have allowed a secretary to copy 'such intimate expressions', and he thus suggests that the author was another Carthusian who knew Maria well.[16] A portion of the text is indeed quite personal. The author records, for example, that 'Mother' Maria admonished him to 'acknowledge certain past faults', and taught him that 'thus far all of [his] life was careless and disordered'.[17] I am not convinced, however, that Kalckbrenner, who devoted significant time, energy, and resources to the promotion of Maria van Hout's teachings, and who had already published several of her letters to him in *Der rechte wech*, would have had the reservations Kettenmeyer suggests in discussing his private interactions with her.[18] Furthermore, the hand is clean and careful enough to indicate that the writer considered it worthy of a broader readership, in spite of the personal elements. Sigrun Haude explains that such collections of 'texts, phrases, and bits of wisdom[...] [with] room for notes', which were common to the Cologne Carthusians, 'not only serve[d] to further one's own spiritual perfection but that of the fellow brethren as well.'[19] That said, the value of the document would be in no way diminished by attribution to a Carthusian other than Kalckbrenner. On the contrary, it would merely expand our understanding of Maria's influence.

---

[15] *Collectanea spiritualia* (Cologne, n.d.). Located in Darmstadt, Hessische Landes- und Hochschulbibliothek, MS 1204.

[16] 'solche intime Aussprachen'; Kettenmeyer, 'Maria van Oisterwijk', pp. 18–19.

[17] *Collectanea*, fol. 33^v–34^r.

[18] Garnefeld's attribution should also be considered seriously. Although Garnefeld did not know Maria personally, he lived in the Cologne Charterhouse during a time in which, according to Kettenmeyer,'Maria van Oisterwijk', p. 12: 'the tradition of the [woman] mystic [Maria van Hout] [...] was still very much alive' (die Tradition der Mystikerin [...] noch sehr lebendig war). In addition, Garnefeld's years in the Charterhouse overlapped with various others who knew both Kalckbrenner and Maria van Hout. See Kettenmeyer, 'Maria van Oisterwijk', pp. 12–13, 18.

[19] Haude, 'The Silent Monks', p. 127.

The author, whoever he was, offers notes and impressions from readings and, significant for our purposes, from his interactions with Maria. He records, for example, that she told him the following parable 'on the fifteenth (Sunday) in the year 1545', which would have been shortly after her arrival in Cologne from Oisterwijk:

> A certain man was going outside to consider the course of the stars, and he fell into a pit. A woman reproved him, saying 'Why do you, a wretch, presume to search into high things, while you neglect all the while your own self and the things around you?' And this parable is particularly applicable to the learned today.[20]

Here Maria employs a time-honoured anti-intellectual parable to lay out her advice to those who would learn the things of God.[21] In fact, although we have no record that Maria knew of Wischaven's letter to Kessel, the exemplum of the astronomer here functions as a sort of interpretation of the strategy Wischaven describes, and thus as advice for men who interact with her. She seems to clarify that her silence in the face of opposition or frustration is not merely a tactic, but indeed a pedagogical and spiritual tool. One can almost imagine that she is recalling interactions with Kessel or other learned religious when she admonishes that 'when you do not understand immediately, then wait patiently, and pray, that you may know the will of God,'[22] or when she explains that 'you will see goodness and love [...] shine forth in all creatures if you are a keen observer.'[23] In Maria's rendition of the exemplum, as is frequently the case in other versions, a woman conveys the message to the wayward man. This detail, along with Maria's comment on the parable's special applicability to 'the learned today', imply rather strongly that the mystic's way of knowing was still considered a predominantly feminine way in Maria's day.

Maria's spiritual and physical ways of knowing merge in a brief but telling editorial passage by Kalckbrenner in *Der rechte wech*. The passage in question is found in the middle of Maria's treatise on the five wounds of Christ, the last of her

---

[20] 'Quidam exiens ad contemplandum cursus syderum cecidit in foveam. Cui exprobavit mulier dicens: Quid tu miser alta scrutari praesumis, negligens interim teipsum et quae circa te sunt. Et haec parabola maxime verificatur apud doctos hodie.' *Collectanea,* fol. 38^r. My thanks to Dr Joachim Vennebusch, Historisches Archiv der Stadt Köln, for generously making his transcription of the Darmstadt manuscript available to me, and to Daniel Hobbins for his reliable (unpublished) translation.

[21] In the *Miller's Tale,* for example, Chaucer has John the Carpenter use this exemplum to rebuke the cleric who lodges him. Geoffrey Chaucer, 'The Miller's Tale'. *The Canterbury Tales* (London, New York: Penguin Classics, 1996) vv. 347–56.

[22] 'Et quando statim non intelligis, tunc expecta longanimiter, et ora, ut voluntatem Dei cognascas.' *Collectanea*, fol. 38^v.

[23] 'Et videbis in omnibus creaturis resplendere bonitatem et amorem [...] si diligens observator fueris'. *Collectanea*, fol. 38^v.

treatises in the book:

> When the aforementioned person shared this exercise with her spiritual son [...] and
> saw that I wrote down and accepted the same with great eagerness, she rejoiced within
> herself and was taken up in God in my presence. And when she came again to her
> outer senses, she said to me: 'When I noticed [...] that you were so well disposed to
> this exercise, God poured such overflowing grace into my heart for your sake that I
> could not bear it, for I had gained a new brother with this exercise, by the love of
> God.'[24]

Kalckbrenner's literal receipt of the exercise in the moment he here describes
instigated a lengthy and important reception among other male religious. And this
broader reception reveals much about the appeal to men of Maria's physical
epistemology.

Physical Ways of Knowing

Maria reports having received her exercise on the five wounds by revelation for a
community of sister religious, perhaps other beguines. This exercise not only makes
known the importance of Christ's passion to Maria's mystical theology, but also
confirms the centrality of the body—both the reader's and the Virgin Mary's—in her
portrayal of salvation. One might say that she elevates the status of the female body
in particular, since she originally wrote for women. While we can consider all of
Maria's treatises in *Der rechte wech* to be devotional literature, since they are all
intended, as she usually states directly, for the edification of her readers, the treatise
on the five wounds is different, since it is also a devotional exercise. In it, Maria
proposes for her readers a series of carefully composed prayers and meditations, as
well as physical tasks, all intended to increase devotion to Christ's passion. In the
spirit of late medieval piety, Maria's exercise urges *compassio* in her readers through
their acknowledgement of sinfulness and their consequent dependence on Christ's
mercy. It also prescribes a quite physical *imitatio*, as the exercise begins and
progresses, through the duplication of Christ's crucified position and Mary's
tormented bearing at the foot of the cross. [25]

---

[24] 'As die vurß persoen disse oeffunge vurß mit iren geistlichen son mit deilte [...] saege
dat ich die selve mit groisser begerten ußschreyff und an nam doe wart sy in sich selven
erfreuwet und in Got up ertzoegen in myner tegenwordicheit. Und doe sy weder tzo yren
ußwendigen synnen quam do sacht sy myr also Do ich mirckte [...] dat yr so gut willich wairt
tzo disser oeffungen doe sturtzte Got ßoe overfloedige gratie in myn hertz van uret wegen dat
ich es nit gedragen kunde umb dat ich einen neuwen broder hain kregen mit diesser oeffungen
mit der lieffden Gotz.' *Der rechte wech,* fol. N1[r].

[25] As described by Martin Elze, '*Compassio* is the means by which the inner person relates
to Christ; *imitatio* the means by which the outer person does so.' [Die compassio ist die
Weise, in der sich der innere Mensch zum Leiden Christi in Beziehung setzt, die imitatio die

Although the purview of this study does not allow a thorough discussion of the role of devotional imagery in Maria's mysticism, even a cursory reading of her exercise on the five wounds makes several features obvious. In harmony with both late medieval religious observance and Catholic teachings of her day, especially in response to Protestant iconoclasm, Maria does not question the use of devotional imagery.[26] Her exercise not only encourages, but assumes the use of the image of the crucifix as a devotional aid. Maria promotes the use of the image and the extension of that image to one's own body to help in reaching a certain knowledge of or union with Christ. At the conclusion of her treatise Maria writes that 'the life and suffering of our Lord is the surest and most useful exercise that one can find'.[27] Since the image of the crucifix is the gateway she suggests to that exercise, it appears that she considers the use of images to be a fundamental aspect of mystical contemplation.[28]

Moreover, she is bold enough to suggest that this approach is not just her own or even a feminine brand of mysticism, but one that can and should be applied by others. Indeed, she sent this exercise with a letter to a neighbouring convent, addressed to the 'honourable mother' and intended 'for the benefit of all your sisters and other good-hearted people'.[29] For these people Maria identifies God as the source of the exercise, declaring with confidence that she had to write, 'even if it sounds daring [...]. But because of my humble love for God and for all of you, I cannot let it be [...]. For [...] God, through his goodness, has given me special grace for your benefit.'[30] Although Maria calls it 'daring', her exercise provides a

---

Weise, in der der äußere Mensch das tut.] Martin Elze, 'Das Verständnis der Passion Jesu im ausgehenden Mittelalter und bei Luther', in *Geist und Geschichte der Reformation,* ed. by Heinz and Klaus Scholder (Berlin: Walter de Gruyter, 1966), pp. 127–51 (p. 128).

[26] For general discussion of Catholic teachings on devotional imagery in the wake of the Reformation see: Walter von Loewenich, 'Bilder, VI: Reformatorische und nachreformatorische Zeit', in *Theologische Realenzyklopädie* VI/3–4 (1980): pp. 546–57, especially p. 555. See also Sergiusz Michalski, *The Reformation and the Visual Arts: The Protestant Image Question in Western and Eastern Europe* (London and New York: Routledge, 1993), especially Chapter 5, 'Symbols and Commonplaces, or the Conceptual Background of the Dispute on Images', pp. 169–94, esp. pp. 193–94.

[27] 'Want dat leven und lyden uns Heren is die sicherste und nutzste oevung die men fyndt'. *Der rechte wech,* fol. N5^r.

[28] For discussion of the relationship between devotional imagery and mysticism in the Middle Ages see Jeffrey Hamburger, *The Visual and the Visionary: Art and Female Spirituality in Late Medieval Germany* (New York: Zone Books, 1998), especially Chapter 7, 'The Visual and the Visionary', pp. 111–48. Also Hamburger, *The Rothschild Canticles: Art and Mysticism in Flanders and the Rhineland ca. 1300* (New Haven: Yale University Press, 1990).

[29] 'eerwerdige moder'; 'tzo behoef allen uren susteren und ander gut willige menschen'. *Der rechte wech,* fol. M7^r.

[30] 'al luidet aventuerlich'; 'Aber durch oitmoedige lieffde tzo got und tzo uch so en darf

somewhat tame contrast to the Passion devotion of Elizabeth of Spalbeek and other thirteenth-century visionaries from the Low Countries. The ecstatic, near frenzied 'performances' of the crucifixion found in the earlier literature becomes a deliberate, devotional routine in Maria's writing, an approach well-suited to sixteenth-century Catholic piety.[31]

The treatise on the five wounds has two sections, both of which Maria calls exercises, but which differ substantially in character. The first and shortest of the two is a prayer cycle consisting of three series of five repetitions each of the Lord's Prayer and the Ave Maria. The second, longer section is also a series of prayers designed to focus the participant on the five wounds of Christ, but it is distinguished from the first by its contemplative, rather than active approach to worship. Maria repeatedly uses the verbs 'anmircken' and 'bedenken' (to notice, consider, contemplate) in this section. While the first exercise revolves around established prayers, in the second, which has a pronounced penitential tone, Maria also provides her readers with prayers that she composed herself. The importance of these prayers to Maria is evident in her prefatory letter, in which she tells her recipients that through the reception and practice of this exercise, 'I shall, I hope, help you to pray.'[32]

Although this second, longer exercise is more contemplative than the first, its focus is no less physical. Maria associates each of Christ's wounds with a virtue, then directs her readers to contemplate their lack of the virtue in question and to recite psalms 'with King David.'[33] She links the Psalmist to the Saviour in the exercise's conclusion by evoking a vivid image of Christ on the cross, playing his

---

ichs niet laissen […]. Want […] [got] hait mich durch syn goetheit sonderlinge gratie gegeven tzo behoef van uch.' *Der rechte wech,* fol. M6[r]. Maria's term 'aventuerlich' is somewhat difficult to translate, but it has the sense, as Willeumier-Schalij indicates, of daring, perhaps even danger. See *Brieven*, p. 46.

[31] For discussions of Elizabeth of Spalbeek and some of her contemporaries see: Walter Simons, 'Reading a Saint's Body: Rapture and Bodily Movement in the *Vitae* of Thirteenth-century Beguines', in *Framing Medieval Bodies,* ed. by Sarah Kay and Miri Rubin (Manchester and New York: Manchester University Press, 1994), pp. 10–23; as well as Walter Simons and Joanna E. Ziegler, 'Phenomenal Religion in the Thirteenth Century and its Image: Elisabeth of Spalbeek and the Passion Cult', in *Women in the Church,* ed. by W. J. Sheils and Diana Wood (Oxford: Basil Blackwell, 1990), pp. 117–126. Carolyn Walker Bynum also discusses Elizabeth in *Holy Feast and Holy Fast: The Religious Significance of Food to Medieval Women* (Berkeley: University of California Press, 1987), esp. pp. 119–122; 256. See also Rebecca Clouse, 'The Virgin above the Writing in the First *Vita* of Bodely, Douce 114', in *Figures of Speech: The Body in Medieval Art, History, and Literature. Essays in Medieval Studies (Online)*, vol. 11 (1984), ed. by Allen J. Frantzen and David A. Robertson. http://www.luc.edu/publications/medieval/vol11/11ch7.html.

[32] 'Ich sal uch helfen bidden hoffen ich'. *Der rechte wech,* fol. M7[r].

[33] 'mit dem koeninck David'. *Der rechte wech,* fol. N2[r].

wounds like a harp to produce the music of the virtues. Here Maria appropriates an age-old crucifixion motif depicting what Bruce Holsinger calls the 'musicality of pain:'[34] 'Therefore […] let us […] play this harp and see how our beloved bridegroom played these five virtues on the cross.'[35] Reminding her readers that she has provided them with an exercise, and not just a discourse for contemplation, she admonishes them to practice their own 'harp' for three days, in representation of the three allegorical nails of faith, hope, and love that held Christ to the cross. Her allusion to the three nails forms a visual outline of the harp. Maria's direct linking of wounds with virtues is a powerful affirmation of the value of suffering and thus of her physical epistemology, namely that bodily pain allows one to understand and imitate God.

Thus, the entire treatise is markedly physical in focus, but the first section, the *Exercise on the Five Wounds,* is of special interest for the current discussion, for it requires active participation. Maria instructs her readers, for example, that the three cycles of five repetitions of the Lord's Prayer and the Ave Maria be directed, respectively, to the Father 'with outstretched arms, standing before a crucifix', then to the Son 'while wringing the hands', and to the Holy Ghost, for which one should 'fall to one's knees on the ground'.[36] Importantly, it is after this exercise that Kalckbrenner interrupts with his account of receiving the exercise. Such placement of his commentary (rather than at the end of the entire treatise, for example), implies that Maria's rapturous experience occurred upon Kalckbrenner's receipt of the *Exercise on the Five Wounds.* Such timing of her rapture might in turn imply a divine seal of approval of the exercise's deliberate physicality. Finally, such divine approval would hardly have surprised a Carthusian, for whom devotion to Christ was 'essential for […] thought and prayer'.[37]

Maria's special focus on the Virgin would also have been familiar to the Carthusians, who had practiced devotion to Mary from the order's beginnings.[38]

---

[34] See Holsinger's discussion of this widespread medieval image of Christ's body as an instrument in *Music, Body and Desire in Medieval Culture: Hildegard of Bingen to Chaucer.* (Stanford: Stanford University Press, 2001), especially pp. 201–208.

[35] 'Alsus […] laist uns […] spelen up disser herpen und besien wie unse lieve brudegam disse funff duechden am Cruytz uß hait gespielt.' *Der rechte wech,* fol. N4^v.

[36] 'mit ausgereckden armen staende vur einem crucifix' *(Der rechte wech,* fol. M7^r); 'mit gewrungen henden' *(Der rechte wech,* fol. M8^r); 'op die knie off tzer eirden vallen' *(Der rechte wech,* fol. M8^v).

[37] The entire passage is as follows: 'Christus als Inbegriff der Liebe Gottes geradezu auch materiell zu "begreifen", is zwar nicht originell, aber dennoch wesentlich für kartäusisches Denken und Beten.' Hermann Josef Roth, 'Kartäuserspiritualität am Beispiel der Kölner Kartäuser um 1500', in *Die Kölner Kartause um 1500,* ed. by Werner Schäfke (Cologne: Kölnisches Stadtmuseum, 1991), pp. 213–224 (p. 216).

[38] Roth, 'Kartäuserspiritualität', p. 216.

Maria's emphasis on Mary as co-redemptrix would also no doubt have enhanced the exercise's appeal as a response to Protestant insistence on Christ as the sole mediator. The second cycle of prayers in the *Exercise on the Five Wounds*, directed to the Son, is distinguished, for example, by its focus on the Virgin's response to Christ's wounds and by the participant's physical imitation of both Christ and Mary. Indeed, Maria begins the treatise by explaining that 'as a daily exercise you should stand under the cross with the mother of God [...]. For whatever the Lord suffered physically, she suffered internally.'[39] Maria's conflation of Mary's suffering with Christ's highlights the role of the human body as an instrument of *imitatio* and ultimately, of salvation. It is also especially understandable in light of the original female audience. Maria directs her women readers to suffer with Christ, and the human mother of God provides the perfect example of a feminine agony, thus offering a gender-related model for experiencing the Passion. In fact, Maria's use of vocabulary signalling the internalized nature of the Virgin's suffering (that she suffered 'van binnen') is reminiscent, as Amy Neff has described, of a host of medieval images, both literary and visual, of Mary's 'swoon'. In these sources, Mary is depicted as suffering the pains of childbirth, and it is through this 'maternal suffering' that she has 'power to bring the individual to salvation.'[40]

The Marian focus in this second set of repetitions in Maria's exercise greatly amplifies the reader's sense of the physical impact of each of Christ's wounds, for they are not merely identified by their location on his body, as in the first cycle, but rather the reader now 'views' them from Mary's perspective. Although there are traditionally seven sorrows of the Virgin, which begin in Christ's infancy, Maria intensifies this section of the exercise by creating of a subset of five sorrows based exclusively on Mary's experience at Golgotha:[41]

---

[39] 'Ir [...] solt dagelichs vur ein oeffunge nemen mit der moder gotz under dat cruitz tzo staen [...]. Want dat der here lichamlich leit dat leit sy van binnen.' *Der rechte wech*, fol. M6[V].

[40] See Amy Neff, 'The Pain of *Compassio*: Mary's Labor at the Foot of the Cross', *Art Bulletin*, 80/2 (1998), 254–73 (p. 265). Some of the sources Neff cites refer to Christ's comparison of the paradoxical pain and joy of childbirth with his death and resurrection as found in John 16. 21–22.

[41] Maria's five sorrows are an expansion of what is generally the fifth sorrow, Mary's standing at the foot of the cross. Joseph Greven, *Die Kölner Kartause und die Anfänge der katholischen Reform in Deutschland* (Münster: Aschendorffsche, 1935), pp. 36–37, and later Roth, 'Kartäuserspiritualität', p. 216, both attribute this innovation of five, rather than seven, sorrows of the Virgin to the Carthusian Johann Justus Landsberg (d. 1539). We should at least consider the possibility, however, that Landsberg, who was apparently well acquainted with Maria van Hout and published a portion of her *Exercise on the Five Wounds* (see note 44), adapted this approach from her. A remarkable vision recorded in the Cologne Charterhouse annals confirms the deep spiritual association Maria must have shared with Landsberg, 'whose soul the holy, illuminated [...] virgin Maria of Oisterwijk saw, [while] in the house in Oisterwijk, soon after [his] death, being borne into heaven by holy angels' (Cujus animam

[Mary] experienced the first sorrow as she saw her dear child lifted up naked between two murderers, with iron nails pounded through his hands and feet, hanging on the cross in inexpressible pain. The second sorrow was when she saw the countenance of her dear child contorted in great pain with deathly colour. The third, as she saw her dear child revived with gall and vinegar in his constant need. The fourth, as she saw and heard his veins tearing asunder and he pled and lamented at being left alone so pitiably in great pain. The fifth, when she saw him die and saw his glorious body shudder and his heart break, the pain exceeded all the pain in both of their hearts[42].

It is thus Mary's common suffering with Christ that creates her intercessory role, or in Maria's words, human beings can ask Christ for mercy 'because of the unspeakable love that he *and* his mother had for us on the cross and because of the inhuman pain that they *both* suffered for our sake' [italics added]. [43] For Maria, the Virgin Mary is here, and consistently in her writings, a model for humanity, including in this role of co-sufferer with Christ.[44]

Of the two hundred or so pages of Maria van Hout's writings, only the *Exercise on the Five Wounds* is known to have enjoyed repeated publication. Although it was

---

mox ab obitu per sanctos angelos in caelum portari vidit in parthenio Osterwickano sancta et illuminata [...] Virgo Maria ab Osterwick), in *Annales Cartusiae Coloniensis 1334–1728*, p. 283. Manuscript copy made before 1749 by the Carthusian Prior Johann Bungartz, currently in possession of the Charterhouse at Marienau. Original no longer extant. Microfilm available in Historisches Archiv der Stadt Köln, GA 132B. Although Landsberg's death occurred before Maria moved to Cologne, and although we have no record of any visits by Landsberg to the Oisterwijk beguine community, the vision implies that the two must have met, or, at the least, corresponded.

[42] 'Dat eirste we had sy doe sy ere lief kynt eirst ansaech tuchsen zwei moerders nackent opgericht und mit yßern negelen durch hende und voeß geslagen am cruytz hangende yn unßprechliger pyn. Dat ii. we do ßy ere lief kint ßach in ßyn angeßicht van groisser pynen ungestalt mit doitliger varven. Dat iii. do ßy ier lieve kint ßaech laven mit gal und essich yn ßyner stetfliger noit. Dat iiii do ßy ßach und hoirt al ßyn adern ußer einandern gain und he suchde und klaichde sich ßo iemerlich verlaissen zo ßyn van großer pyn. Dat v. doe sy im sach sterven und sin herlich licham schudden und syn hertz brechen die pyn gienck boven all in erer beider hertzen.' *Der rechte wech*, fol. M7ᵛ–M8ᵛ.

[43] 'Durch die unsprechliche lieffden de he und syn lieve moder am cruytz tzo uns hadden und durch die unmynslige pine de sy beide umb unsen willen geleden haven'. *Der rechte wech*, fol. M8ᵛ.

[44] Earlier women visionaries also focused their devotions on Mary. Dominican convent chronicles of the fourteenth century, for example, contain repeated examples of women asking to share in the Passion, even asking specifically to suffer as Mary did. See Valerie R. Hotchkiss, '"An Overabundance of Grace": Women's Convent Chronicles in Fourteenth-Century Dominican Cloisters', in *The Unbounded Community: Papers in Christian Ecumenism in Honor of Jaroslav Pelikan,* ed. by William Caferro and Duncan G. Fisher (New York and London: Garland, 1996), pp. 113–126 (p. 120).

originally written for women, through its publication in *Der rechte wech*, it reached an audience of men and women far beyond the small group of original addressees. In addition, the exercise also had a life, both in the vernacular and in Latin, beyond *Der rechte wech*. Kalckbrenner's Carthusian brother, Johann Justus Landsberg, for example, according to Willibrord Lampen, recorded the second, longer portion of the treatise on the five wounds, anonymously, in his *Pharetra divini amoris*.[45] This insured a vast and centuries-long readership for Maria's text, for Landsberg's anthology of meditations enjoyed a diverse publication history well into the nineteenth century.[46]

Carthusian reproduction of the treatise on the five wounds in Latin translation in two quite different formats, both apparently produced during Maria's lifetime, seems to testify of the particular appeal of the exercise's physicality. Kalckbrenner included the exercise in a preface to the letter Maria wrote to him, which he published in Cologne in 1532.[47] In this preface, Kalckbrenner legitimizes Maria's teachings on the five wounds by describing her similarity to Christ: 'For how she suffers to reconcile the world with Him; [...] as if her heart and her hands and feet carried the stigmata of Christ (as if she were a second Catherine of Siena).' He continues: 'she is crucified by burning pains, and finally, how terribly she is continually pierced in her head, as if by a crown of thorns'.[48] One might naturally see the comparison to Catherine of Siena, who was widely venerated for her receipt of invisible stigmata and was already canonized in 1461, as a particularly bold legitimizing strategy for the writings of a woman as obscure as Maria van Hout. On the other hand, Kalckbrenner might also be attempting to use Catherine to diffuse any suspicion of heresy that the more direct comparisons to Christ might imply. It should be noted that Maria herself was not in the least hesitant to compare herself to Christ. In a letter to a sister religious, which Kalckbrenner published in *Der rechte wech*, she

---

[45] Willibrord Lampen, O.F.M., 'Maria van Oisterwijk, Tertiaris van S. Franciscus', *Bijdragen voor de Geschiedenis van de Provincie der Minderbroeders in de Nederlanden*, 9/26 (1957), 219–238. Lampen reprints in his article (pp. 226–34) the third cycle from Landsberg's version of the exercise, which he labels (p. 227) 'a rather free translation of Maria's prayer, but entirely in her spirit' (een nogal vrije vertaling van Maria's gebed, maar geheel in haar geest).

[46] See S. Autore, 'Lansperge ou Landesberg', *Dictionnaire de Theologie Catholique*, VIII/1 (Paris: Librarie Letouzey et Ané, 1924), cols. 2606–2609. Landsberg's *Pharetra divini amoris* was published in 1555/1556 in *Minorum Operum libri XIII posteriores*. Autore discusses the work and its reception in detail. See esp. col. 2608.

[47] For complete reference to the 1532 letter, cited throughout this article as *Frater*, see note 6.

[48] 'Nam quantum per mundi reconciliatione [...], quomodo corde manibus pedibusque (velut altera Catherina Senensis) Christi stigmatibus, id est doloribus igneis crucifigatur, quantum denique in capite veluti spineo serto operto acutissimis doloribus continue compungat.' *Frater,* fol. A1ᵛ.

resolutely lays claim to an intercessory role: '[The Lord] allowed me to see the fall and weakness of mankind, which I had to take upon myself.'[49] Her identification with Christ is strikingly direct in a letter to Kalckbrenner (from which he likely drew his own imagery), also published in *Der rechte wech* 'I am awakened every night around one o'clock, and am so pitifully tormented in my head, hands, feet and heart. [...] And my head feels night and day as if it were pierced through with thorns.'[50] Ultimately, Kalckbrenner's association of Maria both with Christ and with Saint Catherine underscored the physicality of her piety and, crucially, served to assure readers that her writings, unlike others circulating in the day, were orthodox and thus of universal devotional value for those who sought union with God. Indeed, since Protestants rejected such physical forms of devotion, they became increasingly important to the Catholic faithful of both genders.

The *Exercise on the Five Wounds* also appears in the Carthusian Darmstadt manuscript mentioned previously. The manuscript bears a call number from the library catalogue of the Cologne Charterhouse from 1748, indicating that the writings it contained, including Maria's *Exercise,* were read by the Carthusians for at least two centuries.

It is important to consider a few of the distinct characteristics of each of these two re-transmissions of Maria's *Exercise on the Five Wounds.* First, while Maria originally wrote in her Brabant dialect and Kalckbrenner's first production of the text (in *Der rechte Wech)* was similarly in vernacular (Ripuarian), both of the later transmissions of the exercise are in Latin. This naturally limited the audience, but also arguably targeted a learned readership. That this brief, *imitatio*-driven exercise, of all of Maria's texts, was extended to such a readership represents a fascinating melding of two ways of knowing: the physical with the intellectual. Perhaps Latin legitimized the transmission of this physical approach to knowing God when it might otherwise have been met with scepticism.

The dissimilar presentation of the exercise in these two sources also speaks to their distinct purposes. In the letter of 1532, which was printed and thus apparently directed to a learned readership that included and probably extended beyond the Carthusian order, Kalckbrenner's comparison of Maria to Saint Catherine and to Christ intricately establishes her sanctity and thus her legitimacy as an author of spiritual texts. In the Darmstadt manuscript, in contrast, which was likely read primarily by Carthusians in Cologne, the author lets Maria speak to the reader in a voice whose power stems from its intimacy and individuality, and not from its connection to other authoritative voices. Whereas Kalckbrenner seems to elevate

---

[49] '[der Heer] liesz [...] myr sien der mynschen vallen und kranckheit die moist ich up mich nemen'. *Brieven,* p. 74.

[50] 'Alle nacht werden ich wacker umbtrynt ein ure, und werden soe iemerligen gepynigt in mym heufft, handen, voessen und hertz. [...] Und myn heufft is nacht und dach off idt vol doernen stiech [...].' *Brieven,* pp. 90–92.

Maria above the fray of normal life in the 1532 letter, the writer of the Darmstadt manuscript allows her to emerge as a frequent, familiar visitor and as a wise and tender friend. In both cases, the purpose of transmitting Maria's teachings was obviously to strengthen the readership spiritually.[51] In the 1532 letter Kalckbrenner alludes to the contemporary need for such strength in a Church that was increasingly under attack: 'So [Christ] has given them [i.e. friends like Maria] as pillars, through whose prayers the Church is upheld and renewed.'[52]

Thus, although Maria's exercise was originally written for women, this did not restrict its value for a male audience, least of all for the Carthusians. With its concise, cyclical structure, the exercise is reminiscent, on several levels, of the rosary, which is known to have played a significant role in Carthusian devotions. Maria's emphasis on the Virgin as a means to understanding the passion reflects the very essence of the rosary, with its fifteen 'decades' of Ave Marias, each associated with the contemplation of one of the fifteen 'mysteries', which are based variously on events from the life of the Virgin and Christ. Hermann Josef Roth sees the rosary as the fusion of devotion to Christ and to his mother, and, of greater significance for the current discussion, further claims that the rosary has its origins in the Carthusian order.[53] Both the scholarly and pious traditions identify the rosary as a Dominican development. Roth, however, argues that the use of systematic prayer aids is much more characteristic of Carthusians than of Dominicans.[54] The rosary's significance to the Carthusian order in the sixteenth century is depicted in a woodcut of 1515,

---

[51] Sigrun Haude's discussion of the Cologne Charterhouse's significant publishing efforts underscores this. She argues that the Carthusians chose for publication those writings 'which they judged most effective for strengthening the faithful and combatting heretics; foremost among these were their highly prized mystical works'. Haude, 'The Silent Monks', p. 130.

[52] 'Itaque hos dedit veluti columnas, quorum orationibus fulciatur renoueturque ecclesia.' *Frater*, fol. A1^r.

[53] Roth, 'Kartäuserspiritualität', p. 216.

[54] Roth, 'Kartäuserspiritualität', p. 216. Specifically, he argues that two Trier Carthusians, Adolf von Essen (d. 1439) and Dominikus von Preußen (d. 1460), developed a series of systematic devotions from which the rosary evolved, and that their efforts were motivated by a desire to avoid distractions during contemplations of the life and Passion of Christ. Although not addressing Carthusian origins in particular, Michael Carroll affirms that 'the rosary [...] developed slowly, and resulted from the merging of several different traditions.' Michael Carroll, *Catholic Cults and Devotions: A Psychological Inquiry*, (Kingston: McGill-Queen's University Press, 1989), pp. 11–12. See also Anne Winston-Allen's excellent study of the evolution of the rosary. She argues that the rosary 'is not one text, but many: actually multiple versions embedded in a constellation of texts that described, interpreted, and marketed forms of the devotion to users who collectively shaped and selected the ultimate version of choice'. *Stories of the Rose: The Making of the Rosary in the Middle Ages.* (University Park: Pennsylvania State University Press, 1997): p. 8. See pp. 2, 66, 76–77 and 131 for discussion of Carthusian involvement in the development of rosary devotions.

attributed in some sources to Albrecht Dürer, showing a *Schutzmantel-madonna*, flanked by John the Baptist and Saint Bruno, founder of the Carthusian order, shielding a host of praying Carthusians (see Figure 1). At Mary's feet lies another Carthusian who is praying the rosary. Adam Wienand considers it possible that this lying monk might point to a Carthusian origin for the rosary. [55] Whether or not the rosary began in their order, the Carthusians, and the Cologne Carthusians, in particular, would have been especially aware of rosary devotions, since Europe's second rosary confraternity (after that at Douai, France) was established in Cologne in 1475 and 'quickly became the most important of all the rosary confraternities in Europe'.[56]

Maria's entire treatise on the five wounds, especially the exercise portion, conforms to the devotional spirit among the Cologne Carthusians that led to the formation of two other important confraternities. In 1538 Kalckbrenner, together with Landsberg, formed the Confraternity of the Five Wounds (*Fraternitas de quinque vulneribus*), and at the same time the Cologne Carthusians founded the Confraternity of the Co-suffering of the Blessed Virgin Mary (Sodalitas *compassionis BMV*).[57] Thus, Maria's exercise was congruent with the character of Carthusian spirituality of the day, and even seems to have informed it.

---

[55] Adam Wienand, 'Die Marienverehrung der Kartäuser in einem Holzschnitt von Albrecht Dürer dargestellt', in *Die Kartäuser: Der Orden der schweigenden Mönche* (Cologne: Wienand, 1983), pp. 26–27.

[56] Carroll, 'Catholic Cults and Devotions, p. 13. Carroll lists the date as 1474, Winston-Allen as 1475.

[57] Greven, 'Die Kölner Kartause', pp. 41–42.

Figure 1. Woodcut, 1515. Attributed to Albrecht Dürer. Carthusian Madonna with St Bruno and John the Baptist. Copyright: Hamburger Kunsthalle. Photographer: Elke Walford, Hamburg.

Intellectual Ways of Knowing

Several sources indicate that Maria's ways of knowing included not only the contemplative and physical approaches I have described, but also the more standard (one might say masculine) method of knowledge acquisition—reading. Although we know little of what formal education, if any, Maria van Hout acquired, she apparently had sufficient training to be able to write down, in her Brabant vernacular, the exercises and revelations she received. Kalckbrenner's foreward to *Der rechte wech* emphasizes that he was publishing works 'that [Maria] made herself and wrote with her own hand.'[58] We have no indication that she could compose in Latin. The occasional Latin passages in her texts are phrases that she most likely would have acquired from frequent hearing of the liturgy and participation in mass. It is possible, even likely however, judging at least by the influences or sources she mentions, that she could read some Latin. As one might expect, her writings indicate familiarity with the Bible, and she also mentions several early Church Fathers. She apparently also knew Bonaventure's life of Saint Francis.[59] In addition, in her treatises on the Lord's Prayer and the Seven Gifts of the Holy Spirit, she expounds at length on the theme of nuptial mysticism, indicating a deep knowledge not only of the Song of Songs itself, but, in particular, of its medieval interpretations, among them no doubt the writings of Bernard of Clairvaux.

Maria's reading interests were apparently not limited to approved sources. Near the end of her life, she must have sent a request for reading material and for a portable altar to Peter Canisius. In a letter from Bologna dated 17 June 1547 to his Jesuit brothers in Cologne, Canisius indicates his willingness to act as an advocate in this cause for Maria with higher Church authorities:

> Yesterday I presented the case of Maria to the Cardinal [Cervini], and there is good hope for the dispensation of a portable altar, however not for reading heretical books. How greatly I feel the result of your prayers every day, and especially those of Maria, God knows, and my conscience witnesses.[60]

---

[58] '[die] sy [...] selfs gemacht mit yr eygen hant geschreven hait', *Der rechte wech,* fol. A1ᵛ–A2ʳ.

[59] See *Der rechte wech,* fol. F1ʳ–F2ʳ for Maria's account of Francis's stigmatization, which recalls, to a degree, Bonaventure's account, although Maria's explanation of God's purpose for the stigmata is curious. She claims that 'the Lord loved [Francis] so much that he wanted him martyred by no one, for the Lord wanted to do it himself' (der here hadde yn so lieff dat hei ym van niemantz gemartert wolde haven. Dan der Heer woilt dat allein doin). *Der rechte wech,* fol. F1ᵛ.

[60] 'Heri caussam Mariae diligenter apud Cardinalem egi, et bona spes est futurae dispensationis de altare portatili, non autem de legendis haereticorum libris. Quantum ego hic quotidie sentiam vestrarum orationum et praesertim Mariae fructum, Deus (perpetuo benedictus novit et mihi testis) est conscientia,' *Beati Petri Canisii, Societatis Iesu, Epistulae et Acta, Vol. I: 1541–1556,* ed. by Otto Braunsberger (Freiburg: Herder, 1896), p. 251.

The request for the altar implies that Maria was too weak to attend mass in the chapel, yet the book request indicates that she was mentally agile, even this close to the end of her life. (She died about three months after Canisius's letter.)[61] Although we cannot know with certainty, the 'heretical' books she desired to read would almost surely have been connected to the Protestant movements. They might also have been in Latin. Canisius did receive a bull with the dispensation for the altar, but not, however, for the reading material. This rejection is both troubling and unsurprising. It is troubling for its obvious limiting of Maria's realms of inquiry, in spite of her orthodoxy and powerful example. The Jesuits, to be sure, and those Carthusians involved in copying and printing books in Cologne, would certainly have read Protestant and polemical works, since they published refutations of various teachings they deemed heretical. Thus the refusal of similar books to Maria might seem gender-biased. On the other hand, Carthusian publications in the Reformation period were used primarily to combat Protestant teachings and to 'urge their readers [...] toward inner reform'.[62] Thus, with her close ties to the Carthusians, it is not surprising that Maria was denied access to the books she requested, since responses to oppositional texts, not the texts themselves, were circulated among and promoted by the Carthusians. We must still view the refusal as unfortunate, if not even tragic, since one can indeed imagine that Maria's literary and spiritual gifts could have contributed to her own lively and specific responses to various doctrinal debates.

The impressive library at the Cologne Charterhouse kept the Carthusians occupied with more pious readings, a love that Maria apparently also shared. A passage in the Darmstadt manuscript clearly emphasizes the importance of reading within her spirituality: 'When the soul is withered', the author recalls Maria teaching, 'then it sometimes helps to see a good passage from a devotional book so as to rekindle fervour'.[63] Although we do not know whether Maria had direct access to the Charterhouse library, it is hardly a stretch to imagine that if she were willing to write to Italy for permission to read heretical books, she would also have requested and received reading material from next door. Roth indicates that Carthusian

---

[61] Maria's birth year is not known, in spite of the fact that Léonce Reypens in 'Maria v. Oisterwijk', in *Lexikon für Theologie und Kirche*, VII (1962), 43, claims that she was born around 1470. From several accounts of her dealings with the Carthusians and Jesuits, however, one has the impression of a woman of great wisdom, and thus perhaps a woman of advanced age. It is clear, for example, that Maria had been leader of her beguine community for several years before she was finally brought to Cologne. Maria also writes frequently in her letters of physical pain and suffering, which one might associate with aging. However, since she writes of suffering in rather formulaic ways as a sign of God's will, as do even the youngest mystics before her, its connection to advanced age or physical frailty is ambiguous.

[62] Haude, 'The Silent Monks', p. 131.

[63] 'Quando anima est arefacta, tunc iuvat quandoque bonum punctum ex devoto libro videre ad resuscitandum fervorem.' *Collectanea*, fol. 37^v.

libraries were clearly separated into holdings for the monks, who knew Latin and were ordained as priests, and holdings for the lay brothers, which consisted of 'popular devotional writings in the vernacular'.[64] Perhaps the Carthusians circumscribed Maria's realms of inquiry in the same way they did for the lay brothers. The author of the Darmstadt manuscript writes, for example, that Maria 'gathered a foundation of perfection from the life and teaching of [John] Tauler'.[65] He mentions in particular Tauler's sermons. He does not indicate whether or not Maria knew of Tauler's works before her association with the Cologne Charterhouse. If not before, however, then she would certainly have had access to Tauler during her two years in Cologne, as his works, along with those of other fourteenth-century mystics, were on hand in the library of St Barbara.[66]

In spite of such varied evidence of her literacy, it should come as no surprise that Maria repeatedly employs the apologetic cliché of unlearnedness in her writings, including those directed to a female audience. Kalckbrenner also calls her 'unlearned' in his foreword to *Der rechte wech*.[67] Of course, however, such a disclaimer is always also accompanied by a claim to divine inspiration. This combination is a time-honoured trope in spiritual and mystical literature, especially, but not exclusively, that composed by women. Early studies of Maria van Hout and her works seem to have taken these formulaic expressions of ignorance at face value, revealing profound scholarly misogyny, in particular an unwillingness to consider literacy, either Latin or vernacular, as a legitimate source of knowledge for a woman who had not been traditionally educated. In his 1927 study, A. Möllmann, for example, declares bluntly that Maria is 'plain, ignorant, entirely uneducated, [and] primitive'.[68] He calls not only her intellectual, but also her spiritual abilities into question, stating that her 'natural talent is but a poor tool for God's workings'.[69] Wilhelm Oehl states that Maria's writing is uncomplicated by any 'deep insight into the ornate language of the Holy Scriptures and Church liturgy', and that she 'seems to live as if in the depths of the Middle Ages, [...] writing [...] not a word about the

---

[64] Roth, 'Kartäuserspiritualität', p. 213.

[65] 'Ex vita Thauerleri et doctrina hausit fundamentum perfectionis.' *Collectanea*, fol. 34ᵛ.

[66] See James Hogg, 'Die Kartause, Köln und Europa: Gelehrte Kartäuser zwischen Reform, Reformation und Gegenreformation', in Schäfke, *Die Kölner Kartause um 1500*, pp. 169–91 (p. 172). According to Alois Haas, Surius's 1548 Latin translation lent Tauler's teachings 'genuine international status', 'Preface', in *Johannes Tauler: Sermons*, trans. by Maria Shrady (New York: Paulist Press, 1985), pp. xiii-xvi (p. xiii).

[67] 'ungelert', *Der rechte wech*, fol. A2ʳ.

[68] 'schlicht, unwissend, völlig ungebildet, armselig, primitiv'. A. Möllmann, 'Maria van Osterwijk und ihre Schrift "Der rechte Weg zur evangelischen Vollkommenheit"', *Zeitschrift für Aszese und Mystik*, 2 (1927), 319–33 (p. 320).

[69] 'natürliche Begabung nur ein armseliges Rüstzeug bildet für [Gottes] Wirksamkeit'. Möllmann, 'Maria van Oisterwijk', p. 320.

wild battles in the world outside [her convent]'.[70] The patronizing eagerness of these scholars to underscore Maria's simplemindedness belies their underlying desire to establish her difference—necessitated for them by her gender—from the men in her historical context. In the process, however, they miss her influence on those men and her contributions to the context they shared. Many of Maria's teachings did in fact come 'from the depths of the Middle Ages', to use Oehl's formulation. But whereas Oehl used the expression to establish Maria's ignorance, for the Carthusians Maria's connection to the medieval meant that she advanced a familiar, established, and firmly orthodox spirituality that was of critical importance in the context of the Reformation. By neglecting Maria's connection to the world of books and the world of religious controversy in her day, these early twentieth-century scholars thus missed not only central aspects of her mysticism, but also central aspects of her appeal to the male religious of her day. Simplicity, both in Maria's and in Carthusian theology, does not equate to intellectual lack, nor is it a 'poor tool for God's workings', as Möllman describes it, but it must accompany worldly knowledge for spiritual progress to be possible. In the words of the author of the Darmstadt manuscript, one should 'learn simplicity from the child Jesus [and] [...] everywhere in his life, passion and burial'. 'True simplicity', he concludes, '[...] is the foundation of our profession'.[71]

Any assessment of the impact of gender on the acquisition or transmission of knowledge in the Middle Ages or early modern period must admit the many disadvantages, however obvious, that women faced. Feminist scholars of the Middle Ages engage in a critical balancing act as they attempt to distinguish clerical support for the richness of female spirituality from clerical complicity in the establishment and perpetuation of its many strictures.

Maria van Hout's life is no exception. Her tormented relationship with her confessor, as revealed in letters she wrote to him that are included in *Der rechte wech,* is a clear sign that not all clergy shared an appreciation of women's ways of knowing and that some were indeed threatened by them.[72] Maria also alludes to struggles she had with others. In a letter to her confessor, for example, she laments: 'I am well accustomed not to having favourable opinions or words from my superiors all my life'.[73] In a letter to a sister religious, she mourns such

---

[70] 'tiefe Einfühlung in die bilderreiche Sprache der Hl. Schrift und der kirchlichen Liturgie'; 'scheint noch im tiefsten Mittelalter zu leben [...] kein Wort von den wilden Kämpfen draußen in der Welt'. Wilhelm Oehl, 'Maria von Osterwyk', *Deutsche Mystikerbriefe des Mittelalters* (Munich: Albert Langen-Georg Müller, 1931, repr. 1972), pp. 682–720; 835–41 (p. 690).

[71] 'Ex puero Jesu [...] disce simplicitatem. Similiter ubique in vita, passione et sepultura eius. [...] vera simplicitate [...] est fundamentum professionis nostrae.' *Collectanea*, fol. 45ʳ.

[72] See Wiethaus, 'If I Had an Iron Body', esp. pp. 179–81.

[73] 'Ich bins wail gewoen niet vyll suesser ansichten of worden van mynen oversten tzo haven alle myn leeffdage.' *Brieven*, p. 102.

misunderstandings with images of violent self-destruction:

> Dan idt doet mir alszo wee van binnen, als ich hoeren dat yemantz durch mich [...] scandaliziert wurt in worden off in einige andere wyse; weirt myr muglich ich screyde myn ougen usz [...]. Want id is myr niet muglich, dat ich mich altzyt also halden solde, dat idt dem mynschen wail behagen soilde, al mucht ich hemel und erdt dair mit wynnen off verliesen.

> [For it causes me great pain internally when I hear that someone has been scandalized [...] by me in words or in some other way. Were it possible, I would scratch my eyes out. [...] For it is not possible for me to behave always so that it pleases others, even if I could win or lose heaven and earth by doing so.][74]

Maria does not say that these misunderstandings were always with men, thus they were perhaps not only a result of her gender, but also of her unusual visionary gifts, gifts of knowing that certainly set her apart from other religious of both genders.

The Carthusians and Jesuits, in contrast, revered, supported and promoted Maria and her teachings, but even their genuine support could not overcome the gender inequalities that both limited the realms in which Maria could circulate, and dictated the elaborate 'packaging' of Maria in much of their promotion. As I have discussed in detail elsewhere, for example, *Der rechte wech* includes not only Kalckbrenner's Life that amounts to a pre-death sainting, but also a dedication to and response from a prominent Cologne theologian. It is unlikely that the volume could ever have been published without such legitimation. Moreover, all of Maria's writings were published anonymously. Despite the anonymity, though, her gender (not to mention her problematic and 'unofficial' status as a beguine) is alluded to, and is even occasionally emphasized. The editing endeavours of Kalckbrenner and the author of the Darmstadt manuscript also appear to be less intervention than presentation.[75]

The survival of both vernacular and Latin translations of Maria's works attests the breadth of her appeal. The particular care with which her *Exercise on the Five Wounds* was disseminated also points to a concentrated clerical effort to promote her ways of knowing to a male readership and thus to span the gender chasm that apparently loomed increasingly hazardous in the confessional age. The delight with which Maria responded to Kalckbrenner's enthusiastic receipt of her exercise suggests that she probably supported such bridging efforts. Indeed, if there is a constant refrain in Maria's writings, it is of her duty to negate herself and to pray and suffer for all the sheep of God's fold. She explains this as a matter of fact in a letter to Kalckbrenner that he included in *Der rechte wech*:

> Ich unwerdige creatuyr syen dat idt got also van mich belieefft dat ich mit dez son gotz moisz lyden und bidden vur alle mynschen. Und gelich he synen hemelschen vader

---

[74] *Brieven*, p. 82.

[75] See my earlier work on Kalckbrenner's editorship, 'Maria van Hout and her Carthusian Editor', *Ons geestelijk Erf*, 72 (1998), 105–21.

badt vur syn apostolen, dat he die eyn mit im machen woilde gelich im, und dairna ander minschen ouch, also en weisz ich niet bessers tzo bidden und tzo roiffen nacht und dach vur uch allen [...]

[I, unworthy creature, see that God desires that I suffer and pray for all people with the Son of God. And just as he bade his Heavenly Father for his apostles that he might make them one with him, [...] and other people as well, likewise I do not know any better [way] than to pray and to cry out night and day for all of you [...].][76]

Such inclusive language reveals that gender was of little concern to her as she sought to know God's will for others. In this respect, Maria van Hout's epistemologies of the divine offered a vital and universal spirituality to the troubled Church she defended.

---

[76] *Brieven,* p. 90.

Ghostwriting Sisters: The Preservation of Dutch Sermons of Father Confessors in the Fifteenth and the Early Sixteenth Century

THOM MERTENS

In 1963 Paul-Gerhard Völker published a pioneering paper on the form in which medieval German sermons are preserved.[1] He showed convincingly that it was not listeners who recorded the sermons, as was thought until then. In the Late Middle Ages there was simply no kind of shorthand that could be used to note down the sermons while they were being given. Preachers themselves must have done the writing, more than we used to think. While this was no doubt the way in which sermons were usually preserved, Völker saw one exception: manuscripts made out of reverence for the father confessor of a community and destined for use in that community might contain notes taken down during or after the sermons.

The Myth of Sisters with Powerful Memories

Prominent scholars like Kurt Ruh adopted Völker's ideas. In 1981 Ruh provided further proof for his views in an article on German sermon collections.[2] According to Ruh, the preacher himself usually wrote out his sermons or dictated them to a clerk. If somebody else edited them, that person was authorized by the preacher. Rarely did listeners write out sermons from memory. Ruh does not even mention the (im)possibility of *Mitschrift*, writing down sermons at the time they were delivered.

---

[1] Paul-Gerhard Völker, 'Die Überlieferungsformen mittelalterlicher deutscher Predigten', *Zeitschrift für deutsches Altertum*, 92 (1963), 212–27.

[2] Kurt Ruh, 'Deutsche Predigtbücher des Mittelalters', in Kurt Ruh, *Kleine Schriften* (Berlin–New York: Walter de Gruyter, 1984), II, pp. 296–17 (first published in *Beiträge zur Geschichte der Predigt*, ed. by Heimo Reinitzer. Hamburg, 1981, pp. 11–30).

A decade after Ruh's publication, in 1992, Hans-Jochen Schiewer repeated the view of Völker in stronger terms: preachers writing out and editing their own sermons was the normal way of preservation, even in cases we had thought to be exceptions.[3] Schiewer teaches us to mistrust the prologues and epilogues when they declare that sisters wrote out the sermons of their father confessor. We find, for example, a statement like the following:

> Dise bredigen het angnese steffan sahssen dohter gehœrt bredigen vnd het sú behalten in irem herttzen vnd hett sú geschriben vnd det sú abe ir geschrift anderwerbe schriben vnd sint dis die bredigen die hie noch geschriben stont vntz an die bredigen die in dem consilium sint gheschehen zů basel.[4]

> [Agnes, the daughter of Stefan Sachs, heard these sermons preached and kept them in her heart and wrote them down and had them copied after her writing, and these are the sermons that are written here up to the sermons which were delivered before the council in Basel.]

In Schiewer's view we should not take this colophon too literally, because the words *and she kept them in her heart* depict Agnes as an imitator of Mary (and therefore as a devout writer), alluding as they do to the words of Luke 2. 19: 'But Mary kept in mind all these things, pondering them in her heart.'

Schiewer also points out the formal features of the sermons in these collections, maintaining that the texts are as well structured and well formulated as those of ordinary sermons and treatises. If these declarations about sisters writing out sermons from hearing them were true, one would expect to find texts consisting of single points or similarly abbreviated versions. Schiewer wants to put to rest the myth of the 'gedächtnisstarke Nonnen', the myth of the sisters with powerful memories.

Modern research, then, considers it technically impossible for sisters to have written out complete sermons of their father confessor. This view makes the sermon an exclusively male literary genre. As such it fits well into the larger picture of the male exclusiveness of ecclesiastical orders, to which the right to deliver sermons was limited.

Sermon-Preserving Sisters

Statements about sisters noting down sermons of their father confessors—the sort of claims recent research has taught us to mistrust or perhaps even overlook—can be found in the life stories of sisters from the Diepenveen convent, located in the

---

[3] Hans-Jochen Schiewer, 'Spuren von Mündlichkeit in der mittelalterlichen Predigtüberlieferung: Ein Plädoyer für exemplarisches und beschreibend-interpretierendes Edieren', *Editio*, 6 (1992), 64–79 (65–69).

[4] Quoted by Schiewer, 'Spuren von Mündlichkeit', p. 67.

northeast of the Low Countries. Diepenveen was the first (and leading) convent of canonesses of the Modern Devotion.[5] It was founded six hundred years ago, in 1400, by Father Johannes Brinckerinck, who was the confessor of the five Deventer houses of the Sisters of the Common Life. The Sister Book of Diepenveen tells us about canonesses who took notes on a wax tablet during Brinckerinck's *collaties*. These 'collations' were non-liturgical, somewhat informal exhortations or sermons delivered by the father confessor in the afternoon of a Sunday or a feast day. The following is reported about sister Liesbeth van Delft (d. 1423):

> In groter reverencien ende weerdicheit hadde sij hoer oversten ende wat sij hoer segeden, dat nam sij als uut den monde godes. Ende als onse vader collacie dede, soe sat sij ende schrief hem dat uutten monde in hoer tafel. Ende dat meeste dat wy van alsulken schriften hebben, dat heeft sie vergadert.[6]

> [She held her superiors in great reverence and took what they said to her as if from the mouth of God. And when our father (Brinckerinck) gave his exhortation, she sat and wrote it from his mouth on her tablet. And most of what we have of such writings she collected.]

There were other sisters as well who noted down texts from the exhortations. About Alijt Bruuns (*c.* 1450?), for instance, we are told:

> Seer begherlick was sie dat waert gades toe horen inder clacien ende die marclicste[7] punten scrief sie in hoer tafele om die toe ontholden ende na op pappier toe scriven.[8]

> [She had a strong desire to hear the word of God in the exhortation, and she wrote the most notable points on her tablet in order to remember them and afterwards write them on paper.]

And finally Cecilia van Marick (d. 1503) was said to be always very diligent in collecting the exhortations and copying them out, and in other fine points as well.[9]

It is clear, then, that the Sister Book of Diepenveen tells explicitly about sisters taking notes during non-liturgical preaching and copying them afterwards onto paper. But also outside the Sister Book we find clues about the written preservation

---

[5] See for this late medieval religious movement Regnerus R. Post, *The Modern Devotion: Confrontation with Reformation and Humanism* (Leiden: Brill, 1968).

[6] *Van den doechden der vuriger ende stichtiger susteren van Diepen veen ('Handschrift D')*, ed. by D. A. Brinkerink (Leiden: Sijthoff, [1904]), pp. 253–54. Further examples in Thom Mertens, 'Collatio und Codex im Bereich der Devotio Moderna', in *Der Codex im Gebrauch*, ed. by Christel Meyer et al. (Munich: Fink, 1996), p. 177–78.

[7] maclicste *Ms.*

[8] The Diepenveen Sister Book as found in the unpublished manuscript DV, fol. 81^v, quoted by Mertens, 'Collatio und Codex', p. 177 n. 82.

[9] 'plach zeer vlitich toe wesen die clacien toe vergaderen ende uut toe scriven ende ock ander suverlicke punten'. MS DV, fol. 386^v, quoted by Mertens, 'Collatio und Codex', p. 177 n. 82.

of sermons. One example can be found in the sermons of the famous Franciscan preacher Johannes Brugman (d. 1473). It was he who lent his name to the modern Dutch expression *praten als Brugman* [to speak like Brugman, i.e. to speak very ardently]. In one of his sermons he mentions listeners who recollect afterwards some points of a delivered sermon.[10] This activity must have resulted in a series of notes. Völker, Ruh, and Schiewer recognize that some sermons were preserved in this irregular way, but they consider it a marginal phenomenon with no more than local, domestic importance. And they are right. These were sisters who took notes on their own initiative for their own use, and only in a few exceptional cases did their notes survive. We have, for example, an unordered series of three hundred and twelve passages from the collations of Claus van Euskerken (d. 1520), a later father confessor of the Deventer sisters' houses.[11] The exhortations of his predecessor Brinckerinck have been given a superficial associative structure, with the various unconnected points grouped according to theme. The headings in the manuscript suggest that these are eight or nine separate exhortations, but they are in fact just eight or nine broad categories for thematically related textual material. The individual exhortations show practically no structure, thought development, or formal characteristics of a sermon. The exhortations of Brinckerinck, the founder of the women's monastic branch of the Modern Devotion, had a more than local significance, however. Years after Brinckerinck's death the textual material written down by listeners (mainly by Liesbeth van Delft, we may assume) were ordered and supplied with headings by Rudolf Dier van Muiden (d. 1459), one of the later successors of Brinckerinck as rector of the Deventer sisters' houses.[12] But these 'collations' are also irregular in form, despite the order suggested by the headings.

Schiewer's point is that we should exercise caution when ascribing the writing out of sermons to listeners, especially when the sermons have been preserved in a well-ordered and well-disposed form. In such cases we can assume that the preacher wrote out his sermons for the convent himself. Statements in the prologue maintaining that they were written down by a sister should be read very critically. It is simply a myth that there were sisters with such unusually good memories that they

---

[10] 'Gelick als guede menschen wanneer sij wat guets hoeren in colacien, soe pijnt hem een yegelick wat te onthalden, ende wanneer sij dan bij-een sijn, soe seget een yegelick wat hij guets ghehoert hevet [...]'. [As good people, when they hear something good in the collation, each try to remember something, and when they then are together, each one says the good thing he has heard]. Compare Jan Brugman, *Verspreide sermoenen*, ed. by A. van Dijk (Antwerpen: De Nederlandsche Boekhandel, 1948), p. 104, l. 229–32.

[11] 'Goede punten uit de collatiën van Claus van Euskerken (naar hs. no. 686 der Provinciale Bibliotheek van Friesland)', ed. by D. A. Brinkerinck, *Nederlandsch Archief voor Kerkgeschiedenis*, n.s. 3 (1905), 225–395.

[12] Thom F. C. Mertens, 'Postuum auteurschap: De collaties van Johannes Brinckerinck', in *Windesheim 1395–1995: Kloosters, teksten, invloeden*, ed. by Anton J. Hendrikman and others (Nijmegen: Katholieke Universiteit, 1996), pp. 85–97. I am now less hesitant than in 1996 to ascribe this editing to Rudolf Dier van Muiden.

could write out a complete sermon after hearing it. Preachers often used images to structure their sermon and to make it easier for the listeners to understand and remember the content. While it would not have been impossible to reconstruct a complete, highly consistent sermon with the help of images and notes, it would nevertheless have required a great deal of compositional work. In most cases no more was undertaken than the setting down of disconnected points.

Given the arguments of Völker, Ruh, and Schiewer, one is inclined to all but rule out the possibility that listening sisters wrote down complete sermons. The compiled collations of Claus van Euskerken, however, show that such a means of preservation was possible.

The collations of Van Euskerken are preserved in two manuscripts, originating from two different sister houses in Deventer. One manuscript contains only an unordered series of points, as mentioned above. In the other manuscript we have a series of nineteen well-ordered sermons, for the most part complete, and in addition two excerpts. One collection preserves sermons preached in one convent, while the other contains sermons given in the second house. A comparison of the texts has shown that the collection of disconnected points is not derived from the complete sermons found in the other manuscript. There is virtually no overlap between the two collections, and they could not have shared a common textual source.[13]

In the manuscript containing mainly complete sermons, the quires have a highly irregular structure, and the person who copied the text also made important additions in the margin, such as noting down *auctoritates*. At another spot in this manuscript half a page is left open. Of the three points that are announced only two are filled in. Evidently the text was revised and edited by the copyist, who made additions later as well. This manuscript is therefore an autograph, or to state it more cautiously, the copyist assumed the role of author. The headings and subheadings of the sermons were written by this same copyist. We can be sure that this copyist was not Claus van Euskerken himself because he is referred to in the headings and subheadings as 'onse eersame pater [our venerable father]' and 'onse eerweerdige vader [our reverend father]'. The copyist who assumed the role of author must therefore have been one of the sisters. This manuscript clearly conjures up the picture of a sister collecting, copying, and editing the sermons of her father confessor, making not only stylistic improvements but also additions and changes in the content.[14] This means that in the name of their confessor the sisters wrote and edited sermon texts which have all the formal and structural characteristics of sermons and which could thus also lay claim to the authority due to the father confessor.

This manuscript shows that we must be careful when assessing statements in prologues to sermon collections about a sister writing out sermons of the father

---

[13] Thom Mertens, 'Ein Prediger in zweifacher Ausführung: Die Kollationen des Claus von Euskirchen', in *Predigt im Kontext*, ed. by Volker Mertens and Hans-Jochen Schiewer (Tübingen: Niemeyer, forthcoming).

[14] Mertens, 'Ein Prediger'.

confessor for her convent. A literal interpretation should not be rejected out of hand. It is in this light that we should consider the sermon collections of Jan Storm, confessor of the Jericho convent in Brussels. Three of the four extant sermon collections of Storm have extensive prologues in which sisters report who wrote out these sermons and why they compiled the volumes.

Ghostwriting Sisters in the Brussels Jericho Convent

The Jericho convent came about through a merging of two convents. When a monastery of canonesses in Braine-l'Alleud burned down in 1456 (Braine-l'Alleud lies about thirteen miles south of Brussels), the sisters found shelter in the Catharina convent in Brussels. A short time earlier the canonesses of the Catharina convent had fallen into disrepute because of their loose living. In 1457 the convent was re-established under the name 'Maria of the Rose planted in Jericho' (for convenience here abbreviated to Jericho).[15] Soon afterwards the experienced Jan Storm—he had been procurator and prior of a community of canons—became father confessor of this convent, ruling it for thirty-one years until his death in 1488.[16] In both material and spiritual respects, Jan Storm can be viewed as the re-founding father of the Jericho convent.

The sermons of Storm have survived in four collections (see also Appendix A).[17] I list them here in chronological order.

1. *The first collection of Jan Storm's sermons.* The oldest collection was compiled by Maria van Pee in 1466. It contains seventy-seven sermons of Jan Storm that he delivered in the convent Jericho in the years 1459–64. Added to these sermons of

---

[15] *Monasticon Belge*, ed. by Ursmer Berlière et al. (Maredsous: Abbaye de Maredsous, 1890–1993), IV: *Province de Brabant*, 4, pp. 1247–71.—The prologue by Maria van Pee has been published several times: G. C. Zieleman, 'Overleveringsvormen van middeleeuwse preken in de landstaal', *Nederlands Archief voor Kerkgeschiedenis*, n.s. 59 (1978–79), 11–20 (18–19); Gerrit Cornelis Zieleman, 'Das Studium der deutschen und niederländischen Predigten des Mittelalters', in *Sô predigent etelîche: Beiträge zur deutschen und niederländischen Predigt im Mittelalter*, ed. by Kurt Otto Seidel (Göppingen: Kummerle, 1982), pp. 5–48 (38–49).

[16] Ursmer Berlière, 'Storm (Jean)', in *Biographie Nationale* (Brussels, 1866–1985), XXIV (1926–29), pp. 92–93; Floris Prims, 'Drie ascetische schrijvers der Troonpriorij, Jan Storm (d. 1488), Jacob Roecx (d. 1527) en Cornelis Bellens (d. 1573)', *Koninklijke Vlaamse Academie voor Taal- en Letterkunde, Verslagen en Mededeelingen* (1932), 263–85 (pp. 265-73); *Petri Trudonensis Catalogus Scriptorum Windeshemensium*, ed. by Willem Lourdaux and Ernest Persoons (Leuven: Universiteitsbibliotheek, 1968), p. 142.

[17] I am grateful to Patricia Stoop (University of Antwerp) for her help in cataloguing Storm's sermons. See also Maria Sherwood-Smith and Patricia Stoop, *Repertorium van Middelnederlandse preken in handschriften tot en met 1550*, 3 vols (Leuven: Peeters, 2003), pp. 275–82, 410–54, 620–46, 712–16.

Storm is a small collection of eight sermons of other fathers who preached in Jericho. This small collection was finished in September 1467.

The collection by Maria van Pee is preserved in two manuscripts: one was made in the convent Jericho in 1466–67 (possibly an autograph, as the sisters wrote a great many manuscripts[18]); the other comes from another convent where Maria van Pee lived later (probably the convent Vredenberg near Breda).[19]

2. *The Jericho collection*. This collection contains about forty-one sermons delivered in Jericho by several preachers in the years 1468–74. Margriet van Steenbergen compiled this Jericho sermon collection in 1479, copying the sermon texts that has been written out by her fellow sisters Elisbeth van Poelc and Barbara Cuyermans.

3. *The second collection of Jan Storm's sermons*. A second collection of Storm's sermons was compiled in 1507 (almost twenty years after Storm died) by Janne Colijns. It contains forty-four sermons preached by Storm in Jericho, 1468–74. Colijns also includes three sermons that were copied out by Barbara Cuyermans and preserved in the Jericho collection.

4. *The Catharina collection*. The last is a collection of texts compiled for Liesbeth Mols, prioress of Jericho, in honour of Saint Catharine. Among other texts it contains thirteen sermons. Three of them are also found in the first Storm collection of Maria van Pee.

The last collection has no prologue, but those of the other three give us a detailed picture of how these collections were made, of the persons who edited and compiled them and the sources that were used. In each case the sister who compiled the collection also wrote the prologue.

Maria van Pee did the whole job herself, writing out the sermons and compiling the collection. In the case of the other two collections with prologues, other sisters were responsible for writing out the sermons. The sister who undertook the compiling describes in very precise terms the activity of all the sisters involved. The prologue to the Jericho sermon collection by Margriet van Steenbergen illustrates this point.

Men sal weten dat in desen boeke staen XLI sermoenen beghinnende van der heilegher glorioser maghet sinte Katherinen ende alsoe vervolghende djaeromme na dat die daghe volghen, maer niet na den incarnacione dat sij ghepredict waren, alsoe men claerlijc sal vinden gheteekent voer een yeghelijck sermoen in wat jare ende van wien dat sij ghepredict sijn. [...]

Men sal oec weten dat alle dese sermoene sijn ghescreven uut der predicaren monde, alsoe na ende ghelijck als men can, van twee onse religiose susteren, uut

---

[18] Karl Stooker and Theo Verbeij, *Collecties op orde: Middelnederlandse handschriften uit kloosters en semi-religieuze gemeenschappen in de Nederlanden* (Leuven: Peeters, 1997), II: *Repertorium*, pp. 79–90, MSS nos 212–44.

[19] *Monasticon Belge*, IV. 4, pp. 1258–59; *Monasticon Batavum*, ed. by Michael Schoengen (Amsterdam: Noord-Hollandsche Uitgeversmaatschappij, 1941), II, pp. 153–54.

devocien ende warechtegher minnen te gode [...]. Dus hebben sij neerstelijck gheaerbeyt, nacht ende dach ende noch daghelijck doen, soe dat ick in desen boeck maer van haren minsten werke en hebbe na dat sij noch meneghe sermone hebben. [...]

Der eender name es suster Baerbara Cuyermans. Dese heefter hier viere, als die drie van onsen eerwerdeghen pater ende die vierde van den eerwerdeghen provinciael onser liever vrouwen dach in den advent. Die ander es ghenaemt suster Elizabeth van Poelken. Dese heeft alle die andere vergadert.

Nu com ic, suster Mergriete van Steenberghen, [...] ende hebbe [...] desen boeck ghescreven ende vergadert met aerbeyde [...].[20]

[It should be known that in this book are forty-one sermons, beginning with the holy glorious virgin Saint Catharine and continuing through the (Church) year following the order of the days, but not according to the calendar year in which they were preached; thus one will find clearly noted for each sermon in which year and by whom it was preached. [...]

It should also be known that all these sermons have been written from the mouth of preachers, as closely and accurately as possible, by two of our religious sisters, out of devotion and true love for God [...]. Thus they worked diligently, night and day, and they still do every day, so that in this book I have only the least of their work, considering that they have many more sermons yet. [...]

The name of the one is sister Barbara Cuyermans. She has four (sermons) here, three by our reverend father (Jan Storm) and the fourth by the reverend provincial on the day of Our Dear Lady in Advent.[21] The other is called sister Elizabeth van Poelken. She collected all the others.

Now it is my turn, sister Mergriete van Steenberghen; [...] I undertook the arduous task of writing and compiling this book [...].]

The message is clear: Margriet van Steenbergen tells us that she collected a number of sermon texts written out by Elisabeth van Poelken and Barbara Cuyermans, ordered them according to the ecclesiastical year and wrote the manuscript.

Janne Colijns, who compiled the second Storm collection, emphasizes the fact that she herself did not write out the sermon texts, but simply ordered them and wrote the manuscript:

Ic begheere oec dat nyement en meyne maer zeekerlijc weete dat ic, scriverse dees boecks, dese weerdighe sermoenen som selve hoerende niet en hebbe uutghecopiert [...], maer ic heb se alleene vergadert eens deels ende oec des meesten deels uuyt rollen, brieven ende ouden quaternen ghescreven metter hant des selven predicaers. Ende die andere sijn uut ghecopieert van een sijnre gheestelijker dochter ende religioeser suster ons cloesters van Jericho, met namen suster Barbara Cuyermans, die, inden heere ghestorven, voertijts mijn meerstersse van scrijven gheweest is [...].[22]

---

[20] Ghent, Universiteitsbibliotheek, MS 902, fol. 1^v–2^r. For the translation of the complete text of the prologue see Appendix B of this article.

[21] Immaculate Conception of Mary, 8 December.

[22] Brussels, Koninklijke Bibliotheek, MS II 298, fol. 4^v–5^r.

[I also want nobody to surmise, but everybody to know for certain that I, writer of this book, did not copy out these noble sermons, some of which I heard myself, [...] but that I only collected them, partly and mostly from scrolls, leaves, and old quires handwritten by the preacher himself. And the other sermons were copied out by one of his spiritual daughters and a religious sister of our convent of Jericho, namely sister Barbara Cuyermans, who, deceased in the Lord, was formerly my writing mistress.]

These prologues therefore tell us in very exact terms, using first and last names, who played which part in writing out and compiling the sermons. The detailed nature of the information suggests precisely that this is not simply a literary stylization of the listener's role, as the criticism of the sisters with powerful memories would have us believe, but that the sisters were actually responsible for these written texts.

The detailed information also enables us to sketch an intellectual profile of the sisters who put together these collections. Not all the names mentioned can be traced in the sources about Jericho. A few are known to us, however. Maria van Pee was the first important prioress of the convent after it was transformed into the new foundation. Two prioresses preceded her, but they remained in office for only a short time. Elisabeth van Poelk(en) succeeded Maria van Pee as prioress following the short priorate of another sister. There was also a prioress Janne Colijns, but the only source that mentions the year of her death reports that prioress Janne Colijns died in 1491, in other words long before our Janne Colijns composed the second collection of Storm's sermons, in 1507. This means either that there were two Janne Colijns in the convent, or that the year of prioress Janne Colijns's death is reported incorrectly. Barbara Cuyermans was her 'writing mistress', which means—I would assume—not only that she taught young sisters to write, but also that she would organize the writing activities in the convent. She must in any case have been a gifted person in writing and editing new texts. Margriet van Steenbergen is not mentioned in these sources, but research on the unpublished manuscripts of the convent might shed more light on her.

Obviously a writing mistress, the most likely person in the convent to be producing written texts, would have been involved in writing out sermons. A striking fact is that two or three of the sisters mentioned were prioresses. The writing out of sermons was not, however, a task of the prioress, for the sermons date from either before or after their term of office. Probably the same qualities that made these women suitable for a leadership function also equipped them for the writing out of sermons.

Gender and Ghostwriting

In early Christian times preaching was the task of the bishop, occasionally also of the priest or a layman authorized by the bishop. Differentiation in the Church hierarchy and concern about orthodoxy led in the course of the third century to preaching being restricted to the bishop. The following century, however, brought such an expansion of Christianity that the bishop more and more frequently was compelled to delegate this task to priests. The sermon was primarily the right and the task of the bishop, aided by other clerics with major orders, namely priests and deacons.[23] Considering that major orders were open only to men, preaching was clearly a matter of gender.

While the preaching of sermons was limited to clerics with major orders, the recording of this activity in writing shows a paradox. The sermons from the Jericho convent are preserved under the name of the preacher, but at the same time the sisters make it clear that they have been responsible for editing these sermons. Most surprising of all, perhaps, is that they have placed themselves totally in the role of the father confessor and write in his name and with his authority. The sisters do not write in a *reportata* style with formulas such as 'he said', but instead completely simulate a preaching situation. They present an 'I' who addresses the listening sisters with authority:

Van onser vrouwen ontfanckenisse dat IIII^{de} sermoen Anno LXII

Ave, gracia plena dominus tecum—Luce I. Achterghelaten alle ander disputacie die arguacie in bringhen mochten om te ondersueken oft Maria in erfsonden ghewonnen was, soe neme ic alleen vore tghene dat tot minnen ende devocien trecken mach toter glorioser moeder ende maghet Maria. Van 'Ave gracia plena' hebdi hiervoer ghehoort. Daerom late ic nu ende neme alleene dat woort dat onse moeder die heyleghe kerke daer toeghedaen heeft, dat es 'Maria'.[24]

[The fourth sermon on the Annunciation. Anno [14]62

Ave, gratia plena dominus tecum—Luke 1. Leaving out of consideration all other discussion which would present arguments to investigate whether or not Mary was conceived in original sin, I shall deal only with that which can draw us in love and devotion to the glorious mother and virgin Mary. You have heard before about 'Ave gratia plena'. Therefore I will not go into that now but only the word that our mother the holy Church has added to it, namely 'Mary'.]

This example clearly shows that the sermons are written in the first person singular, the 'I' referring to the preacher who determines how the topic of the sermon will be treated. Here he limits himself to 'that which can draw us in love and devotion to the glorious mother and virgin Mary'. An interesting point in this passage is that it then refers back to the previous sermons: 'You have heard before about "Ave gratia plena".' This is an allusion to the sermons which *in this volume* immediately precede the sermon at hand but which were actually preached years earlier, namely on the same feast day in 1459, 1460(?), and 1461. The reference, in

---

[23] *Lexikon des Mittelalters*, ed. by Robert-Henri Bautier et al. (Munich: Artemis & Winkler, 1977–1998), VII (1995), col. 171–72; *Lexikon für Theologie und Kirche*, ed. by Michael Buchberger et al. (Munich: Herder, 1993-), VIII (1999), col. 527.

[24] Brussels, Koninklijke Bibliotheek, MS 4367–68, fol. 13^r.

other words, is to the series of sermons as compiled by Maria van Pee and not to the sermons as they were delivered at one-year intervals. This means that the person responsible for making the reference is the editor of the sermons, Maria van Pee. This quotation makes clear the extent to which the person of the preacher and that of the editing sister have merged in the written record of the sermons.

Where did the sisters derive the right to assimilate so completely the authority of the father confessor in their writing? The prologues provide no answer to this question: no arguments are presented for taking over the role as such, and authority is simply not an issue. The sisters do try, however, to follow the original wording as closely as possible. Margriet van Steenbergen writes, for example: 'Men sal oec weten dat alle dese sermoene sijn ghescreven uut der predicaren monde, alsoe na ende ghelijck als men can, van twee onse religiose susteren [It should also be known that all these sermons have been written from the mouth of the preacher, as closely and accurately as possible, by two of our religious sisters]'.[25] And Maria van Pee regrets that she did not succeed in rendering everything completely verbatim:

> Maer dat ic uuten gronde mijns herten beclage, es dat ic soe plomp van begripe ben dat ic alle die scoene redenen ende auctorijteyte der heiligen welke hi in sinen sermoenen alligeerde, niet en heb connen van woerde te woerde onthouden om te scriven soe hi se schone uutleide. Maer alleen soe heb ic den bloeten sin daeraf ghepijnt te onthouden soe ic naest conste [...]. Hier om soe biddic eenen yegeliken die in dit boeck selen lesen dat sijt mijnre plompheit vergeven als si die poenten oprecht niet en vinden overgeset, want minen sinnen veel te hoege was alle dingen soe schoene ende cuystelijc te bescriven als sij uutgeleit ende gepredict waren, noch oec voer gheen vermetelheit en houden dat ic mi bestaen hebbe des ic oprecht niet volbringen en mochte, want ict noyt en begonste om yemen daermet te believen dan alleen tot mijns selfs orbore ende salicheit.[26]

> [But what I regret from the depths of my heart is that I am so dull of understanding that I was not able to remember word for word all the beautiful arguments and the quotations of the saints to which he alluded in his sermons in order to write them as beautifully as he formulated them. But I only attempted to remember the bare meaning as accurately as I could [...]. Therefore I ask all those who will read this book to forgive my dullness if they find that the points have not been rendered perfectly, for it was far beyond my understanding to write everything as beautifully and exquisitely as it was formulated and preached; and not to consider it audacious of me that I dared to undertake something which I could not complete perfectly, for I in no way began it in order to please others but only for my own benefit and salvation.]

These passages make it clear that Maria van Pee's efforts were aimed at rendering the sermon verbatim. It is also evident that the literal or correct rendering of the

---

[25] Ghent, Universiteitsbibliotheek, MS 902, fol. 1[v].

[26] Brussels, Koninklijke Bibliotheek, MS 4367–68, fol. 3[v]–4[r]; compare Brussels, Koninklijke Bibliotheek, MS IV 402, fol. 2[v]–3[r].

sermon was not only a matter of memory but—to an even greater degree—of intellect.[27] Margriet van Steenbergen also in the first place praises her fellow sisters who wrote out sermons for their understanding and secondly for their memory: 'Sij sijn wonderlijck verlicht in claerder verstannissen ende onthoudender memorien [They are wonderfully enlightened with a clear understanding and a retentive memory]'.[28] The main structure of the sermon can be easily remembered from the image or the biblical words that form the point of departure. More difficult to remember are the points of the subdivisions and most difficult of all is the argumentation using *auctoritates*, quotations from the Bible and great Christian writers. It is precisely in this last area that Maria van Pee admits her shortcoming. Nevertheless she did not limit her texts to the main points, but included extensive quotations and arguments. This is where intellectual capacities come into play. What we cannot rule out is that the sisters themselves supplied a great deal of the argumentation with the help of *auctoritates*, probably using the same heuristic handbooks as the preachers.[29] In the sermon collection of Claus van Euskerken mentioned above we can see that the editing sister continued to add new *auctoritates* in the margin after writing out the sermon. Elsewhere in the manuscript she left a number of lines open for a subsection that still had to be worked out. All this means that although the 'skeleton' of the sermon was the work of the preacher, the sisters who did the writing were to a large extent responsible for the 'flesh' that brought these bones to life. The assimilation of the preacher's role extended not only to formulating and editing the sermon text but evidently also included some inroads into the area of *inventio*.

All of the prologues mention the fact that the texts preserve sermons actually delivered in the Jericho convent. None of the texts, then, were composed by a preacher in sermon style only for the purpose of reading rather than for delivery from the pulpit. This means that the sisters must have played a large role in producing these sermon collections. Only Janne Colijns claims to have used textual sources written by the preacher himself. We can assume that she nevertheless had to do a fair amount of editing on most of them, for in the heading of one sermon she

---

[27] Despite the recent interest in the art of memory in the Middle Ages, little is known about the concrete training of memory as part of a normal school curriculum or about the way in which texts, either read or heard, were committed to memory. Compare nevertheless the *Tractatus de arte memorativa* of Goswinus de Ryt, chancellor of Brabant (born in Brussels 1436, d. 1465), Chapter 12: *De artificiali memoria oracionis prolixe, premeditate vel audite statim ab alio*, edited and commented on by Sabine Heimann-Seelbach, *Ars und Scientia. Genese, Überlieferung und Funktionen der mnemotechnischen Traktatliteratur im 15. Jahrhundert* (Tübingen: Niemeyer, 2000), pp. 68–67, 180–202 (196–97).

[28] Ghent, Universiteitsbibliotheek, MS 902, fol. 1[v].

[29] Compare, for example, Richard H. Rouse and Mary A. Rouse, *Preachers, Florilegia and Sermons: Studies on the Manipulus florum of Thomas of Ireland* (Toronto: Pontifical Institute of Mediaeval Studies, 1979), pp. 1–90.

mentions the exceptional fact that the text of this sermon was completely written out by Father Storm: 'Een schoen sermoen van sinte Marien Magdalenen dat welke ons ghelaten heeft onse eerwerdighe pater Storm, met sijns selfs hant van woerde te woerde ghescreven. [A fine sermon on saint Mary Magdalene which our reverend Father Storm left us, written word for word with his own hand.]' [30]

The fact that sisters wrote out the sermons of their father confessors was not seen as a problem as long as they did their best to render the sermon verbatim. In the absence of any developed form of shorthand, however, a truly verbatim rendering was not possible. Attempts to produce a literal text would encounter the greatest difficulties when it came to argumentation in sections and subsections. Any failures here were, as we have seen, attributed to one's own intellectual shortcomings. An additional excuse offered by Maria van Pee is that she noted down the sermons for herself and not in the first place for others. The fact that the sisters took over the role of their father confessor in writing out the sermons was not perceived as a problem. Other sources also make it clear that the sisters wrote down the sermons on their own initiative and in the first place for their own use. [31] If, however, they subsequently did not keep the sermons for themselves but made them public in their convent, some justification was necessary. The question of authority, which never arose for the writing out of sermons, did become an issue if they were made public. [32] What arguments did the sisters use to justify their decision to publish?

Men sal oec weten dat alle dese sermoene sijn ghescreven [...] van twee onse religiose susteren, uut devocien ende warechtegher minnen te gode omdat sij gode daer ten yersten inne eeren souden ende haerder zielen zalicheit inne werken souden ende om alle dat goet datter namaels af comen soude, dat sij daer in deylachtich wesen mochten. [33]

[It should also be known that all these sermons were written [...] by two of our religious sisters, out of devotion and true love for God, so that they in the first place might thereby honour God and bring about the salvation of their soul, and that they might share in the good that would come of it later.]

They wrote, in other words, to honour God but also to increase their own merits for the next life by sharing in the merits of those who, thanks to these written sermons, would perform good works. Maria van Pee comes with a similar argument:

---

[30] Brussels, Koninklijke Bibliotheek, MS II 298, fol. 227[r].

[31] Mertens, 'Collatio und Codex', p. 177–78, compare especially n. 85.

[32] The collations of Brinckerinck were edited and published as a collection by a priest who based his work on the notes of a sister (compare Mertens, 'Postuum auteurschap'). This instance also shows that the publishing of sermon material was clearly one step beyond the writing out. In this early example the two steps were taken by different persons, the first by a nun and the second by a priest. The second step was therefore taken by a person who had the authority to preach.

[33] Ghent, Universiteitsbibliotheek, MS 902, fol. 1[v] (quoted in part above).

Ende want ic mi selven zeer trage ende wederstravich ter dueght kinne, god beteert, soe hebbic dit werck in doppenbaer vergadert opdat ic ghenieten mach der gheender dueght die hier haer profijt in doen selen ende dat ic bi haren vercrighen mach dat mi uut mijns selfs crancheit ontbrect.[34]

[And because I know myself to be very slow and averse to virtue—may God better this—I have compiled this work in public so that I may enjoy the virtue of those who will profit from this and so that I may obtain through them what I lack out of my own weakness.]

And Janne Colijns makes it clear that the father confessor also shares in these merits: 'Oec soe beruert my speciaelijc totten love ende weerdicheit des ghedinckelijken predicaers die vermeerdinghe sijns toevallenden loens. [Also the enlargement of the reward due to this memorable preacher motivates me in particular to praise and honour him.]'[35]

There is an authority vacuum between the spoken sermon, which is the work of the preacher, and the written text, which is the work of the sisters. This vacuum is filled by keeping the written text as close as possible to the spoken one. The sisters' strategy here was to adopt a highly imitative form, a consistent sermon fiction that created as little distance as possible. To the extent that the sisters were unable to realize this imitation, they appealed to their readers' good will, pointing out their own intellectual limitations and the fact that they had written out these sermons in the first place for themselves. The subsequent step of compiling and publishing them in the limited circle of their own convent is motivated by the goals they wished to attain, namely to honour God and, together with their beloved father confessor, to share in the rewards that would come from the reading of these sermons. The most obvious motive, that of edifying the community, is not mentioned explicitly.

Prologues with detailed descriptions of what the sisters did and why are exceptional. In most of the sermon collections from outside the Jericho convent the sisters have disappeared entirely behind the name of the preacher. In some cases we know from other sources that sisters took notes of sermons. It can be demonstrated that Claus van Euskerken's sermons, for example, were edited by an anonymous sister.[36] In rare cases the prologues speak at some length about all the effort put into these collections. In the Jericho convent the sisters worked together intensively in building up their library, revealing in the process a strong preference for the sermons of their own father confessor.[37] Perhaps they described their own role so precisely in the hope of enlarging their reward.

---

[34] Brussels, Koninklijke Bibliotheek, MS 4367–68, fol. 4[r].

[35] Brussels, Koninklijke Bibliotheek, MS II 298, fol. 4[r].

[36] See the section above on 'Sermon-Preserving Sisters', for the narrative sources and the preservation of Van Euskerken's sermons.

[37] Stooker and Verbeij, *Collecties op orde*, I: *Studie*, p. 230; II: *Repertorium*, pp. 79–90, MSS nos 212–44.

Conclusion

It was long assumed that the vernacular sermons of the Late Middle Ages were generally written out by women, until Paul-Gerhard Völker showed in 1963 that most sermons must have been written out by the preachers themselves, an exception being those noted down by sisters as a gesture of veneration for their confessors. As the years went by, Völker's ideas found more and more support, and eventually even prologues which maintained that sisters had listened to and written out the sermons of their father confessor, were interpreted in this light. Narrative sources, codicological evidence, and detailed prologues to sermon collections make it clear, however, that in a number of cases sisters did write out and edit the sermons of their confessor and in doing so tried to assimilate his style and authority completely.

In the unusually detailed prologues to the sermon collections from the Jericho convent we can distinguish three gendered roles involved in the production of the sermon texts: that of the father confessor, of the sister who wrote out the sermons, and of the sister who compiled and edited them.

The father confessor delivered sermons in the church of the convent. He was entitled to do so because of his higher ecclesiastical ordination as a priest, and it was his task to preach, as rector and confessor of the convent. Writing out his sermons was not part of his task, nor would he have had time for it, busy as he no doubt was with the temporal government of the recently re-established convent.

The sisters' motive for copying out the sermons was a personal one, namely to better interiorize the content. There was no obligation whatsoever on behalf of the community to do this. The decision to publish the results of their efforts in their community had to be expressly motivated, however, and they declared that their father confessor would in this way share in the eternal reward for the good works that would come from the reading of his sermons. The sisters who copied out the sermons would also share in this eternal reward.

Copying out sermons from memory required special mental qualities. One had to have a keen mind in the first place and an unusually good memory. The high-level intellectual capacities required for writing out sermons after hearing them without using notes may have predisposed these sisters to become leaders of their convent. This would explain why at least two of them became prioresses.

A third consideration concerns the role of the sister who compiled and edited the collection. This seems to have demanded lesser intellectual capacities. Maria van Pee combined the two roles, but in the case of the later collections the roles were divided. Writing out sermons from notes made by the preacher, as Janne Colijns probably did, seems to have been a great deal easier than writing them out from memory.

The sermons copied out by sisters under the name of their father confessor reveal a complex authorship. Writing under the name of the confessor implied writing under his authority. Nevertheless, there are no signs of explicit authorization of the sermons by the father confessor. One can imagine that the sisters consulted their confessor on the sermons they had written out, but this was not necessarily the case.

Janne Colijns compiled and edited her collection of Storm's sermons long after his death. And she gives no hint at all of regretting the fact that she could not turn to him for help or for his authorization.

In copying out the sermons of their father confessor, the sisters took over his role completely. This is the most striking aspect of their work. They wrote complete, well-structured texts in which an authoritative 'I' speaks to the beloved sisters. They took up their role as genuine ghostwriters, and precisely because they played it so convincingly, modern researchers have disbelieved the claims made in the prologues that a sister wrote the sermons.

APPENDIX A: THE COLLECTIONS CONTAINING JAN STORM'S SERMONS

1. First Collection of Jan Storm's Sermons

Sermons written out, compiled and edited by Maria van Pee Can A (1465–80 prioress in Jericho, d. 1511)
Contents:
1. introduction to the prologue
    prologue by Maria van Pee
    77 sermons by Jan Storm Can A (d. 1488) given 1459–64 in Jericho
    collection finished (before) 10 August, 1466
2. 8 sermons by several preachers in Jericho (Godevaert Kemp Can A; a Franciscan observant; the first Dominican subprior, Aert O.P.)
    collection finished (before) 6 September, 1467
Manuscripts:
1. Brussels, Koninklijke Bibliotheek, 4367–68 (Jericho, 1466–67)
2. Brussels, Koninklijke Bibliotheek, IV 402 (Vredenberg near Breda? 1486)

2. Jericho Collection
Collection compiled and edited by Margriet van Steenbergen
Sermons written out by Barbara Cuyermans (4) and Elisabeth van Poelc (the other sermons)
Contents:
prologue by Margriet van Steenbergen
about 41 sermons delivered by several preachers 1466–78 in Jericho, including 3
  sermons by Jan Storm, written out by Barbara Cuyermans (d. before 1507)
Manuscript: Ghent, Universiteitsbibliotheek, 902 (Jericho, 1479)

3. Second Collection of Jan Storm's Sermons
Collection compiled and edited by Janne Colijns Can A (probably)
Sermons written out by Barbara Cuyermans, Can A Jan Storm Can A, Janne Colijns Can A(?) using scrolls, leaves and quires of the late Jan Storm.
Contents:
prologue by the editor (Janne Colijns Can A?)
44 sermons by Jan Storm (1468–74), including the 3 sermons by Storm written
  out by Barbara Cuyermans (d. before 1507) also preserved in the Jericho
  Collection)
Manuscript: Brussels, Koninklijke Bibliotheek, II 298 (Jericho, 1507, by Janne
  Colijns Can A)

4. Catharina collection
Collection compiled and edited by an anonymous sister, commissioned by prioress
Lijsbeth Smols (d. 1538) for the Jericho convent
Sermons written out by Maria van Pee (3 sermons from the first collection)
Contents: mostly texts on Saint Catharina, including the 3 sermons delivered by Jan
    Storm on the feast of Saint Catherina (from the first collection by Maria van Pee).
Manuscript: Brussels, Koninklijke Bibliotheek, 1683–87 (Jericho, early 16th century)

Appendix B: The Prologue of Sister Margriet van Steenbergen

The prologue to the Jericho collection (Ghent, Universiteitsbibliotheek, 902, fol. 1ʳ–
2ʳ) is extremely detailed and clarifies exactly which part was played by the various
sisters in putting together the collection of sermons. For this reason the prologue is
quoted here in its entirety.

> **Hier beghint een sympel voerredene van den navolghenden boeke**. Men sal weten
> dat in desen boeke staen XLI sermoenen beghinnende van der heilegher glorioser
> maghet sinte Katherinen ende alsoe vervolghende djaeromme na dat die daghe
> volghen, maer niet na den incarnacione dat sij ghepredict waren, alsoe men claerlijc
> sal vinden gheteekent voer een yeghelijck sermoen in wat jare ende van wien dat sij
> ghepredict sijn. Mer alle gader sijn sij gepredict in die kerke ons cloesters van
> Jhericho,[38] dwelck ghesseten es in der goeder liever stat van Bruesele bij der kerken
> vander heilegher maghet sinte Katherinen.
>
>   Dese werdeghe sermoenen sijn ghepredict van persoenen uut drierley ordene, als
> uut onser ordenen ons werdeghen vaders sinte Augustijns, die welke sijn gheweest ons
> eerwerdeghe pater her Jan Storm, wijlen eer gheweest prioer van den Troene, in welck
> cloester dat hi profes es. Dander es gheweest sijn vleesschelijcke broder her Willem
> Storm, oeck wijlen eer gheweest prioer van Onser Vrouwen Marien Bethleem.[39]
> Welck sermoene dat sijn gheweest, sal men vinden inder rubriken voer den
> sermoenen. Dander ordene sijn die predicaren die haer woenstede hebben hier in der
> selver stat. Die derde ordene sijn van sinte Francissicus die observancie houden,
> woenende buten der stat te Botendale.
>
>   Alle dese sijn alsoe werdeghen verlichten ende belefden mannen gheweest dat sij
> welna alle in den staet van prelatueren waren oft cort inne gheset worden, ghelijck als
> wel blict in der leerringhen van den sermoenen, soe dat wij wel moghen segghen dat
> sij sijn inghegaen die alder vetste weyden der heilegher scrieftueren ende hebben daer
> ghepluect te menegher steden die alderschoenste open bloemen ende dierbare
> ghesteynte van perlen der notabelder leeringhe, gheauctorizeert bij meneghen leeraren
> der heilegher kerken, ende hebben ons *(1v)* dus ghemaect een suete electuarie ende

---

[38] Jherico *MS*

[39] Bethleem [added in the margin].

welriekende specie ons ziele mede te medicineren als sij zieck es oft flau, ic meyne als wij traghe oft onlustich sijn ten duechden.

Dese selve specie es ons oec dienende in eender spijsen onser zielen, soe sij se ons notabelijc bereyt hebben, die ons sterckheit gheven mach in allen becoringhen ende tribulacien, het sij van binnen oft van buten, van wat zijden dat sij aenvallen.

Het es oec, ten derden male, een specie van crachteghen ontstekene onser edelder zielen in der minnen ons liefs heren ende ons daer uut met vieregher begheerten tot hem ons op te heffen ende met meneghen verlanghen uut gronde ons herten tot hem te suchten. Want hi es almoghende ons te hulpen in allen, volle goet ons willichlijck te gheven sijn gracie ende die ewilike onvganckelike blijsscap, hem selven onser zielen ghevende te loene na dit aerm bedroefde leven.

Men sal oec weten dat alle dese sermoene sijn ghescreven uut der predicaren monde, alsoe na ende ghelijck als men can, van twee onse religiose susteren, uut devocien ende warechtegher minnen te gode omdat sij gode daer ten yersten inne eeren souden ende haerder zielen zalicheit inne werken souden ende om alle dat goet datter namaels af comen soude, dat sij daer in deylachtich wesen mochten. Dus hebben sij neerstelijck gheaerbeyt, nacht ende dach ende noch daghelijck doen, soe dat ick in desen boeck maer van haren minsten werke en hebbe na dat sij noch meneghe sermone hebben. Sij sijn wonderlijck verlicht in claerder verstannissen ende onthoudender memorien, dwelck sij oec met werdegher dancbaerheit onsen lieven here wederghevent met neersteghen aerbeyde ende met stichteghen duechdeliken leven. God sij ghebenedijt ende gheloeft.

Der eender name es suster Baerbara Cuyermans. Dese heefter hier viere, als die drie van onsen eerwerdeghen pater ende die vierde van den eerwerdeghen provinciael onser liever *(2r)* vrouwen dach in den advent. Die ander es ghenaemt suster Elizabeth van Poelken. Dese heeft alle die andere vergadert.

Nu com ic, suster Mergriete van Steenberghen, ende wil sijn een beclyevende[40] saeyken haerder alder aerbeyt dier in gheproficieert hebben, ende hebbe daeromme ter eeren ende ten ewighen love gods ende ter zalicheit mijnder zielen ende alle der gheender dier noch goet uut werken selen, desen boeck ghescreven ende vergadert met aerbeyde, in cleynen gherieve ende in groter tribulacien opdat ic van dier sueter electuarien ende specie voer ghealligeert nu soude beghennen te smaken metter hopen die ewilike loene die te vercrighen sijn met neersteghen ende volherdenden aerbeyde. Daeromme dese werdeghe spijse cuuwende in daecheliken voersiene ende studerende, soe hebbicker dus vele ghescreven. Want ick en hadde maer voer ghenomen te scriven die sermoene vanden eerwerdeghen gaerdiaen brueder Dyonijs van Hollant, der welker ic hebbe XVII. Dese man was alsoe luter ende recht godminnende dat hi mijn herte wonderlijke zere bewechde ende recht raecte, sodat[41] ic ghevoelde die woerde Davids daer hi seet: 'Dat woert gods es als een vierich schielt', ende noch dat hi seet: 'Lieve here, dijn woert heeft mijn herte verlicht ende het is een lanteerne minen voeten ende een claer licht minen toepaden.'

Nu biddic eenen yegheliken die in dese werdeghe sermone sal comen te lesen, dat hi sijn oeghen slae op enich poent met ghemerke dat hem beweghe toter minnen gods

---

[40] in fine writing in the margin 'beclyevende' [?]

[41] sodat: reading of 'so' is uncertain

ende dat behoude in sijnder memorien, want van der minnen gods heeft men den weseliken loen inden ewighen leven ende het es die meeste blijscap. Tot welker blijsscap ons bringhen moet die vader, die sone ende die heileghe gheest. Amen.

[Here begins a simple prologue to the following book. It should be known that in this book are forty-one sermons, beginning with the holy glorious virgin Saint Catharine and continuing through the (Church) year following the order of the days, but not according to the calendar year in which they were preached; thus one will find clearly noted for each sermon in which year and by whom it was preached. But all of them were preached in the church of our convent Jericho, which is located in the good, beloved city of Brussels, near the church of the holy virgin Saint Catharine.

These worthy sermons were preached by persons from three orders. From the order of our venerable father Saint Augustine it was our reverend Father Jan Storm, former prior of Ten Troon,[42] in which monastery he also made his profession. The other was his brother in the flesh, Willem Storm, also former prior of Our Lady Mary of Bethlehem.[43] Which sermons those were can be found in the rubrics preceding the sermons. The second order was that of the preachers who have their place of residence in this same city. The third order was that of the observants of Saint Francis who live outside the city in Botendale.

All of these were such worthy, enlightened and experienced men that they almost all held the office of prelate or were placed in that office a short time later; this is also evident from the teachings of the sermons, so that we can say that they entered the lushest meadows of Holy Scripture and plucked from many places there the most beautiful open flowers and precious stones, pearls of noble teaching, authorized by many teachers of the Holy Church; and they thus made for us a sweet delicacy and fragrant herb to medicate our soul if it is sick or weak, I mean if we are sluggish or unmotivated with respect to virtue.

This same herb also serves us in the food for our soul that they have so carefully prepared for us, food that can give us strength in all trials and tribulations, whether from inside or from outside, from whatever side they attack us.

In the third place, it is also a herb that can powerfully ignite our noble souls in the love of our dear Lord, and out of this raise us up to him by ardent desires, to sigh for him with many a longing from the depths of our heart. For he is all-powerful to help us in all things, full of the goodness to willingly give us his grace and eternal undying joy, giving himself as a reward to our soul after this poor, sad life.

It should also be known that all these sermons have been written from the mouth of preachers, as closely and accurately as possible, by two of our religious sisters, out of devotion and true love for God, so that they in the first place might thereby honour God and bring about the salvation of their soul, and that they might share in the good that would come of it later. Thus they worked diligently, night and day, and they still do every day, so that in this book I have only the least of their work, considering that they have many more sermons yet. They are wonderfully enlightened with a clear understanding and a retentive memory, which they, with due thankfulness, give back

---

[42] In Grobbendonk near Herentals.

[43] In Herent near Louvain.

to our dear Lord with diligent work and an edifying, virtuous life. God be honoured and praised.

The name of the one is sister Barbara Cuyermans. She has four (sermons) here, three by our reverend father (Jan Storm) and the fourth by the reverend provincial on the day of Our Dear Lady in Advent.[44] The other is called sister Elizabeth van Poelken. She collected all the others.

Now it is my turn, Sister Mergriete van Steenberghen; I want to be a small sprouting seed of all the efforts of those who have contributed to it. For this reason, to the glory and eternal love of God and for the salvation of my soul and of all those who will yet perform good works because of it, I undertook the arduous task of writing and compiling this book, with little (bodily) comfort and great tribulations, so that the sweet delicacy and (healing) herb alluded to earlier would now begin to taste good, in the hope of gaining the eternal reward with diligent, persevering effort. For this reason I copied so many of them, chewing this worthy food in daily ponderings and study. For I had intended to write only the sermons of the reverend guardian, Brother Dionysius of Holland, of which I have done seventeen. This man was so pure and upright in his love of God that he moved my heart wondrously and touched it so directly that I felt the words of David when he says, 'The word of God is as a fiery shield', and again when he says, 'Dear Lord, thy word has brought light to my heart, and it is a lamp to my feet and a light to my path.'[45]

Now I beg everyone who comes to read these worthy sermons that he direct his eyes attentively to any point that may move him to the love of God and that he keep it in his memory, for one has the true reward of the love of God in eternal life, and that is the greatest joy. To which joy the Father, the Son, and the Holy Ghost must bring us. Amen.]

Translated by Myra Scholz

---

[44] Immaculate Conception of Mary, 8 December.

[45] Compare Psalm 118 (119). 114 (?), 105.

[46] Jherico MS

[47] Bethleem [added in the margin]

[48] [in fine writing in the margin] beclyevende(?)

[49] sodat [reading of 'so' is uncertain]

[50] In Grobbendonk near Herentals.

[51] In Herent near Louvain.

[52] Immaculate Conception of Mary, 8 December.

[53] Compare Psalm 118(119). 114 (?), 105.

What Francis Intended: Gender and the Transmission of Knowledge in the Franciscan Order*

LEZLIE KNOX

A t the beginning of the Cinquecento Sister Battista Alfani, a Poor Clare in the convent of Monteluce in central Italy, prepared a vernacular translation from the Latin of the *Legenda sanctae Clarae Virginis* for her community.[1] It was not slavishly literal. She also frequently added stories that present Clare as more

---

* Throughout this essay I have referred to the female Franciscan Order as the 'Poor Clares' both for convenience and consistency with the common English designation. That term, however, is not actually an appropriate reference before 1263 when Pope Urban IV promulgated his Rule for the *Ordo sanctae Clarae*. An introduction to the complex history of how the women's religious movement in central Italy (such as the *povere donne* associated with Clare of Assisi as well as the Order of San Damiano, organized by the Roman curia) were incorporated into the Franciscan Order is given by Maria Pia Alberzoni, *La Nascità di un'Istituzione: L'Ordine di S. Damiano nel XIII secolo* (Milan: Edizioni CUSL, 1996). For helping me to clarify my ideas about Battista's story, I would like to thank in particular Dorsey Armstrong, Jason Glenn, Mark Jordan, Rachel Koopmans, Anneke Mulder-Bakker, and John van Engen. Except where noted, all translations are my own.

[1] Battista Alfani, *La Leggenda della Serafica Vergine Santa Chiara,* preserved in Florence, Biblioteca Nazionale Centrale Magliabecchiano XXXVIII, 135 (hereafter abbreviated as *VSC*). Giuseppe Cozza-Luzi described the manuscript: 'Il codice Magliabecchiano della storia di S. Chiara. Lettera a Luigi Fumi', *Bollettino della Società Umbra di Storia* Patria, 1 (1897), 417–426. Zeffirino Lazzeri edited the text from four manuscripts as *La vita di S. Chiara. Raccolta a traditta da tutte le fonti conosciute e completata col testo inedito del processo di canonizzazione per un Francescano toscano del Cinquecento* (Quaracchi: Collegio S. Bonaventurae, 1920). Battista's identity as author was first suggested by Giovanni Boccali, 'Due opere pittoriche di Raffaello Sanzio e notizie storiche nelle cronache delle clarisse dell'Umbria', *Studi Francescani*, 85 (1988), 81–93, see p. 87 and note 32 especially.

enterprising and more distinctly Franciscan in her spirituality than the standard portrait of an enclosed contemplative offered by the thirteenth-century legend.[2] One even places Clare in the midst of the friars' debate over the role of academic study in the Franciscan Order.

> One day the most devoted mother Saint Clare asked the Guardian at Santa Maria degli Angeli to send a brother to preach to them. It so happened that just then in the friary there was a master in Sacred Theology whom many have identified as the Irrefutable Doctor, Master Alexander of Hales. He was most famous for his learning and for his holy way of life, having entered the Order of Saint Francis as a respected doctor and master of great excellence. Because of his devotion to Francis, [Alexander of Hales] had come to Assisi and stayed for a long time at Santa Maria degli Angeli. In fact, he had been there long enough that he was able to speak and preach in Italian. Thus, when Saint Clare asked for a preacher, Father Guardian was able to send that master to the convent of San Damiano to preach the word of God to those holy sisters. He went there and began to preach and speak magnificently about God. But when he was in the middle of the sermon, Brother Giles–who also was there to hear the sermon–suddenly stood up, animated by the Holy Spirit and inflamed with divine love. He said, 'Be quiet, Master, for I wish to speak.' Filled with true humility, [Alexander] at once uttered no more words and humbly sat down. Completely inflamed, Brother Giles spoke some words about God of such sweetness and consolation that all of the minds of the listeners were wonderfully consoled and brought to amazement. When Giles finished speaking, he said to the Master, 'Stand up and finish the sermon which you began some time ago.' What a mirror of humility! The master in Holy Theology at once raised himself and finished the sermon to the great consolation and good example of all those who were present. Once he had finished the sermon, the preacher departed. Then the holy mother Saint Clare, with joy exulting in her spirit, turned to the friars who were still present and said, 'O Brothers, I tell you that I have seen here today many marvellous things. Today the desire of my father Saint Francis was achieved. I remember that many times he said these words: "I want to see such great humility in my Order that when a brother who is a master in Holy Theology is preaching and a lay brother interrupts wishing to speak, that he should humbly yield to the simple lay brother." Today I saw that happen before my eyes and I say to you truthfully, I was more edified by the humility of that brother, the master preacher, than if I had seen a dead man resurrected.[3]

---

[2] *Legenda sanctae Clarae Virginis. Tratta dal Ms. 338 della Bibl. Comunale di Assisi*, ed. by Francesco Pennacchi (Assisi: Metastasio, 1910) (hereafter cited as *LCl*). This edition was reprinted in *Fontes Franciscani*, ed. by Enrico Menestò and others (Assisi: Edizioni Porziuncola, 1995), pp. 2415–2450 (hereafter cited as *FF*). In a recent study, Mario Natali has identified similar passages that suggest Battista was also using the Mariano of Florence's *Libro delle degnità et excellentie del Ordine della Seraphica madre delle povere donne Sancta Chiara d'Assisi*, the first 'history' of the Franciscan nuns, which Fra Mariano composed between 1516–1519 (see note 9 below). Mario Natali, 'La *Leggenda della Seraphica Vergine Chiara* di Suor Battista Alfani', *Collectanea Franciscana*, 70 (2000), 169–84.

[3] *VSC* 94r–95v: 'Havendo una volta la devotissima madre Santa Chiara fatto pregare il

This episode clearly responds to the fundamental problem faced by the Franciscan Order: how were the followers of Francis of Assisi expected to live out their vocation in light of his ideals? Specifically, the exemplum's male protagonists respond to the question of how academic study could be part of their religious identity. They represent two traditions of acquiring sacred knowledge: book learning and divine inspiration. Alexander of Hales was the Franciscan Order's most famous academic recruit, his entry a coup for the Franciscans who, like the rival Dominican Order, actively recruited at the universities. Alexander was already a famous master at Paris when he became a friar and soon after was appointed to organize the order's houses of study. He therefore epitomized the increasingly clericalized Order of Friars Minor in which study was understood to support their apostolic mission as preachers. But the growing importance ceded to academic learning was opposed by lay brothers like Giles, who famously complained that 'Paris destroyed Assisi.'[4] According to Bonaventure, Giles lacked a formal education but was distinguished by

---

guardiano di Santa Maria degli Angeli, che gli mandassi qualche se frate à predicare. Et essendo all'hora in quel loco uno maestro in santa Teologia, il quale da molti si siene che fussi lo inrefragebile Dottore Maestro Alessandro di Ales, famosissimo in scientia et in santità di vita el quale per questa via era venuto all'ordine di Santo Francesco essendo esso dottore et maestro di grande eccellentia, et estimatione. Et in processo di tempo per devotione di Santo Francesco venne Ascesi et dimorò in Santa Maria degli Angeli lungo tempo, tanto che potessi parlare et predicare in lingua italiana et domando santa Chiara un predicatore, il padre Guardiano mandò il detto maestro al monastero di Santo Damiano à predicare la parola de Dio à quelle sante suore, il quale essendo andato. Et havendo incominciato à predicare et molto magnificamente parlando de Dio era quasi nel mezzo del suo sermone, il suo frate Egidio era quivi presente à udire la predica, subito si levo su in fervore di spirito, et infiammato del divino amore disse à quel maestro, taci maestro. Imperoche io voglio parlare io. Et quel maestro pieno di vera humilità, subitamente si fermò et non disse più parola, ma humilmente si pose à sedere. Et frate Egidio tutto infocato disse alcune parole de Dio di tanta dolcezza, et consolatione, che tutte le mente degli auditori furono mirabilmente consolate et dicio maravigliate. Et havendo frate Egidio compiuto il suo parlare disse à quello maestro, levati sù et fornisci il tuo sermone che incominciasti all'hora. Quello specchio di humilita maestro in santa Teologia subito si levo sù. Et compie la sua predica, in gran consolatione et buono esempio di tutti quelli li quali furono quivi presenti. Et essendo espedita la predica et partito il predicatore, la devotissima madre santa Chiara, con gaudio esultando in spirito disse a gli frati che erano quivi presenti: O frati io vi dico che hoggi ho veduto cose maravigliose. Hora è adempiuto il desiderio del mio padre Santo Francesco. Imperoche io mi ricordo che piu volte mi disse queste parole, io desidero di vedere tanta humilta nello ordine mio, che predicando il frate il quale è maestro in santa Teologia, et alle parole d'un frate laico volendo esso predicare, cessi humilmente dalla sua predicatione, et dia loco al semplice frate laico. La qual cosa veramente hoggi è stata adempiuta dinanci à gli occhi miei, et dicavi in verita frati miei che più mi ha edificato hoggi la humilità di questo frate, et maestro predicatore, che se io gli havessi veduto resuscitatre un morto.'

[4] *Dicta Beati Aegidii Assiensis* (Quaracchi: Collegio S. Bonaventurae, 1905), p. 91.

his humble and obedient nature. The *Speculum perfectionis* extolled his contemplative life and proclaimed that 'the mind elevated to God possessed its highest perfection' in Brother Giles.[5] The exemplum's central idea thus seems obvious: Alexander of Hales demonstrates the proper humility that academic learning was supposed to adopt when confronted with prophetic knowledge.

The story is complicated, however, by its gendered context. The cloister at San Damiano is the setting and the enclosed nuns are the immediate audience of the exemplum. Clare interprets the episode for all those present, including a group of friars whom she addresses directly at the end. She is able to do so because her privileged relationship with Francis allows her to act effectively as the 'magister' and ratify the importance of inspired knowledge within the Franciscan tradition. This active female presence juxtaposed with the friars suggests that the exemplum is also questioning who possessed the authority to transmit knowledge–clerics or visionaries, friars or nuns. Sacred prophecy was open to both holy men and holy women, but women were usually not entrusted to interpret it.[6] Yet as Anne L. Clark, John Coakley, and others have demonstrated, some clerics recognized that mystical experiences gave such women access to a type of divine understanding that they could not achieve through their academic studies of theology.[7] This move privileged women's role as mystics, but we would be wrong to assume that academic learning and prophecy were simply gendered as masculine and feminine respectively. Indeed, Battista's story dismisses the possibility of any simple gendered binary between friars and nuns concerning the authority of knowledge by setting the encounter between Alexander (academic and cleric) and Giles (lay brother and mystic) against the commentary from Clare (enclosed contemplative and *magistra*). Her account suggests that the authority of divine knowledge was still being negotiated among both male and female members of the Franciscan Order in the late fifteenth century.

---

[5] See the *Legenda Maior*, 4 in *Opera Omnia S. Bonaventurae* (Quaracchi: Collegio S. Bonaventurae, 1898), VIII; *Speculum perfectionis*, 85, reprinted in *FF*: 1849–2053.

[6] See Alcuin Blamires, 'Women and Preaching in Medieval Orthodoxy, Heresy, and Saints' Lives', *Viator*, 26 (1995), 135–52. For medieval women and mysticism generally, see Peter Dinzelbacher, 'Rifiuto dei ruoli, risveglio religioso, ed esperienza mistica delle donne nel Medioevo', in *Movimento religioso e mistica femminile nel Medioevo* (Turin: Edizioni Paoline, 1993), pp. 31–89.

[7] Anne L. Clark, *Elisabeth of Schönau: a Twelfth-Century Visionary* (Philadelphia: University of Pennsylvania Press, 1992); John Coakley, 'Friars, Sanctity and Gender: Mendicant Encounters with Saints, 1250–1325', in *Medieval Masculinities*, ed. by Clare Lees (Minneapolis: University of Minnesota Press, 1994), pp. 91–110, and 'Gender and the Authority of Friars: the Significance of Holy Women for the Thirteenth-Century Franciscans and Dominicans', *Church History*, 60 (1991), 445–60. See also the recent collection of essays, *Gendered Voices: Medieval Saints and their Interpreters*, ed. by Catherine M. Mooney (Philadelphia: University of Pennsylvania Press, 1999).

Moreover, by presenting this episode in the context of Clare's biography–which to the best of my knowledge is a unique occurrence–Battista also seems interested in making some implicit claims about the female order relative to the friars.[8] Specifically, whereas the friars had come to live out their Franciscan vocations as trained preachers, she seems concerned with how the women would define their identity as Franciscans. Although the confrontation that arose in the decades following the death of Francis of Assisi (1226) between an anti-intellectual ideal that claimed to be true to his ideals and a more moderate outlook that encouraged education is a topic well known to scholars, the ways in which female Franciscans, and especially the Poor Clares, were part of this conflict remain mostly unexplored. Presumably, these women had little interest or stake in the debates over whether it was licit for the Friars Minor to pursue academic study. Clare of Assisi and other enclosed women were not supposed to go out and preach to convert the world. Rather, they were to stay behind cloister walls and pray for it. Two problems emerge, however, if scholars accept this representation uncritically: cloistered women not only appear excluded from the Order's intellectual life if that category is restricted to academic training, but also and more problematically, they seem separated from the main concerns of the Franciscan Order. Battista's story challenges that assumption. Its historical and literary contexts also encourage us to think more broadly about how it demonstrates a female Franciscan's view of the stakes involved in the transmission of knowledge.

The Confrontation in Historical Context

More than other religious orders in the later Middle Ages, the Franciscans had to confront the role of academic study as a part of their institutional self-consciousness.[9] As with his spiritual ideal of poverty, Francis's own response was

---

[8] I have looked for references to this story in the standard Franciscan annals and chronicles (e.g. in Luke Wadding's *Annales Minorum*), as well as in Latin and vernacular versions of Clare's legend. It is not surprising that the more literal translations of the thirteenth-century text do not include it (for example BNCF, Magliabecchiano, XXXVIII, 55, ed. by Guido Battelli, as Tomaso da Celano, *La Leggenda di Santa Chiara d'Assisi*. (Milan: Vita e Pensiero, 1952)) but its absence in other later medieval *vitae* may suggest that Battista and her community had particular interest in the story. For example, neither a contemporary vernacular legend (dated 1494), composed by Ugolino Verino for the sisters at Santa Chiara Novella (BNCF, Landau Finaly 251, fols 81ᵛ–121ᵛ), nor Mariano of Florence's 1519 history of the Order of Saint Clare, *Libro delle degnità et excellentie del Ordine della seraphica madre delle povere donne Sancta Chiara da Asisi* [sic], ed. by Giovanni Boccali (Florence: Edizioni Studi Francescani and Assisi: Edizioni Porziuncola, 1986) include the story. I have not yet made a systematic comparison with sermons devoted to Clare.

[9] For the relationship between intellectualism and Franciscan institutional identity see Roberto Lambertini, *Apologia e crescita dell'identità francescana (1255–1279)* (Rome:

ambivalent. Frustrated by trying to manage the growing order, he complained bitterly about friars who wanted to have books and houses of study rather than to embrace their vow of simplicity. Yet he also respected those brothers who had studied theology and he recognized that the friars needed academic training supported their pastoral duties. He therefore was willing to allow study as long as it did not conflict with the brothers' avowed humility.[10] Nonetheless, after Francis all of the Order's ministers general were well-educated men who encouraged academic study and enacted legislation granting scholars extra privileges.[11] As external attacks on the friars' involvement with studies escalated during the 1240s and 1250s, educated masters like Alexander of Hales, Hugh of Digne, and Bonaventure defended study as neither inappropriate for the Friars Minor nor a violation of their vow of poverty. Indeed, it was necessary for preaching. There is no reason to assume that these learned brothers were dissembling when they defended learning as a part of their religious identity, but their actions laid the groundwork for later internal condemnations of the Order's clericalization.

To the fourteenth-century Franciscan Spirituals it was clear that the Order of Friars Minor had moved far away from Francis's intentions. Angelo Clareno, for example, identified the pursuit of academic glory as a symptom of institutional dissolution.[12] The most radical sources from these circles even created an image of Francis as a vehement critic of learning. The *Speculum perfectionis* (*c*. 1318), a compilation of stories about Francis derived from earlier biographies and the testimonies of his closest companions, explained that Francis's attitude toward education was linked with his understanding of the friars' vocation.

Istituto Storico Italiano per il Medio Evo, 1990).

[10] The complexity of the question of studies in the Franciscan Order cannot be adequately represented here. See a fuller discussion with relevant bibliography in Maranesi, pp. 20–66; and Roest, pp. 1–4.

[11] Including privileges such as separate cells and exemption from attending chapter; see 'Statuta generalia Ordinis edita in capitulis generalibus celebratis Narbonae an. 1260, Assisii an. 1279 atque Parisiis an. 1292', ed. by Michael Bihl, in *Archivum Franciscanum Historicum*, 34 (1941), 13–94 and 284–358.

[12] Angelo Clareno, *Liber chronicarum sive tribulationum ordinis minorum* (Assisi: Edizioni Porziuncola, 1999), p. 333. 'Ex quibus omnibus tempore huius fratris Crescentii, qui praedecessoris sui fratris Heliae sectatus est affectus et mores, quaedam insatiabilis et curiosa cupiditas sciendi, apparendi, habendi, acquirendi, mutandi loca solitaria, paupercula, et aedificandi sumptuosa, procurandi legata et sepulturas, et clericorum iura subripiendi, addiscendi scientias saeculares, et in his scholas multiplicandi suborta crevit in tantum, praesertim in Italiae partibus, ut non erubescerent fratres pro suis vitis implendis, palam pecuniam procurare et recipere, et litigia in curiis contra quascumque personas aliquid eis debentes facere et movere.' For the Franciscan Spirituals, see now David Burr, *The Spiritual Franciscans: From Protest to Persecution in the Century after Saint Francis* (University Park: Pennsylvania State University Press, 2001).

It grieved blessed Francis when brothers sought learning which inflates (*scientia inflativa*) while neglecting virtue, especially if they did not remain in that calling to which they were first called. He said: 'Those brothers of mine who are lead by curiosity for knowledge (*scientiae curiositate*) will find themselves empty-handed on the day of reckoning [...].' He did not say these things out of dislike for the reading of Holy Scripture, but to draw all of them back from excessive concern for learning. Rather he wanted them to be good through charity rather than be dilettantes through curious learning[13]

In isolation this anecdote does not appear especially provocative, but the rubric for this passage asserted: 'How [Francis] foresaw and predicted that learning would be an occasion of ruin for the Order (*Qualiter praescivit et praedixit quod scientia debebat esse occasio ruinae ordinis*).' The Spirituals emphasized his love of humility and simplicity as the antithesis of academic pride. Another chapter in the *Speculum perfectionis* told how a Dominican theologian sought out Francis and asked him to explain a passage from Scripture to him. He at first demurred, citing his lack of learning, but complied when pressed. The Dominican was awed and told Francis's companions, 'My brothers, the theology of this man, held aloft by purity and contemplation, is a soaring eagle, while our learning crawls on its belly on the ground.'[14] To be sure, the Spirituals generally overstate Francis's opposition to learning and their perspective never came to dominate the institutional Franciscan Order. Nonetheless, their stories are important because they represent how a debate about the role of studies existed outside the Order's institutional hierarchy. The *Speculum perfectionis* and similar texts such as the *Fioretti* (a vernacular collection of stories about Francis) circulated widely among both male and female Franciscans. But we do not have much direct evidence about how the sisters viewed these debates or even participated in them. That is, we do not unless Battista's story represents an actual event.

Alexander of Hales entered the Order in 1236 or 1237 and died in 1245, which limits the time for an encounter between him and Giles. The Franciscan annalist Niccolò Papini claimed that the incident must have occurred in 1242 when Alexander presented a commentary on the friars' rule to the General Chapter meeting in Bologna. He posits that the Parisian master may have travelled to Assisi as well at this time.[15] The Quaracchi editors of Alexander's commentary on the Sentences reject this suggestion and propose instead 1239 when he might have attended that year's chapter meeting in Rome. The editors acknowledge, however, that there is no independent evidence for Alexander of Hales's presence in central

---

[13] *Speculum perfectionis*, 69, translated in *Francis of Assisi: Early Documents,* ed. by. Regis J. Armstrong and others (New York: New City Press, 2001), III, pp. 314–15.

[14] *Speculum perfectionis*, 53, translated in *Francis of Assisi*, III, p. 296.

[15] Nicolò Papini, *Index onomasticus Scriptorum universae Franciscanae familiae* (1828) cited in Alexander of Hales, *Glossa in quatuor libros sententiarum Petri Lombardi* (Quaracchi: Collegio S. Bonaventurae, 1951), I, p. 55*.

Italy in that year or any other outside the story which Battista Alfani incorporated into her translation at the end of the fifteenth century.[16] It thus seems unlikely that this story reports an actual event, particularly if we examine it didactic purpose.

The story's textual genealogy begins only in the second half of the fourteenth century. These reports, however, are much less specific or descriptive than Battista's version. The first recognizable account appears in the biography of Giles of Assisi presented in the *Chronica XXIV Generalium* (*c.* 1369).[17] It may be drawn from a story that was circulating orally since an earlier vita of Brother Giles does not report it.[18] The brief narrative focuses on humility, specifically that Giles found that virtue so pleasing that he wished others to demonstrate it as well.[19] The educated friar is simply referred to as an English master in theology. That description certainly could refer to Alexander, but equally to other brothers such as Haymo of Faversham, a master at Oxford and Paris who was elected Minister General in 1240, or even Radulphus, Bishop of Hertford, whom the following entry identified as an Englishman and master of theology.[20] Direct references to Alexander of Hales in the *Chronica XXIV Generalium* do not allude to the incident rendering it unlikely that the author intended to portray him as one of the protagonists.

Bartolomeo of Pisa's *De conformitate* (1399) also records the story of the sermon preached before Clare and her sisters. He actually recounted it twice as happens with

---

[16] *Glossa*, 55* and 74*.

[17] *Chronica XXIV Generalium Ordinis Minorum*, in *Analecta Franciscana sive Chronica aliaque varia documenta ad historiam Fratrum Minorum spectantia edita a Patribus Collegii S. Bonaventurae* (Quaracchi: Collegio San Bonaventura, 1995), III, pp. 74–115.

[18] There are two recensions of Giles's *vita*: the earlier 'Shorter Life' attributed to Brother Leo (Francis's companion) and the later 'Longer Life' which exists only in the *Chronica XXIV Generalium*. The most recent edition of the earlier text is printed in Rosalind B. Brooke, *Scripta Leonis, Rufini et Angeli sociorum S. Francisci*, corrected edition (Oxford: Clarendon Press, 1990 (1971), pp. 316–49.

[19] *Chronica XXIV Generalium*, p. 81: 'Qualiter magister quidam in theologia praedicans ad praeceptum eius tacuit, et de verbis sanctae Clarae. Et quia sibi summe placebat virtus humilitatis, ipsam in alio voluit experiri. Cum enim semel quidam frater Anglicus, sacrae theologiae magister, in monasterio sancti Damiani, presente sancta Clara et fratre Aegidio, praedicaret et in sermone aliquantulum processisset, cum fervore dixit sibi frater Aegidius: "tace magister, tace, quia ego volo praedicare." Ille vero statim tacuit. Et frater Aegidius dixit illi magistro: "Perfice nunc, frater, sermonem quem coepisti." Et magister ille suam praedicationem resumpsit et complevit. Quod cum vidisset beata Clara, exsultans in spiritu dixit: "Hodie completum est desiderium sanctissimi Patris nostri Francisci mihi aliquando dicentis: 'Opto multum ego, fratres meos clericos ad tantam humilitatem venire, quod magister in theologia ad vocem laici praedicare volentis a praedicatione cessaret.' Dico vobis, fratres, ait sancta Clara, quod ne plus me aedificavit magister sua humilitate, quam si vidissem eum mortuum suscitatem."'

[20] Compare *Chronica XXIV Generalium*, pp. 218–20.

other events in this long work (1136 pages filling two volumes of the *Analecta Franciscana*). The first version again appears within Giles's biography, specifically that he wished a learned master to demonstrate the virtue of obedience.[21] In a later book, Bartolomeo retold the story to show how an anonymous master demonstrated the virtue of humility.[22] Neither version names Alexander of Hales or even identifies the master of theology as English. Nonetheless, the second example suggests circumstantially that contemporary readers might associate the anonymous master with Alexander. The preceding episode appears to be an account of his entry into the Order of Friars Minor and debate over whether he should become a Franciscan or a Dominican.[23] Both chronicles therefore seem to have taken a potentially charged account of a confrontation between academic and inspired knowledge, which perhaps was circulating orally, and neutralized it by presenting it as an exemplum about humility and obedience.

---

[21] Bartolomeo of Pisa, *De conformitate vitae beati Francisci ad vitam Domini Iesu*, in *Analecta Franciscana*, IV and V (IV, p. 208: 'Semel frater Aegidius obedientiam volebat experiri cuiusdam fratris in sacra theologia magistri, qui sanctae Clarae praedicabat et eius sororibus. Cui praedicanti dixit frater Aegidius: "Tace magister; quia ego volo praedicare"; qui statim tacuit. Et postquam frater Aegidius in fervore spiritus eructavit melliflua, dixit magistro: "Perfice nunc frater, sermonem, quem incepisti," et sic fecit. De quo beata Clara exsultans dixit: "Hodie completum est desideratum beati Francisci mihi aliquando dicentis: "opto multum, fratres meos clericos ad tantam humilitatem venire, quod magister in theologia a voce laici volentis praedicare a praedicatione cessaret," Dico vobis, fratres, ait sancta Clara, quod plus me aedificavit magister sua humilitate, quam si vidissem eum mortuum suscitatem."'

[22] *De conformitate,* in V, p. 144: 'Procedente autem tempore, dictus magister ob reverentiam beati Francisci venit Assisium, et ibi commoratus est et stetit tanto tempore, quod bene poterat lingua Italica praedicare. Cum autem semel beata Clara, quae tunc vivebat, mandasset guardiano, quod mitteret sibi aliquem fratrem ad praedicandum, guardianus praefatum misit magistrum ad monasterium sanctae Clarae ad praedicandum. Cumque incepisset praedicare et de Deo eructaret magnifice, sanctus frater Aegidius, qui erat laicus et tunc in dicto erat monasterio et sermonem audiebat, subito surrexit totaliter spiritu inflammatus et dixit ipsi magistro praedicanti: "Magister, tace, quia ego volo aliquantulum loqui." At ille cum hoc audisset, sermone dimisso et caputio capite informato, sedit humiliter. Cumque frater Aegidius fuisset locutus ad libitum, dixit tandem dicto magistro: "Surge frater, et sermonem tuum perfice." At ille surrexit illico et sermonem inceptum complevit. Sermone autem completo et magistro foras egresso, dixit beata Clara fratribus, qui ibidem aderant: "Dico vobis, fratres, quod hodie vidi mirabilia. Dixit enim mihi aliquando beatus Franciscus, pater et dominus meus, quod tantam humilitatem desiderabat in ordine suo, quod si unus magister in theologia loqueretur, ad mandatum unius laici etiam taceret. Quod hodie completum est in oculis meis. Et dico vobis fratres, quod magis sum aedificata de humilitate illius fratris, quam si vidissem eum mortuos suscitare."'

[23] The anonymous story in *De conformitate*, V, p. 309 should be compared to *De conformitate*, IV, p. 429 and the *Chronica XXIV Generalium,* p. 281 where Alexander of Hales chooses between the Dominicans and the Franciscans.

Battista knew Bartolomeo of Pisa's work and cited it as her source for two stories, which she added to the miracle collection at the end of Clare's legend.[24] But unlike either chronicle, her presentation focuses more directly on the problem of studies because she incorporated the story into a chapter focusing on sermons and preaching. Battista's story does not condemn academic learning, of course, but we should consider whether she was interested in making some point about the role of learning in the Franciscan Order. Her community, Santa Maria de Monteluce, was part of the Regular Observance, a fifteenth-century reform movement. Like the earlier Franciscan Community represented by Bonaventure and his successors, Observant Franciscans accepted study as necessary to support preaching, a point to which the last section will return. First, though, it is necessary to consider whether Battista was interested in presenting a certain image of Clare, which serves to comment on the transmission of knowledge.

In the fourteenth-century chronicles, Clare's participation in the episode was almost an afterthought. She came to the centre, however, when the story was part of the narrative of her life. In Battista's legend the presence of the famous Alexander of Hales and the saintly Brother Giles draw attention to a story in which Clare plays an important role commenting on the nature of Franciscan life and especially the role of learning. This change alters earlier readings of Clare's life. A comparison of this chapter in the Latin *Legenda sanctae Clarae Virginis* and Battista's translation demonstrates that whereas the thirteenth-century text had emphasized her silence and enclosure, Battista modified this image by presenting Clare as a vocal reformer who participated in the friars' debates concerning institutional self-formation and Franciscan identity.

Rewriting Clare

Vernacular translations of the legend of Saint Clare circulated widely in the later Middle Ages, partly in response to renewed interest in the Franciscan Order's spiritual origins.[25] This interest was particularly acute for the Poor Clares, who Battista addressed in her prologue.

> For the comfort of these beloved and most devoted daughters of our glorious mother blessed Clare, we will describe in the vernacular the life of that Blessed One written by Father Thomas [of Celano],[26] along with some other things worthy of recollection

---

[24] *VSC*, 148r: 'Due altro miracoli narrerò qui li quali mette maestro Bartolomeo da Pisa nel libro delle Conformità in questa forma.'

[25] See Felice Accrocca, 'I Codici romani della 'Legenda di Santa Chiara in Volgare', in *Collectanea Franciscana*, 63 (1993), 55–70.

[26] Thomas of Celano, Francis's first biographer was identified by contemporary Franciscans as the anonymous author of Clare's Latin legend. Scholars continue to debate that

drawn from the chronicles of the Order, including those findings of the bishop of Spoleto, that is from her [canonization] process.[27]

The process survives only in a fifteenth-century vernacular translation preserved at Monteluce.[28] The record, which includes the testimonies of fifteen of Clare's companions, represents one way in which a tradition of stories about her survived outside of the official legend which Pope Alexander IV had commissioned for her canonization in 1255. Indeed, Battista's modification of the thirteenth-century legend with stories drawn from the process and other sources suggests the Poor Clares were not wholly satisfied by the portrait of their founder in that Life.

Compared to the assured personality who emerges from Clare's own writings and from the testimonies at her process, the Latin legend offers a generic account of a female saint.[29] The sterile quality of the thirteenth-century text had resulted from specific circumstances. During Clare's lifetime the friars fought the incorporation of new convents into the Franciscan Order, complaining that their growing pastoral responsibilities to enclosed women took them away from preaching and teaching.[30] Moreover, as the friars accepted modifications to their observance of poverty in the years following Francis's death, they begrudged Clare's insistence that communities of enclosed women could live without material support. They saw her attempts to secure the right for women to adopt apostolic poverty as a criticism of their own, now more relaxed, way of life.[31] Yet even as the friars were reluctant to support a Saint Clare who represented the early Franciscan ideals, the papacy enthusiastically endorsed a sanitized version of her life as a model for the growing number of women

---

attribution.

[27] *VSC* 2ʳ: 'Onde à consolatione delle dilette et devotissime figliuole di questa nostra gloriosa madre beata Clara descriverremo in questa vulgare la vita d'essa Beata, scritta per el sopradetto frate Tommaço alcune altre cose degne di memoria cavate delle cronache dell'ordine, inserendo ancora quelle relitte del Vescovo di Spoleto, cioe del suo processo.'

[28] 'Il processo di canonizzazione di S. Chiara', ed. by Zeffirino Lazzeri, *Archivum Franciscanum Historicum*, 13 (1920), 403–507, now reprinted in *FF*, pp. 2255–2507.

[29] For a comparison of Clare's self-representation and the resulting saintly image, see Catherine M. Mooney, '*Imitatio Christi* or *Imitatio Mariae*? Clare of Assisi and her Interpreters', in *Gendered Voices*, pp. 52–77.

[30] Investigations of this problem include Herbert Grundmann, *Religious Movements in the Middle Ages: The Historical Links between Heresy, the Mendicant Orders, and the Women's Religious Movement in the Twelfth and Thirteenth Centuries*, 2nd rev. ed. trans. by Stephen Rowan (Notre Dame: University of Notre Dame Press, 1995).

[31] Thomas of Celano's two biographies of Francis demonstrate the shifting attitude toward Clare and her followers. In 1228 he praised Clare (1 Cel 18) but by 1247, he no longer mentioned Clare by name and emphasized Francis's withdrawal from the enclosed women at the end of his life when he came to resent the friars' obligations toward female communities (compare 2 Cel 204–207). Both texts are easily accessible in *FF*.

who were seeking to live out a religious vocation.[32] These two problems influenced Clare's canonization. The friars' complaints meant that she could not be presented as a moral authority on Francis's spirituality. Her life was refashioned according to the paradigm of a consecrated virgin, which in turn served the Church's needs and supported the curia's efforts to normalize the women's religious movement in central Italy along traditional monastic lines.[33] While Battista did not overtly challenge this portrayal, she altered the narrative to underscore the close bond between Francis and Clare, as well as the latter's role in shaping the Franciscan Order.

Battista emphasized Clare's devotion to Francis's ideals. While the thirteenth-century text had made only passing reference to Clare's attempts to secure the right for women to live in complete apostolic poverty, Battista referred to the Privilege of Poverty which Clare had obtained for San Damiano.[34] She translated Clare's Testament and Benediction, texts which were modelled on Francis's writings, and also referred to her formula Lives, which Clare had modelled on the Regula Bullata, Francis's rule for the brothers.[35] She also stressed the personal closeness between the two founders of the Franciscan Order.

> For the love of Jesus Christ blessed father Francis promised to sustain all those who were present in every affliction and fatigue, as well as all those other [sisters] who would come to make a profession in that order, so that they would never lack for his spiritual conversation or the aid and perpetual sustenance of his friars. Francis diligently did this while he was alive. When he was nearing his death, he ordered the friars that they should always do so in the future, saying that the same spirit had called the friars as [had] those holy women.[36]

---

[32] Clare was the only enclosed woman canonized between 1198–1431, see André Vauchez, *Sainthood in the Later Middle Ages,* trans. by Jean Birrell (Cambridge: Cambridge University Press, 1997).

[33] For the monasticization of the women's religious movement in Italy, see, for example, Luigi Pellegrini, 'Female Religious Experience and Society in Thirteenth-Century Italy', in *Monks and Nuns, Saints and Outcasts: Religion in Medieval Society. Essays in Honor of Lester K. Little,* ed. by Sharon Farmer and Barbara H. Rosenwein (Cornell University Press, 2000), pp. 97–122.

[34] *VSC*, 109^v. This was the 1228 privilege granted by Pope Gregory IX, not the 1216 one attributed to Pope Innocent III, which Werner Maleczek has demonstrated convincingly is a 'forgery', see below.

[35] *VSC*, 113^r–121^r (*Testament* and *Benediction*) and 123^v–124^v (*formula vitae*).

[36] *VSC*, 100^{r-v}: 'Per amore de Jesu Cristo, à sostenere ogni afflitione et fatica, et di non volere mai piu mancare alli comandamenti suoi, esso beato padre Francesco promisse alloro che erano presente, et alle altre che hanno à venire che faranno professione in tale ordine, et conversatione il suo et de suoi frati adiutorio, et consiglio perpetuo, et cosi fece lui questo diligente mente, per insino che visse. Et essendo presso alla morte comando alli frati che cosi facessino semper per lo advenire, dicendo che un medesimo spirito haveva chiamato gli frati et le povere monache di questo secolo.' This passage echoes 2 Cel 204.

Another story told how Clare and a companion travelled to Santa Maria degli Angeli for a meal with Francis and the friars.[37] The brothers and their way of life had received little attention in the thirteenth-century legend. Francis hardly figures in that text after Clare was settled at San Damiano, nor is there mention of texts of consolation or counsel which Battista confirmed he gave to Clare and her companions.[38] The accumulation of these stories confirms Clare's authority to comment on the nature of the Franciscan vocation, an image of her distinctly lacking in the Latin *Legenda sanctae Clarae*.

The chapter on Clare's love of preaching clearly shows how Battista modified the thirteenth-century text.[39] The chapter begins with a description of Clare's concern to secure preaching for the sisters. While the Latin legend dispatched this information in a single sentence, her translation expanded this theme by elaborating on Clare's love of sermons and by describing specific events. For example, Battista inserted a story that told how when Francis once came to preach at San Damiano, his sermon on the Holy Name of Jesus greatly moved all the sisters. Clare was most affected, so that she appeared inflamed by the Holy Spirit as a result of his words.[40] She also reported that Clare especially enjoyed sermons on Christ's Passion and was often moved to tears out of empathy. Battista next presented a miracle story drawn from the *Legenda*: one time the Christ Child appeared standing next to Clare while Brother Philip of Atri preached to the nuns. The thirteenth-century legend had treated that episode briefly but Battista's description drew out its impact on the

---

[37] *VSC*, 84ᵛ–85ʳ, compare *Actus Beatus Francisci et Sociorum Eius* 15, in *FF*, p. 2118 (this source was translated into the vernacular where it was known as the *Fioretti*).

[38] Battista however wrote: 'Dappoi che il beatissimo padre serafico Francesco hebbe fatto le laude del signore di tutte le sue creature cioe sole, lune, et stelole et altre cose, fece anche alcune sante parole con modo di Canto, per consolatione et edificatione delle povere donne inclaustrate suore de santa Chiara' (*VSC*, 101ʳ).

[39] *VSC*, 90ᵛ–96ᵛ compares to *LCl* 37.

[40] *VSC*, 91ʳ⁻ᵛ: 'Nelle quale predicatione di tanta spirituale giocondità et letitia era ripiena et per la recordatione del suo diletto Jesù per tale modo le interne dolcezze et spirituali delitie et gusti divini assaporava, che etiamdio gli segni esteriori il dimostravano et massime nelle predicatione del suo santo maestro Santo Francesco. Onde una voltra infra l'altre, essendo ancora molto giovane, prima che infermassi advenne che udendo la predica del suo serafico padre Santo Francesco il quale come huomo la cui mente et conversatione era sempre in cielo, predicava con tanto eccessivo fervore, che pareva più cosa celestiale che humana, mandando fuora quelle parole infocate, tutte piene di Spirito Santo et in quella predicatione spesse volte nominava il santo nome di Jesù, il quale santissimo et mellifluo nome, esso benedetto padre lo esprimeva con tanta dolcezza di parole, et con tanta suavità di voce che à tutti gli auditori pareva che penetrassi, et liquefacessi il cuore, ma la devotissima vergine Santa Chiara per quella santa predicatione essendo sopra tutti gli altri infiammata et accesa del divino amore pareva quasi ebbra di Spirito Santo.'

sisters based on Sister Agnes's testimony at the canonization process.[41] This attention to the community at San Damiano set up the story about Alexander and Giles. She then concluded the chapter with another account drawn from the Latin legend describing how Clare threatened a 'hunger strike' after the friars withdrew from sisters' communities until the pope ordered them to resume pastoral visits. Battista's translation thus presents the same events as her source, but her expansion of the narrative through both additional examples and expanded details changed the impact of the chapter by focusing on the women's perception of events.

The Latin *Legenda sanctae Clarae* depicts the nuns as passive listeners to clerical authority. The benefits accrued from listening to sermons were meant to be individual and internal as in this description of Clare's appreciation of preaching from the same chapter.

> Although she was not educated in the liberal arts, [Clare] nevertheless enjoyed listening to the sermons of those who were because she believed that a nucleus lay hidden in the text that she could subtly perceive and enjoy with relish. She knew what to take out of the sermon of any preacher that might be profitable to the soul, while knowing that to pluck a flower from a wild thorn was no less prudent than to eat the fruit of a noble tree.[42]

This passage distinguishes between academic education and divine knowing. Clare clearly possesses the latter, but since its benefits are personal the Latin legend also demarcates the ways in which the friars and nuns were expected to live out their vocations as preachers and contemplatives respectively. Although the Friars Minor were required always to remain in the sight of their brother companions when they visited a convent, the *Legenda sanctae Clarae* did not refer to the presence of X's *socius* or the other friars who lived adjacent to San Damiano to provide spiritual care to the sisters.[43] Their absence from the text suggests the sisters' distance from the external world and therefore also from the concerns of the Friars Minor such as the debates over the place of study. The previous chapter in Clare's Latin legend already

---

[41] Sister Agnes was the tenth witness, see *FF*, 2491.

[42] *LCl* 37: 'Licet autem litterata non esset, litterariorum tamen gaudebat audire sermonem, rata quod in testa verborum nucleus lateat, quem ipsa attingebat subtilius et sapidius degustabat. Novit de cuiuslibet sermone loquentis elicere quod anime prosit [...].' I have used Regis Armstrong's translation in *Clare of Assisi: Early Documents* (St. Bonaventure, NY: Franciscan Institute Publications, 1993), p. 289.

[43] The witnesses at the canonization process made several references to the 'begging brothers', see *FF* pp. 2460–2461 (witness 1:15), 2470 (3:13) and 2479 (5:5). A reference in the earliest Life of Anthony of Padua also describes the early female houses as a sort of double community: 'Erant enim ibi fratres prope monasterium Dominarum pauperum commorantes et, iuxta consuetudinem ordins, divinis illis administrantes.' See *Vita Prima di S. Antonio o "Assidua" (c. 1232)* ed. by Vergilio Gambosa (Padua: Edizioni Messaggero, 1981), p. 363.

had called her the teacher of the uneducated (*magistra erat rudium*) and identified the subject of her 'teaching' as silence and rejection of the secular world in favour of the love of Christ and the cloister.[44] Battista's addition of the story in which Clare interprets the exemplum to be enacted before the women, refocused this message.

Perhaps, the most important part of the story for the nuns who read or listened to Battista's legend were the closing sentences where Clare instructs the brothers about Francis's attitude toward learning. She is not silent but speaks directly to the friars assigned to San Damiano. Enclosure therefore did not isolate her or her sisters from the Friars Minor or their concerns. Her explanation of Francis's hopes that academic learning would yield to divine inspiration and devotion proclaims her authority to speak about the Franciscan vocation. By inserting this episode into Clare's Life, and specifically into this chapter, Battista was affirming that women had a stake in the friars' way of life, much as Clare herself had asserted throughout her lifetime. Battista's story thus empowers its female readers by inserting Clare into the centre of debates about the nature of Franciscan life in contrast to her official hagiographical image. It also represents a positive model of interaction and shared vocation amongst the friars and nuns which the thirteenth-century *Legenda sanctae Clarae* lacked. This particular image of Clare would have had particular resonance for the nuns at Monteluce who were Battista's primary audience and who were directly engaged in the process of transmitting knowledge throughout the order.[45]

Learning and the Poor Clares

Monteluce became well known during the fifteenth century for its role in spreading Observant reform throughout Central Italy.[46] After adopting the Observant rule in

---

[44] Compare *LCl* 36.

[45] Other manuscripts of Battista's text show the sisters' were circulating works from their scriptorium. Besides the Magliabecchiano manuscript, the Clarisses at Santa Chiara Novella in Florence and in Coverciano each preserved a copy (both still in the sisters' possession). Florence, Archivio di Stato, MS 699 is a copy of the Santa Chiara Novella manuscript produced in Monteluce's scriptorium. For these manuscripts, see Accrocca, 'I Codici Romani', p. 58. Mario Natali has identified two additional manuscripts: Genoa, Biblioteca d'Università, MS F.I.16 and Venice. Biblioteca Nazionale Marciana, MS It. V17. See Natali, pp. 169–70 note 2.

[46] Monteluce's history is relatively well studied; see for an introduction (with references to relevant primary sources and studies) Stefano Felicetti, 'Aspetti e risvolti di vita quotidiana in un monastero Perugino riformata: Monteluce, secolo XV', *Collectanea Franciscana*, 65 (1995), 553–642 and Peter Höhler, 'Il Monastero delle Clarisse di Monteluce in Perugia (1218–1400)', in *Il Movimento religioso femminile in Umbria nei secoli XIII–XI*. Atti del Convegno internazionale di studio nell'ambito delle celebrazioni per l''VIII centenario della

1448, sisters from Monteluce helped reform other houses as well as establish new communities under the Observance[47] They undertook this task in partnership with the friars at nearby Monteripido who had made Perugia the intellectual centre of the Franciscan Regular Observance. Like the earlier Franciscan Community, the Observants accepted academic study as necessary for their pastoral mission. Bernardino of Siena, the charismatic preacher and leading reformer, had established a studium generale at Monteripido in the early 1440s. Although that site had once been a favoured retreat of the cantankerous Brother Giles, the Observants rapidly built up a large library reflecting their acceptance of study as compatible with their vocation and indeed necessary to train effective preachers.[48] Personal connections between the brothers and members of the university community further supported an elevated intellectual culture in the friary. Monteripido, in fact, soon became a centre of study and teaching as well as of literary production.[49] So did Monteluce.

A *Memoriale* begun by Battista Alfani as a record of the convent's reform testifies to the high level of education possessed by some of the Poor Clares and also to the active role of their scriptorium.[50] By the mid-fifteenth century Monteluce was considered one of the most prestigious religious houses in Perugia. It attracted the daughters of the ruling families, elite professors, and wealthy citizens. These women were likely to have already received some education when they entered the convent and thus they were well prepared for copying and even translating texts. Battista, the daughter of a wealthy merchant, is typical in this regard. Noting her death in 1523, the *Memoriale* praised:

> Besides her piety, she was learned in knowing how to understand and write books. For the comfort of her sisters, she wrote the book of the holy fathers all with her own hand, and the legend of our holy mother Clare. She copied many more books, editing and

nascita di S. Francesco d'Assisi. Città di Castello, 27–28–29 ottobre 1982, ed. by Roberto Rusconi (Florence: La Nuova Italia Editrice, 1984), pp. 161–82. Also see briefly Jeryldene Wood, *Women, Art, and Spirituality: The Poor Clares of Early Modern Italy* (Cambridge: Cambridge University Press, 1996), pp. 99–112.

[47] On Monteluce and reform, see specifically Antonio Fantozzi, 'La riforma osservante dei monasteri delle clarisse nell'Italia centrale. Documenti sec. XV–XVI', *Archivum Franciscanum Historicum*, 23 (1930), 361–82; 488–550.

[48] Mario Fois, 'La Questione degli studi nell'Osservanza e la soluzione di San Bernardno da Siena', in *Atti del Simposio Internazionale Cateriniano-Bernardiniano* (Siena: Accademica Senese degli Intronati, 1982), pp. 477–97.

[49] For examples see Ugolino Nicolini, 'I Minori Osservanti di Monteripido e lo 'Scriptorium' delle Clarisse ndi Monteluce in Perugia neo secoli XV e XVI', *Picenum Seraphicum*, 8 (1971), 100–131.

[50] *Memoriale di Monteluce. Cronaca del monastero delle Clarisse di Perugia dal 1448 al 1838* (Assisi: Edizioni Porziuncola, 1983). Felicetti discusses the registers's documentation of learned activities, see pp. 629–40.

organizing them in chapters as one can see. She was directed to do this by the reverend father generals, from whom she received praise that they were exceptionally fine. She made many other books on diverse matters, including this *Memoriale* which she recorded and organized in her own hand all the way to this point.[51]

The texts she worked on included a copy of Domenico Cavalca's *Vitae patrum*, works on Christ's Passion and on the Virgin's sorrows composed by Fra Gabriele of Perugia, as well as Lives of Christ and of the Virgin and a verse Passion. [52] The subjects clearly demonstrate that the scriptorium supported the sisters' devotional lives. It was also a way to obtain financial support for the community. The friars at Monteripido helped the nuns secure commissions for prayer books; for example, an entry in the register of *Entrate e Uscite* records the sale of a breviary to Angnolo Alfani by his sister, Battista, which may be identified as the prayer book now preserved at the Biblioteca Comunale Augusta in Perugia.[53] The surviving manuscripts demonstrate, moreover, that the Clarisses applied their role as scribes to spreading the spiritual ideas of the Observant reform. Copies of the Rule of Saint Clare, which governed Observant convents, and the Lives of noted Franciscan holy women circulated from this house.[54] The only existing manuscripts of Clare's Testament and Benediction, as well as the canonization process, all can be traced to Monteluce's scriptorium. If Werner Maleczek is correct that these two texts actually date from the middle of the fifteenth century, perhaps as products of Monteluce's scriptorium along with the fabricated 1216 Privilege of Poverty, then we have even more evidence of the intellectual abilities and agility of Battista's community.[55] The

---

[51] *Memoriale di Monteluce*, pp. 124–25: 'Et oltra lo spiritu, era docta in sapere intendere et scrivere libri, et a consolatione delle soi figliole scripse lo libro delli sancti padri tucto da suo mano, la legenda della nostra madre sancta Chiara: la retrasse de più libri, aseptolla et compusela distinta in capitoli, come appare. La qual cosa li fo commandata dalli reverendi padri generali, che li arechavano li dicti libri, et da loro do poi reveduta et commendata, che stava benissimo. Fece più librecti de diversi cose, et etiam questo Memoriale fo facto tucto et aseptato per sua mano per fine a qui.'

[52] *Memoriale di Monteluce*, pp. 107–108.

[53] See also Perugia, Bibl. Com. MS 1299, cited in Nicolini, 'I Minori Osservanti', p. 109.

[54] Compare *Memoriale di Monteluce*, p. 94. Recording the death of Sister Maria de Bartholomeo of Perugia, the chronicle noted: 'Questa fu donna molto suffitiente, docta de lectere et de scrivere; scripse uno breviario, et doi Regule vulgare, cioè la Regula nostra, una in carta bambagina, la quale se usa in in leggere ad la mensa. L'altra scripse in carta pecorina, la quale ne vulghariçò el sancto padre beato Bernardino da Feltro per nostra consolatione.'

[55] Werner Maleczek, *Chiara d'Assisi: La Questione dell'autentictià del privilegium paupertatis e del Testamento* (Milan: Edizioni Biblioteca Francescana, 1996), a corrected translation of the original German article which appeared in *Collectanea Franciscana* in 1995. In brief: he argues that the 1916 Privilege of Poverty attributed to Pope Innocent III was a forgery based on the lack of thirteenth-century documentation and its internal inconsistencies with contemporary practices in the papal chancery. Since Clare's Testament and Benediction

circulation of texts by and about Clare clearly shows the Perugian communities' interest in their founder and her efforts to shape the Franciscan Order, as well as how they were involved in the transmission of knowledge about their origins.

 A mutual commitment to living out Francis's ideals was the lived experience of their community at the heart of the Observant reform movement in central Italy. While the friars preached, the enclosed nuns copied the texts that promoted reform and guided spiritual life within both male and female communities in the Franciscan Order. The Observant nuns' work in their scriptorium provided a means of transmitting religious ideas comparable to sermons delivered by the friars. Battista's story thus may offer a gloss on how contemporary Poor Clares understood their identity as members of this religious order. These enclosed women had access to both prophetic knowledge and written texts. When Clare told the friars that Alexander's humility in yielding to Giles fulfilled Francis's intention that academic learning would always yield to divine grace, this also alluded to the spiritual ideal embraced by the fifteenth-century Observant sisters whose enclosed life combined contemplation and intellectual endeavour.[56] Her proclamation that Francis had wanted academic learning to yield to humility reminds the brethren that contemplation, the defining characteristic of the nuns' life, was an important part of the Franciscan charism. Perhaps Battista was even suggesting that if women could acquire the most profitable forms of learning, divine knowledge, than there was no reason to block them from more conventional forms of intellectual life.

 The story about Alexander, Giles and Clare which Battista Alfani included in her *Leggenda della Serafica Vergine Santa Chiara* demonstrates how the Poor Clares viewed their own stakes in the Order's debates over education and their institutional identity. Her representation of Clare may have empowered women to speak out about the nature of their vocation including the role of intellectual life, a topic generally gendered masculine in the Middle Ages. This Clare was not merely 'the teacher of the unlearned' as another thirteenth-century Life called her—a description

---

appear to rely on this text and since there are no thirteenth-century manuscripts, he argues they also are likely a creation of a fifteenth-century scriptorium, perhaps Monteluce's. While his argument about the 1916 Privilege has been accepted by some scholars, his claims about Clare's writings have been less well received. Those who favour their authenticity point out that both texts are consistent with her ideas and that both the Process and the Latin Legend allow for this possibility; see Attilio Bartoli Langeli, *Gli autografi di frate Francesco e di frate Leone,* CC Autographa Medii Aevi, 5 (Turnhout: Brepols, 2000), pp. 77–130 especially.

[56] In contrast, John of Capistrano's commentary on the Rule of Saint Clare, the monastic legislation adopted by Observant convents, makes clear that the friars continued to view the Poor Clares primarily as enclosed contemplatives. Although not meant as a prescriptive text, John's text was particularly influential and perceived as authoritative since he was currently Vicar General of the Observant branch of the Franciscan Order. See,'Explicatio Primae Regulae S. Clarae auctore S. Ioanne Capistratensis (1445)', ed. by Donatus van Andrichem, *Archivum Franciscanum historicum,* 22 (1929), 337–57 and 512–29.

that Battista's translation crucially omitted.[57] Friars and nuns might live out their vocations in different ways, but ultimately they were inspired by and responsible to the same idea.

---

[57] Although the information is basically the same, Battista omits that phase, *VSC*, 88^r–^{v}: 'Perche questa prudentissima et gloriosa vergine Santa Chiara nel palazzo del magno imperator Jesù Cristo era degnamente preposta et fatta Abatessa, madre, et maestra delle novitie et semplice giovanette con tal dottrina et ammaestramento le informava et di tanto cordiale amore le amava, come propria madre, raccogliendole tutte nel seno della sua viscerosa pieta materna, che per parole non sarebbe possibile poterlo esprimere. Ammaestrava le prima a dovere discacciare dalla mente loro ogni mondano strepito, acciochè liberalmente si potessino aciostare à gli intimi segreti dello altissimo signore Iddio.'

A Textual Community in the Making: Colettine Authorship in the Fifteenth Century*

BERT ROEST

For centuries the historiography of the early female Colettine reform was in the hands of church historians and hagiographers. Although many of them were concerned with the establishment of historical facts, they worked from a pious vision of male and female sainthood, in which the Colettine reform had a 'natural' place. These scholars shaped the actions and motivational forces of the protagonists (i.e. Colette of Corbie, her confessors/counsellors and the religious authorities) according to the hagiographic categories that since the late Middle Ages ruled official canonization procedures; categories that hammered out the thoughts, feelings, motivations and deeds congruous to male and female sainthood and its circumstances. History itself, insofar as it was not presented as a dialectic between divine intervention and the omnipresence of sin, receded into the background. It became the stage on which models of sainthood were enacted.

The apex of such pious historiography came in the second half of the nineteenth century, with the re-assertion of Catholic conservatism, more often than not in alliance with reactionary nationalism. Attempts were made to represent Colette as a typical protagonist of French Catholic virtue, and to connect Colette with Jeanne d'Arc, that other emblem of nineteenth-century French nationalist Catholicism. Together, Colette of Corbie and Jeanne d'Arc could function as the Catholic nationalist antidotes to the maiden of the French revolution.[1]

---

*With thanks to The Dutch Royal Academy of Arts and Sciences for financial support.

[1] Jacques-Théodore Bizouard, *Histoire de Sainte Colette et des Clarisses en Franche-Comté* (Besançon: P. Jacquin, 1888); Bessonet Favre, *Jeanne d'Arc tertiaire de saint François* (Paris: Gedalge, 1896), pp. 35–36; Alphonse Germain, *Sainte Colette de Corbie* (Paris: C. Poussielgue, 1903). In the introduction of his 1912 edition of Colette's Lives, Ubald d'Alençon concedes that the connection between Colette and Jeanne d'Arc is invention rather than history.

With the pioneering works of d'Alençon, Lippens, and de Sérent, who still cherished a pious Catholic vision of the past, the history of the early Colettine movement received a secure documentary footing. Their works laid the basis for more secular historical studies, like those of Elizabeth Lopez, the most prominent Colette scholar to date.[2] These studies sketch a detailed picture of the early Colettine movement. Some major problems, however, have remained with regard to the interpretation of events, predominantly in relation to the gendered roles of the main protagonists.

At first sight, a flat description of the events delivers a straightforward historical narrative. The young and religiously inclined maiden Colette (born in 1381 and orphaned after 1399), subsequently aligned herself with the beguines and the Poor Clares of the royal convent of Moncel. As these communal forms of female religious life did not satisfy her, Colette, supported by the Franciscan guardian Jean Pinet, took the vows of the third order of Francis, and embarked on a career as a recluse in Corbie (1402–1406). During this period, she became acquainted with other reform-minded Franciscans in Corbie and Hesdin, among whom was Friar Henry de Baume. In 1406, Colette was allowed to leave her cell, to travel with Friar Henry de Baume and several high aristocratic female supporters to Pope Benedict XIII in Nice, who gave Colette permission to establish a reformed convent of Poor Clares.[3] In addition, she received permission to establish or to reform other religious convents and to draw on male Franciscan communities to assist her in these matters.[4] The pope also assigned Henry de Baume with the task of guiding Colette in all her efforts.[5] After some abortive attempts, Colette and Henry succeeded in establishing a reformed Colettine convent in Besançon in 1410. Thereafter, things were definitely on the upswing. With high aristocratic sponsorship no less than eighteen convents were established before Colette's death; convents where the sisters devoted much of their energy to an elaborate liturgy, prayer sessions, penitential activities, and devotional exercises centring on the suffering Christ.[6] She died in 1447.

---

[2] See in particular Elisabeth Lopez, *Culture et sainteté, Colette de Corbie (1381–1447)*, C.E.R.C.O.R., Travaux et Recherches (Saint-Étienne: Publications de l'Université de Saint-Etienne, 1994).

[3] *Bullarium Franciscanum*, VII (Rome, 1904), no. 1004.

[4] *Bullarium Franciscanum*, VII (Rome, 1904), no. 1015.

[5] To assist these reformed houses, Henry received the power to act as Visitor General. He also became Vicar General of the male reformed Franciscan convents from which confessors and priests serving the female Colettine communities were to be drawn. Hence the Colettan friars came into existence.

[6] See for details Antoine de Sérent, 'Une nouvelle vie de Sainte Colette', *Études Franciscaines*, 17 (1907), 426–42, as well as the work of Lopez mentioned in n. 2, and her article 'Sainte Colette' in *Sainte Claire d'Assise et sa postérité*. Actes du Colloque international organisé à l'occasion du VIIIe Centenaire de la naissance de Sainte Claire, ed. by G. Brunel-Lobrichon and others (Nantes: Association Claire Aujourd'hui, 1995), pp. 193–217.

Both the hagiographic tradition and much traditional Catholic scholarship on Colette and her movement assign a pivotal importance to Colette's overwhelming personal sanctity. Her sanctity ensured all (male) initiatives, which were fully subservient to the divine goal embodied by the female saint. Although the female saint hardly ever is presented as an independent agent, her overwhelming sanctity was the stimulus and focal point for male service and action. With John Moorman as notable exception,[7] modern scholars who try to move beyond the 'naïve' hagiographic accounts, tend to see the emergence of the Colettine movement foremost as the outcome of male planning, turning the pious wishes of female religious ecstasy into a religious programme for female religious life. Whatever Colette's own intentions might have been, the realization of the Colettine reform would have been a male-controlled undertaking, and the ingredients of Colettine devotions, religious practices and literary activities would have been shaped by the admonitions and spiritual treatises of Henry de Baume and subsequent Franciscan confessors and priests of the Colettine communities.[8]

Taken as ideal types, both the hagiographic vision and its modern counterpart alienate the activities of Colette and her sisters from their primary historical subject—or at least reduce these activities to powers beyond their direct control. Either grace-driven sanctity or dominant male intervention seem to carry the day. This is unsatisfactory from a historian's point of view. If the narrative's central characters are driven by forces or signifiers beyond their control, history relapses into a form of cultural semiotics. More to the purpose of my direct argument, the

---

Although Colette herself did not have an aristocratic background (her father was carpenter at the Benedictine abbey of Corbie), she was from early on able to enlist the support of important noble families in France and Burgundy, starting with Blanche de Genève, sister of the late Pope Clement VII. On the high aristocratic background of many Poor Clares (Damianites, Urbanists, Colettines, and Observant Poor Clares) and their benefactors, see apart from the works of Lopez also Jacques Guy Bougerol, 'Il reclutamento sociale delle Clarisse di Assisi', in *Les ordres mendiants et la ville en Italie centrale, v. 1220–1350*, published in the *Mélanges de l'École française de Rome, Moyen Age—temps modernes*, 89 (Rome, 1977), 629–32.

[7] Moorman did not have any qualm to acknowledge Colette's capacities. John Moorman, *A History of the Franciscan Order. From its Origins to the Year 1517* (Oxford: Clarendon, 1968), p. 554: 'She was, in fact, a leader—a woman of great force of character, determined, competent, autocratic, and self-confident. What she wanted she normally got; and she held the love and loyalty of those over whom she ruled by the austerity of her life, her obvious piety, and her administrative ability.'

[8] Hence, Lopez hammers on Henry de Baume's role as theologian and spiritual author, and as organiser of the Colettine way of life. Elisabeth Lopez, 'Frère Henry de Baume (*c.* 1367–1440): La vie et les écrits d'un franciscain réformateur', *Revue Mabillon*, n.s. 5 (=66), (1994), 117–41. In modern studies informed by categories of gender, the issue of male control has lead to comparable conclusions with regard to the *Handlungsfähigheit* and self-expression of late medieval female religious in general.

posited subjugation of female action and initiative does not provide access to the actual negotiation of religious action and self-expression *in situ*, in which the human agents work with and confront the behavioural constraints and socio-religious teachings of their own time.

The latter problem provides the focus of the present article: the question how Colette and her sisters were able to negotiate their understanding of their religious ideals, by tracing their literary activities and the ways in which they accessed a shared religious understanding.

Colettine Literature and Religious Self-Representation

To trace the literary culture of Colettine sisters, several sources are at our disposal. Most important are the various dossiers in the archival collections of the Poor Clares in Besançon, Ghent, Amiens, and Poligny. They contain a wide range of devotional texts, statutes, admonitions, letters and saints' Lives, most dating from the fifteenth century and bearing testimony of the literary world of Colettine religious life.

For the present purpose a sufficient number of texts and extracts from these archival collections have been edited.[9] Among these edited materials, we can point to many letters written by Colette or by other sisters (either personal letters or letters dealing with the management of Colettine convents), as well as to letters written to Colette or other Colettine sisters by male counsellors and confessors (like Henry de Baume, Pierre Salmon, François Claret and Pierre de Reims), order officials, high church dignitaries and lay benefactors. Second, there are several Lives of Colette and Henry de Baume, her first male counsellor and confessor. A third category consists of a corpus of devotional texts that are predominantly ascribed to Henry de Baume and Colette of Corbie; texts overtly written for the edification of the Colettine sisters. A final group of texts is formed by the constitutions of Colette and Henry, respectively written for the Colettine sisters and the Colettan friars who served them. Hence, we are dealing with a variety of texts both of male and female authorship. At present only the letters and the Lives will concern me.

Colette's surviving letters to other Colettine sisters, most of which date from the 1430s and 1440s, are fully geared to implement a specific religious behaviour. These letters are, in fact, hortatory letters and letters of moral support, stressing the importance of devotion, humility, patience, silence, and obedience. These virtues are depicted as constituting elements to become a 'bonne fille'[10] and amount to a

---

[9] See for an initial overview of edited materials *Les vies de Sainte Colette Boylet de Corbie*, ed. by Ubald d'Alençon, *Archives Franciscaines*, IV (Paris, 1911), pp. xxvii-xxviii.

[10] Compare the letter to sister Loyse Bassande in Auxonne, *Lettres de Ste Colette* (Paray-le-Monial, 1981), p. 6; the letter to Marie Boen of Ghent (*c.* 1442), *Lettres de Ste Colette*, p. 32–34; the letter to the abbess and the sisters of Besançon (July 1446), *Lettres de Ste Colette*, pp. 46–49. Compare the letter to sister Loyse Bassande in Auxonne.

programme of religious perfection. The most encompassing programme of Colettine religious perfection is unfolded in Colette's so-called testament, a long letter written near the end of her life.[11] This testament, which circulated among Colettine communities, contains a systematic exposition of an ideal religious educational programme for women. Its main elements are the uncompromising exercise of obedience, poverty, chastity, and penitence (fasting and bodily discipline), the devotion to total enclosure,[12] prayer, and meditation (on the death of Christ and his sufferings), attempts to focus the eyes as often as possible on the community's cemetery, and total attention to the Divine Office.

A straightforward reading would suggest that Colette exhibited great care to represent herself and her sisters as weak and undignified members of humanity, in accordance with established theological representations of the feminine. When she writes to outside benefactors of the Colettines, whether they be kings or the merchants of Ghent who provided funds for building a Colettine convent in that city, Colette presents herself as 'la plus indigne serviteresse de Jésus-Christ et très inutile orateresse'.[13]

However, there is a strong sense that the weak can be strong and powerful to withstand temptation by adhering to the religious programme just mentioned.[14] It seems that in this vision of female evangelical perfection through religious education, the wished for feminine qualities by male educators and confessors are fully incorporated, to become building blocks for the creation of a confident Colettine self-image. When Colette deemed it necessary, she did not hesitate to give spiritual counsel of her own to her male confessors.[15] In relation to her male confessors and advisors, Colette was also perfectly capable of expressing her own will as sufficient cause for getting things done.[16]

---

[11] Published in the *Seraphicae Legislationis Textus Originales* (Quaracchi: Collegio S. Bonaventurae, 1897), pp. 298–307, and translated in *Lettres de Ste Colette*, pp. 54–66.

[12] Enclosure as the grave in which the soul descends to obtain salvation. This theme might be inspired by Colete's recluse background.

[13] Her own letters are rhetorically geared to the needs of her addressees. If necessary, Colette was able to compose carefully. Compare the circular letter that she wrote to the Colettine convents on the death Henry de Baume, *Lettres de Ste Colette*, pp. 17–19.

[14] For example in a letter to the sisters of Ghent (*c.* 1442): 'Nonobstant que vous soyez faibles et débiles, ce n'est pas en la puissance de l'ennemi d'enfer de vous vaincre, si vous ne voulez être vaincues [...]'.

[15] Witness the letter to Pierre de Reims (*c.* 1439), *Lettres de Ste Colette*, pp. 22–23, where she asks him ('with all the power of her poor soul'): 'que vous mettiez toute la peine que vous pourrez d'aimer Notre Seigneur. Embrasez votre coeur en la benoîte Passion de Notre benoît Sauveur. Portez et sentez ses peines come vrai enfant. Allez partout après lui par ardent désir et méprisez toute autre amour que la sienne.'

[16] In a letter to Friar Jehan Lanie du Puy (*c.* 1447), in which she discharges him from being confessor and announces his successor, she is fully confident that everyone will agree with the

The surviving letters towards Colette of Corbie written by Church dignitaries and order officials, mostly written to the mature abbess, are very interesting in themselves. The male authors of these letters predominantly ask Colette to use her spiritual and moral influence on their behalf. She is asked either to intervene with the pope, the French king, or other powerful agents, or to use her spiritual allegiance with the Divine. Almost without exception, these letters address Colette as a spiritual mother.[17] A good example is the letter of Cardinal Julien Césarini, legate of Pope Eugenius IV, who presided over the council of Basel. He wrote in February 1436 to Colette, asking her intervention to restore Bishop Bernard to the episcopal see of Albi.[18] The cardinal addresses her as the venerable and religious lady Colette, 'comme à une mère honorée', begging her to counsel and press the king to act on these matters. The topos of the mother is taken up in another letter, where Cardinal Julien presents himself as a loving son to his beloved mother, in need of her spiritual support and prayers. In return, as her beloved son, he sees it to be his role to provide for his mother's spiritual necessities, donating her twelve Rhine florins for clothing.[19] Successful mature female religious apparently could take on this role of spiritual mother. The surviving letters between Colette and these male authority figures indicate that Colette knew how to use this role for her own objectives.

The letter collections not only contain letters from and to Colette of Corbie, but also letters by other sisters, such as Agnes de Vaux,[20] Elisabeth of Bavaria, Guillemette de Gruyère,[21] and Catherine Rufiné. Several of these letters provide concrete evidence for autonomous female authorship, unfiltered by male scribal mediation. They also exhibit the interesting topos of writing as a major means to store and recreate the experiences and the lived history of the Colettine sisters, to

---

new arrangement and will care for him, as that is her will and pleasure: 'J'envoie au Puy, mon père, frère Jehan Frosseau pour être confesseur, car j'ai entendu que vous ne pouvez plus bonnement faire l'office et ne doutez pas que tout le plaisir qu'il pourra vous faire, lui et les soeurs, on vous le fera; car c'est là mon plaisir et ma volonté qu'il soit fait ainsi.' *Lettres de Ste Colette*, p. 53.

[17] The mature Colette is addressed as spiritual mother by male Church dignitaries, as well as by Franciscan friars. It is definitely spiritual motherhood as understood by Rosalynn Voaden in her study *God's Words, Women's Voices. The Discernment of the Spirit in the Writing of Late Medieval Women Visionaries* (York: York Medieval Press, 1999), passim. See also note 66.

[18] *Lettres de Ste Colette*, pp. 10–12.

[19] *Lettres de Ste Colette*, pp. 13–16.

[20] See the letters of Agnes de Vaux (*c.* 1458), some of which are edited in *Règle de Ste Claire* (Desclée, 1892), pp. 286–88.

[21] For the seemingly unedited testimonies of sister Elisabeth of Bavaria and Guillemette de Gruyère, abbess of Hesdin, see: *Archives of the Poor Clares of Amiens*, Liasse 23, mémoires d'Hesdin, no. 11.

build proper knowledge and a proper communal religious disposition. These latter writings bear witness to the formation of a collective cultural memory by the sisters. An interesting example is Catherine Rufiné's letter to sister Marie de Berghes in Ghent.[22] This letter, written around 1492, not only mentions the opening of Colette's tomb, where the prospective saint was found in the odour of sanctity, but also deals with female writing as such. It offers a glance into the exchange of letters between sisters of different convents, and it provides an instance of female editorial comment on another woman's compositions, in this case a description of the opening of Colette's tomb on the authority of Jacques Bernard, at that time official Visitor of the Franciscan order.

In the beginning of her letter, Catherine thanks Marie for various letters (and relics), and apologizes for her inadequate response: her quill and hand are getting tired easily.[23] This reference to writing is taken up again at the end, where she again mentions pain in her hand: she has not written such a long letter for some time.[24] In addition, Catherine gives Marie editorial advice concerning the latter's literary representation of the opening of Colette's tomb, thereby acting as an effective proof reader and showing a keen sense of how to write politically effective hagiography, with as ultimate purpose Colette's official canonization.[25]

On Marie's request, Catherine provides her with additional information about the early history of the Colettine movement, referring explicitly to the sayings and writings of other sisters (such as Perrine de Baume), thereby revealing the existence of a strong commemorative literary culture in her own Colettine community, aiming

---

[22] Historians have used this letter to obtain information about the opening of Colette's tomb (1492). The letters of Catherine Rufiné, and her additional souvenirs (written *c.* 1492) on the first disciples of Colette (the original of which is lost) are edited by Ubald d'Alençon, 'Documents sur la réforme de sainte Colette en France', *Archivum Franciscanum Historicum*, 3 (1910), 82–86. In the historicist view of d'Alençon these letters are only interesting insofar as they establish actual facts concerning the life, death, and cult of Colette.

[23] 'Tres chiere et bien amée mère et seur en nostre signeur, tres humblement me recommande toujours à vos devots prieres et chierement vous mercie de vos charitables lettres et ossi de tres dignes reliques dont m'avez fait tres singulier plaisir, et pour brief à cause que ma plume et ma main seront bien tost lassées et ma teste encore plus tost [...]'. D'Alençon, 'Documents sur la réforme', p. 82.

[24] 'Plusieurs ans a que n'escripsi si longe lettre.' D'Alençon, 'Documents sur la réforme', p. 86.

[25] 'Parlerai tout premier de la matiere dont m'escrisies, par vostre humilité puis qu'il vous plest savoir mon povre avis, c'est que en l'escripture ce qui y est me samble tres bien, mes je cuide que le nom de nostre pere visiteur et de vostre pere confesseur qui là l'ont mis en enclos y debvroit escript. Ossi quant on ouvera le dit plonc s'il sont encore brunet, ja soit ce que ce n'est que de la terre, il porra sambler que ce mot: "souveraine beauté" seroit trop dit et souffiroit dire: "En par [...] entiereté et beauté", et ne causeroit nulle dubieté as lisans ne nul contredit as veans.' D'Alençon, 'Documents sur la réforme', p. 85.

for the creation of a *kulturelles Gedächtnis*.[26] These references are embedded in a narrative of concern about the loss of knowledge through negligence and the importance of writing for maintaining knowledge of the past.[27]

Notwithstanding disparaging remarks of nineteenth- and twentieth-century editors, who miss structure and a consistent scholastic terminology, letters like these were written in an elegant vernacular and sometimes even in Latin. They mirror the level of vernacular literary prowess of contemporary lay aristocratic women; in itself probably a testimony to the predominantly aristocratic background of many fifteenth-century Colettines and other Poor Clares. For them, as for their lay sisters, mothers and nieces, letter writing was a matter of course. It enabled women to maintain long-distance relationships and friendships, and to strengthen the communal religious bonds between various communities, creating a textual community with a unified outlook.[28]

Next to such letter collections, we find another group of texts, namely the late medieval Life of Colette of Corbie and her confessor Henry de Baume. Most famous of these is the Life produced by Pierre de Reims (or Pierre de Vaux), Henry de Baume's successor as Colette's main confessor and counsellor. It is important to note that he wrote the Life on the eve of Colette's death, on the request of the Franciscan provincial or Minister General. [29] It is, therefore, first and foremost an Order's Life, composed to enlist Colette into the body of Franciscan saints, next to Francis, Clare, Anthony, and Louis of Toulouse. This would explain why the text is modelled along the lines of Bonaventure's *Legenda major*.[30]

---

[26] On commemorative practices and the creation of a *kulturelles Gedächtnis*, see Otto Gerhard Oexle, 'Memoria als Kultur', in *Memoria als Kultur*, ed. by Otto Gerhard Oexle, Veröffentlichungen des Max-Planck-Instituts für Geschichte, 121 (Göttingen: Vandenbroeck & Ruprecht, 1995), pp. 9–78.

[27] 'Par neglicence de mettre les choses oyes en escript, en puis avoir beacop oublié, mes les seurs de Hesdin ont esté plus sages [because they wrote] car tantost apres que nostre bone mere seur Agnes leur fut ostée et menée Arras, considérans que de toutes leurs anciennes elles n'avoient mais que la bonne mere seur Hughette et seur Perrine de bame, elles s'avisèroient que sur la vie de nostre tres sainte mère ja faite [by Pierre], elles y ajousteroient en plusieurs pas aucunes des choses que elles et moi avons maintes fois oy dire par cy devant à nos anssiennes meres, du quel livre nous avons la copie en nostre convent.' D'Alençon, 'Documents sur la réforme', pp. 85–86.

[28] On medieval female epistolary culture, see Albrecht Classen, 'Emergence from the Dark: Female Epistolary Literature in the Middle Ages', *Journal of the Rocky Mountain Medieval and Renaissance Association*, 10 (1989), 1–15; *Dear Sister. Medieval Women and the Epistolary Genre*, ed. by K. Cherewatuk and Ulrike Wiethaus (Philadelphia: University of Philadelphia Press, 1993).

[29] *Les vies de Ste Colette*, pp. xxii-xxiii. Look there for information on later Lives, translations and re-workings.

[30] With, according to the editor, additional reminiscences from the legends by Thomas of

Pierre relates the life and miracles of Colette of Corbie from the perspective of the learned confessor who has been a direct or indirect witness of the deeds he relates. In accordance with then-current traditions in official Lives, the narrator's voice in the text (with exception of the introductory passage) normally does not refer to itself in the first person. Pierre presents his story as a transparent 'petite extraccion de la tres parfaitte et saincte vie de tres venerable et devote religieuse et de memoire glorieusse nonmée seur Colette de l'ordre de ma Dame Saincte Clare'.[31] According to the narrator, the Life was ordered and licensed by Franciscan order superiors. The writing was motivated not by a concern to amplify the greatness of Colette herself, but by the pious wish not to lose the memory of the graces that the Lord by his sovereign goodness had deemed to exhibit in Colette during and after her earthly existence.[32]

Pierre carefully depicts Colette as a small virgin and small servant of the Lord (*petite ancelle, petite serviteresse de notre Seigneur*).[33] As such she had left her natural female weakness behind, to serve the Lord under his guidance and protection as a chosen virgin; a status she already had reached through vigorous asceticism and self-mortification as a young recluse, even before she embarked on the renovation of the order of Poor Clares. In this way, she would have been almost from the outset beyond bodily temptations and wrong inclinations.[34] As a virgin-saint chosen by God, her major virtues were chastity and virginity, in importance only equalled by the love of poverty.[35] If we believe Pierre's account, the virtue of chastity was so important that the young Colettine order at first only accepted true virgins. Widows who had given birth would not have been welcome. When, 'due to the wisdom of God,' non-virgin postulants began to be admitted, Colette was not as intimate with

---

Celano and the *De conformitate* of Bartolomeo of Pisa.

[31] *Les vies de Ste Colette*, p. 3.

[32] *Les vies de Ste Colette*, p. 3.

[33] 'en laquelle je l'appelle la petite ancelle, c'est-à-dire la petite serviteresse de notre Seigneur pour chartaine cause qui est à ma cognoissance. Car je scay que devant Dieu plusieurs fois elle a esté ainsy ditte et nonmée [...].' *Les vies de Ste Colette*, pp. 3–4.

[34] *Les vies de Ste Colette*, p. 23. This aspect of her sanctity is dealt with in additional detail on pp. 103–110.

[35] *Les vies de Ste Colette*, p. 54. 'De ceste belle et plaisante vertus de chasteté [presented as the most fundamental virtue for a female saint] fust moult noblement parée et ordonnée le cuer et le corps de la petite ancelle de notre Seigneur. Par tous les tamps de sa vie elle volut hair et fuyr tous vices et tous pechiés et par especiael elle eust ungne grande orreur et abhominacion des pechiéz charnelz contre lesquelz elle garda sy nettement et sainctement les sens du corps qui sont les portes du cuer et les cloy sy estroittement que onques depuis qu'elle eust cognaissance de Dieu par consentement ne parvint jusques à elle vain delyt ne charnel plaisir.' On her love of poverty, see pp. 46–50.

these latter sisters as with her virgin followers.[36] Purity seems to have held a particular fascination for Colette, or at least for the narrator, who later tries to counterbalance it with the story of a vision in which Colette encountered the mother-saint Anne, showing her glorious offspring. Thereafter, Colette's inhibitions against non-virgin sisters would have abated.

The principal occupations of the *petite ancelle* of the Lord would have been prayer and the praise of God in a liturgical context, as well as the utmost devotion to the Passion of Christ and the Eucharist.[37] Personal and intercessory prayer is presented as the perfect occupation of enclosed nuns, who are literally barred from the world. The devotion to Christ's Passion and the connected Eucharist devotion turned the reception of the body and blood of Christ into an ecstatic moment, and enticed the female saint to undergo self- and divinely-inflicted bodily suffering.[38]

In accordance with the then-current discourse on female religious learning, Pierre's Life of Colette emphasizes the familiar route that leads from the right virtues (following the commandments with total humility, chastity, and obedience, the practice of poverty, prayer, and the willingness to suffer for Christ) and evocative devotions towards the host and the mass, to prophetic gifts and the grace to perform miracles.[39] There is a typical emphasis on infused knowledge as opposed to acquired knowledge through scholastic training, and the male narrator plays down Colette's formal education.[40]

As Colette was not just a virtuous saint but a renovator, who founded a range of new convents during her lifetime, the narrator has to incorporate her reforming activities. Not surprisingly, the narrative emphasizes the will of God to solve the practical impediments and obstacles to Colettine reform programme, and to give at the right moment *clere congnoissance* to the male authorities needed to get things done.[41] In this way, it is not necessary to tackle the problem of female action.

Pierre de Reims was a dominant figure in the Colettine movement as Colette's confessor and as supervisor of the Colettine communities. No wonder that ecclesiastical authorities and Colettine sisters alike regarded his narrative as authoritative. Hence it was copied and used in the Colettine convents. External and

---

[36] *Les vies de Ste Colette*, pp. 60–61.

[37] *Les vies de Ste Colette*, pp. 64–68 and 88–90.

[38] *Les vies de Ste Colette*, pp. 102, 109–115.

[39] *Les vies de Ste Colette*, pp. 115–17.

[40] 'Sa petite ancelle […] eust petite science acquise, mais de science infuse elle fust plenturussement remplie, c'est assavoir de la grace du saint esprit par laquelle elle congnoissoit clerement les chosses qui estoient passées qu'elle n'avoit oncque veu ne sceu, et les chosses secretes qui estoient presentes et celles qui estoient advenir.' *Les vies de Ste Colette*, pp. 116–17. See also pp. 121–27.

[41] Hence God gives 'clere congnoissance' to the pope to proper understand and accept the mission of 'La glorieusse ancelle de notre Seigneur.' *Les vies de Ste Colette*, p. 36.

internal manuscript evidence shows that the Life was kept in the Colettine houses and transcribed in combination with other hagiographic texts and devotional works.[42] As such, the text was formative in the constitution of the Colettine literary self-representation. Yet Pierre de Reims's narrative was not the single constitutive text in this regard. Also important was the Life written by Perrine or Petronilla de Baume, a relative of Colette's confessor and co-operator Henry de Baume.[43]

Perrine wrote or dictated her work around 1474, when she was in her sixties.[44] In contrast with the Life written by Pierre de Reims, the narrative voice in Perrine's work speaks consistently in the first person. More often than not the narrator presents itself as a direct eyewitness. If not, the narrator invokes the authority of others: Colette herself, her confessors Henry and Pierre, other friar-confessors, and fellow sisters. Also contrary to Pierre's Life, Perrine's narrative is not set up according to existing and authoritative models of 'official' hagiographic writing. Perrine's story is literally a memoir. She does use parts of Pierre's legend, which she cites regularly and for some parts follows almost literally. Yet her account seems to be the result of an autonomous urge for commemoration and history in the Besançon convent. Of fundamental importance is the female narrator's self-presentation as a transparent medium of witnessed events.[45]

In Perrine's story, Colette is not so much the little lamb of the Lord, but *notre glorieuse mere soeur Colette*. She is claimed as 'our own leader'. At the same time, there is great concern to display Colette's adherence to the model of feminine sanctity. Perrine emphasises Colette's shame to go out and meet people. Enclosure is a running theme. This urge for total enclosure is connected with Colette's unsurpassable humility. Whereas Perrine describes Colette as her glorious leader,

---

[42] In all twelve manuscripts, among which some interesting early copies. *Les vies de Ste Colette*, pp. xliii–xliv.

[43] Three manuscripts still survive, one dating from 1492. Perrine was a close companion of Colette for almost thirty years, travelling with her and fulfilling several functions (such as mistress of novices). Perrine had at least one older sister who had joined the order at an early stage (Mahaut de Baume). The sources also mention the presence of the nun Katherine de Balme in Besançon, maybe of the same family.

[44] According to the letters of Catherine Ruffiné mentioned above, Perrine's reminiscences were known and read by her sisters. The letters of Catherine Ruffiné also indicate that Colettine nuns regularly engaged in the actual composition of letters and other texts. This information notwithstanding, subsequent (male) editors of Perrine's text have assumed that Perrine's memoirs must have been written down by her confessor François de Marez; a conclusion that might need reconsideration. See also AASS, *VII: Martii tomus primus*, cur. *Joannes Carnandet* (3rd edn, Paris-Rome: Victor Palmé, 1865), pp. 532–33.

[45] 'Chy apres ensieult la declaration de che je, soeur Perrine de Basme, de l'eage de LXVI ans [...] scay tant avoir vue et ossy oy dire et experimenté plusieurs fois de la saincte honorable vie et conversation tres religieuse de la dicte glorieuse vierge soeur Colette [...]' *Les vies de Ste Colette*, p. 202.

she takes care to note that Colette presented herself as the *indigne serviteresse et inutille orateresse*.[46] She was so humble that she did not want her life and sayings being used as an example.[47] Next to her humility, Colette is continually presented as a *vraie amateresse de saincte povreté*,[48] whose life was formed by a great zeal for total enclosure, liturgical chant, the Eucharist, Passion devotion and fierce bodily penitence.[49] There also is a strong emphasis on (predominantly vocal) prayer, whether or not in a liturgical context, and accompanying penitential exercises. Prayer is presented as 'sa principale occupacion ou mentelement ou vocalement', and as the key to solve difficult questions and overcome doubts.[50] In Perrine's account, as well as in other devotional texts read and copied in Colettine communities, learning to pray is a cornerstone of Colettine religious education.

Perrine's memoir relates that sanctity leads to wisdom, a theme in complete accordance with the Franciscan hagiographic tradition. Throughout her flow of recollections, Perrine provides the reader with examples of Colette's infused knowledge about the thoughts and sins of other people. She disseminated this knowledge in her writings, which were cherished like relics by their recipients.[51] This was first of all knowledge about the state of grace of her companions: the sisters that shared her enclosed existence, as well as the male confessors.[52] The text exploits

---

[46] *Les vies de Ste Colette*, pp. 207, 241 (and elsewhere).

[47] But she would not hesitate to use her full authority to ensure that this did not happen. When Friar Henry secretly composed a booklet on her graces and life: 'Sy appella le dict bon pere et le reprind tres asprement de ce qu'il avoit ainssy escript à sa loenge, elle soy disant grande pecheresse toutte defectueuse et plus digne de confusion que aultrement. Sy demanda ce dict livret, lequel luy fust bailliet, et elle incontinent le getta au feu et l'ardist, ad fin qu'il n'en fust nulle memore jamais.' *Les vies de Ste Colette*, p. 207.

[48] *Les vies de Ste Colette*, p. 219.

[49] There are many examples of her astounding devotion to Christ's Passion, the crucifix and the sign of the cross, replete with '[...] l'abondance des larmes et les piteulx pleurs et gemissemens [...]', fierce forms of self-torture and other forms of bodily penitence. This is matched by a supreme love for the blood and body of Christ, and a veneration of the host and the altar. Colette's love of enclosure (the chosen grave) also expresses itself in her love of solitude. *Les vies de Ste Colette*, pp. 232–34, 242, 250, 266.

[50] 'En touttez adversitez et doubtez son refuge estoit au sacrefice de saincte oreison'. *Les vies de Ste Colette*, pp. 222–25. It would seem that the emphasis was more on vocal than on mental prayer with mystical overtones. Lopez, 'Sainte Colette', p. 207 therefore suggests not to see Colette's doctrine of prayer as a precursor to that of Teresa of Avila.

[51] Henry de Baume would have reverred letters of Corbie as relics and divine messages. *Les vies de Ste Colette*, p. 249: '[...] ilz recheupt ses lettres moult reverentement à genoulx en les baisant'.

[52] *Les vies de Ste Colette*, p. 241: 'Item tesmoigne que chest vray que touttes les soeurs qu'ilz morroient et trespassoient se venoient monstrer et presenter à nostre dicte glorieuse mere, car je luy ay oy dire à elle meismez: "Une soeur est trespassée, il me fault aller dire mes

the theme that such infused knowledge gave Colette a privileged position with regard to male authority figures.[53] It also comprised a deep insight into the nature of the divine presence in the host and other theological matters. In relation to this, the text deals with Colette's state of tranquil ecstasy (both in her cell and on the road), while she was contemplating divine truths.[54] Furthermore, she had a prophetic knowledge concerning the future of the Church and the world.[55] Her knowledge extended to the fate of popes and antipopes and the fate of the General Council of Basel.[56] In that context, the memoir refers to Colette's interaction with high church leaders. The surviving letters to Colette by such church dignitaries shows that this was not just a hagiographic topos.[57]

In the circumference of these different kinds of knowledge, Perrine's account sketches an ambivalent picture of Colette's learning. On the one hand, the text provides references to her schooling before embarking on a religious career.[58] On the other hand, all testimonies of Colette's superior knowledge are presented as divine gifts.[59] It seems clear that we are dealing with two kinds of knowledge: basic reading and writing skills that (aristocratic) girls could learn in school or at home versus important theological and spiritual knowledge that must be infused, as women did

---

patre nostres pour elle." Mon pere frere Henry sy le m'a dist plusieurs fois.'

[53] *Les vies de Ste Colette*, p. 251.

[54] She and her confessor travelled totally in divine rapture, so as to be untouched by and oblivious of the world through which they travelled in a sort of mental enclosure: 'Item quant elle alloit par les champs pour fonder ou visiter aulcuns convens de la dicte ordre, ou sus ung quar ou sus une beste, elle estoit comme toujours ravie.' *Les vies de Ste Colette*, p. 236.

[55] *Les vies de Ste Colette*, p. 213: 'Item je, soeur Perrine dessus nommée [...] oys dire que mon dict pere frere Henry de Basme disoit devant lez soeurs du dict convent, que nostre dicte glorieuse mere en une vision espantable avoit congneu generalemnt tous les estas de l'esglise et de la secularité.'

[56] *Les vies de Ste Colette*, p. 268–69.

[57] It is difficult to obtain a concrete picture of Colette's direct or indirect role at the Council of Basel. She corresponded with several dignitaries, urging them to bring the schism to an end. There is no real evidence to support the tradition that Colette convinced Amadée VIII of Savoy (Pope Félix V) to renounce the tiara, although she certainly was opposed to his papacy and urged the Colettine sisters of Vevey and Orbe not to recognize him, notwithstanding the fact that Amadée was the official protector of these convents. Compare Lopez, 'Sainte Colette', p. 212.

[58] 'Je luy ay oy dire que quant en son josne eage elle alloit à l'escolle, elle donnoit volontiers aulx povres enffans che qu'elle portoit l'escolle pour mengier [...]' *Les vies de Ste Colette*, p. 220.

[59] 'Nostre gl. Mere soeur Collette eust pou de science acquise; mais de science infuse elle en fust plaintureusement remplie par la grace de benoit sainct esprit. Par laquelle elle cognoissoit clerement plusieurs choses etpresentes et advenir [...]' *Les vies de Ste Colette*, p. 257.

not have access to higher theological schooling. At the same time, this dichotomy of acquired versus infused knowledge was a very influential *docta ignorantia* theme in Franciscan circles ever since Bonaventure's epistemological and mystical treatment of Francis of Assisi's *speculatio* in the *Legenda major* and in the *Itinerarium mentis in Deum*. In the case of Colette it had a special significance, however, as the other road to such theological knowledge ordinarily was closed to women. Whatever the source of her knowledge, Colette was not modest about it.

Several times she said to her sisters in confidence: 'I tell you, my sisters, that our Lord has given me the grace to bestow on me at the age of nine as much knowledge about religion as Saint Francis had when he was thirty or forty years old.'[60]

At least within her own community, her knowledge was not something to hide, and the way in which Colette's knowledge was referred to vocalized self-confidence and pride within the boundaries set for female expression of learning.

Aside from Perrine's commemorative narrative, there survive personal testimonies on Colette by Aleyde de Sanchines (1493),[61] as well as the anonymous *Vita Fratris Henrici de Balma*, a late fifteenth-century vernacular product of a sister from Besançon. That latter saints' Life is interesting as a female representation of a male confessor.[62] The text is written for a female audience engaged in the search of evangelical perfection.[63] This seems to have had direct repercussions for the representation of the male confessor-saint. Just like Pierre de Reims had made Colette into a receptacle of divine grace, so too Henry is here depicted as such a receptacle, whose examples, writings and admonitions can provide consolation and direction to the nuns. It indicates that within female religious communities the saint

---

[60] 'Plusieurs fois elle disoit à ses religieuses familierement: 'Je vous dis, mes soeurs, que nostre Seigneur m'a faict ceste grace qu'il m'avoit donnée aussy grande cognaissance de la religion com seigneur sainct Franchois en l'eage de IX ans comme il avoit à XXX ans ou XL.' *Les vies de Ste Colette*, p. 260.

[61] AASS *[...]–: Martii tomus primus, cur. Joannes Carnandet* (3rd edn., Paris-Rome: Victor Palmé, 1865), pp. 594–96.

[62] *Vita Fratris Henrici de Balma*, ed. by Ubald d'Alençon, *Archivum Franciscanum Historicum*, 2 (1909), 601–607. Lippens writes: 'Cette soi-disant biographie est le type des *vitae* ou *legendae* médiévales, qui n'apportent rien de ce que nous, lecteurs du XXe siècle, y cherchons.' Hugolin Lippens, 'Henry de Baume coopérateur de S. Colette. Recherches su sa vie et publication de ses Statuts inédits. Une contribution à l'histoire de la réforme dans l'Ordre des Frères Mineurs au XVe siècle', *Sacris erudiri*, 1 (1948), 234–35.

[63] Hence it also describes the essence of Colettine life. *Vita Fratris Henrici de Balma*, ed. by Ubald d'Alençon, p. 603. In agreement with papal licence, the sisters (of Besançon): 'vivant en subjection et obeissance sans avoir nul propre ni domination en ce monde, vivant en chasteté et perpetuelle clausures, estant constantes de l'abstinance de ne mangé chair, jeusner toutz les iours, de la nudité et froidure des pieds, de la dureté du toucher, la pauvreté et rudesse du vestir, estre constante de vivre pauvrement des petites viandes qui leur sont administreés et donées pour dieu, avec labeur jour et nuit spirituelz et manuel […]'.

as vessel of infused knowledge was not a model limited to females. Henry is
described in the same evocative and effeminate language as Colette is described in
the memoirs of sister Perrine.[64] Again, just as in the letters mentioned before, there is
an outspoken emphasis on writing as the guarantor of the collective memory that
sustains the community of nuns. It is writing—the writing of Henry himself (his
many admonitions), the copying process of Henry's letters by the nuns of Besançon,
and the independent writing of the nuns in which such deeds are recounted—that
provides spiritual consolation.[65] Writing is complementary to the collection of
relicts: just as the morsels of Henry's writing continue to work in the community, so
do the relicts of his body. They both make the absent present and they feed the
process of commemoration and identity formation.

Writing and Identity

Scholars nowadays emphasize that religious programmes and programmatic
literatures (such as saints' Lives), reflect ingrained power structures and ruling
gendered discourses. This leads to questions as to what extent religious women had
power over their own language, to what extent female literary articulation was
encased in discourses of subjugation beyond female control. If women were
deprived of their own subjectivity, they either were always at the mercy of a male
subjectivity, or they were consciously or unconsciously forced to adopt a feminine
subjectivity that was a male construction. Insofar as real mysticism was a sought loss
of subjectivity in the union with the Divine, a transcendence of this subjectivity
dilemma might be found in some female mystic texts.[66] In most other cases,

---

[64] *Vita Fratris Henrici de Balma*, p. 605.

[65] *Vita Fratris Henrici de Balma*, p. 601: 'Sensuit ung petit traicté de la devoste memoire et
saincteté de vie et mantion des vertus innumerables que notre seigneur par sa grace a mis au
tres glorieux et sainct pere frere Henry de Baulme. [...] aussi verres, s'il plait à la devotion du
lisant, aucunes epistres et lettres qu'il [Henry] a envoyé et escript de sa propre main tant en se
couvent de Besançon comme en d'aultres qui sont gardees et tenues comme reliques bien
dignes et pour ce les avons icy copiees de mot à mot pour la consolation des bons qui desirent
profiter en vertu.' *Vita Fratris Henrici de Balma*, p. 604: '[...] parce qu'il ne pouvoit estre
tousiours present pour les enflammer en l'amour de Dieu et de leur saincte vocation par ses
divines et douces parolles qui estoient comme dars et glaives aigus tres persant et navren leur
coeurs de l'amour et doulceur de nostre seigneur, lesdictes religieuses a ceste cause
augmentoient de plus en plus leur bon courage et vouloir de servir à Dieu en leur austere vie et
penitence de leur regle qui leur estoit comme delice; en son absence la saincte main ne cessoit
d'escripre des lettres et epistres plaines d'amour et doulceur de Dieu et salutaires monitions.'

[66] The Helfta visionaries employed images drawn from biological *female* characteristics
rather than culturally determined and pre-programmed *feminine* characteristics such as
compassion and nurturing. These latter characteristics were almost commonplace in later
medieval devotional works designed to stimulate affective piety. Rosalynn Voaden, 'God's

however, the enactment of religious life as well as the religious language in female communities would have been shaped by pre-given templates of the feminine; templates that originated in gendered representations controlled by male-dominated discourses of power.[67]

From this perspective, the feminization of religious language and the appropriation of specific devotional and ascetical models and practices by the female religious is not an indication of emancipation, but of an increasing incorporation of religious models by which female religious expression was brought under control. This process was stimulated by the circumscription of female learning and female access to the basic texts of Christian faith and knowledge. This is not to say that there did not exist highly educated nuns. Neither can we explain the work of later medieval mystics without some access to religious learning. Yet the downplaying of female religious learning by religious authorities and the propagation of feminine docility and humility might have promoted the conscious anti-intellectual and uneducated self-representation of later medieval nuns, if only to forego criticism. Elements of this are present in the letters and Lives portrayed in the above. Colette and her sisters were clearly concerned to display their learning as infused and not as acquired. In this, they followed the prerequisites of a given feminine subjectivity.

The closure of Latin education did not stop female access to vernacular literacy.[68] This was even stimulated by male confessors and male religious educators. Hence, we see a quick proliferation of vernacular devotional literature for women. This production can be divided into literature produced by women and a corpus of literature produced by men. In either case, scholastic theological knowledge (present in Sentences Commentaries and *Quaestiones* literature) was not made available.[69]

Almighty Hand: Women Co-writing the Book', in *Women, the Book and the Godly*, ed. by Leslie Smith and Jane H .M. Taylor (Cambridge: Brewer, 1995), pp. 55–66.

[67] Weinstein, Bell, and Bynum distinguish between the masculine type of saint (acting in the outside world) and the androgynous or feminine (rather than female) saint, characterized by penitential asceticism, private prayer, mystical communion with the Godhead and charity. This latter type could hold for males and females alike, yet was used for women in particular. See for more information Daniel Bornstein, 'Women and Religion in late Medieval Italy: History and Historiography', in *Women and Religion in Medieval and Renaissance Italy*, ed. by Daniel Bornstein and Roberto Rusconi (Chicago & London, 1996), pp. 1–27.

[68] See Doris Ruhe,'Mönche, Nonnen und die ideale Frau. Zur Herausbildung des weiblichen Erziehungsideals im Mittelalter', in *Strukturen der Gesellschaft im Mittelalter. Interdisziplinäre Mediävistik in Würzburg*, ed. by Dieter Rödel and Joachim Schneider (Wiesbaden: Reichert, 1996), pp. 50–66; Marie-Luise Ehrenschwendtner, 'Puellae litteratae: The Use of the Vernacular in the Dominican Convents of Southern Germany', in *Medieval Women in their Communities*, ed. by Diane Watt (Cardiff: University of Wales Press, 1997), pp. 49–71.

[69] Georg Steer, 'Die Rezeption des theologischen Bonaventura-Schrifttums im deutschen Spätmittelalter', in *Bonaventura. Studien zu seiner Wirkungsgeschichte*, ed. by Ildefons

What got translated were texts of basic religious instruction, devotional exercises, and affective mysticism; texts that could be used to uphold approbated tenets of feminine sanctity. All of this ties in with the topos of infused knowledge in the Lives of female saints, as well as with the emphasis on self-mortification, prayer and Passion devotion.[70]

Female vernacular literacy was under severe control. At the same time, female writing and reading also gave women their own outlet. It has been argued that even then they needed a male scribe, whether or not their confessor, to write it all down in the 'right' language.[71] Yet we have seen that in Colettine communities the female author could be free from such direct mediation, even if the vocabulary and the available models were mainly derived from a male-controlled discourse of feminine religious life. I would agree with Bornstein, who argues that the existence of male-made models for women should not blind scholars to the active participation of women in generating these models or to the manifold ambiguities inherent in the process of modelling.[72] Within strict limits, the emerging feminine vernacular religious discourse in Colettine houses can be seen as a renegotiation of religious identity, through an exploration and exploitation of available and sanctioned feminine religious models. Colette was able to make her male entourage listen to her (divinely inspired) voice. She succeeded in creating communities, the authority structure of which gave her more power than was usually bestowed on a female abbess or prioress—as can be seen in her relations with confessors and counsellors, as well as with higher ecclesiastics. Within these communities, the literary production of the nuns, as much as that of the manifold male authority figures, shaped the women's discourse.

Vanderheyden, Franziskanische Forschungen, 28 (Werl: Dietrich-Coelde, 1976), pp. 146–56.

[70] See also Ann M. Hutchison, 'What Nuns Read: Literary Evidence from the English Bridgettine House, Syon Abbey', *Mediaeval Studies*, 57 (1995), 205–22; Katherine Gill, 'Women and the Production of Religious Literature in the Vernacular, 1300–1500', in *Creative Women in Medieval and Early Modern Italy: A Religious and Artistic Renaissance*, ed. by Ann Matter and John Coakley (Philadelphia, 1994), pp. 64–104; Anne Clark Bartlett, *Male Authors, Female Readers: Representation and Subjectivity in Middle English Devotional Literature* (Ithaca: Cornell, 1995); John Coakley, 'Friars as Confidants of Holy Women in Medieval Dominican Hagiography', in *Images of Sainthood in Medieval Europe*, ed. by Renate Blumenfeld-Kosinski and Timea Szell (Ithaca: Cornell, 1991), pp. 222–46.

[71] Rosalynn Voaden, 'God's Almighty Hand: Women Co-writing the Book', in *Women, The Book and the Godly*, pp. 55–65.

[72] Bornstein, 'Women and Religion', pp. 20–27 suggests that during the Avignon papacy and the Great Schism the validity of male institutional authority had weakened. This engendered willingness to listen to female, divinely inspired, voices calling for reform (within the interpretory matrices of the dominant gendered discourse). When male institutional order was restored, the eccentric female model could more easily be rejected. From this perspective, the Colettine reform might have been a 'niche' operation, in a time of discredited masculine authority.

No doubt many elements of this discourse cohered with sanctioned feminine models of sanctity. Yet these models and their discourse did not exhaust women's understanding of their religious life, as accredited meanings of words never have total control over human thought and experience. Moreover, the construction of subjectivity is a complex process of confrontation and socialization, in the process of which is carved out the sense of self and of individual and communal identity.[73] Fifteenth-century Colettine communities seem to have been relatively successful in developing their own sense of identity and integrity through their own epistolary activities and their active participation in the production of commemorative texts. They used the given models to establish a textual community with a special form of commemorated knowledge. It provided Colettine nuns with an identity that they could call their own.[74]

---

[73] Margaret R. Miles, *Carnal Knowing. Female Nakedness and Religious Meaning in the Christian West* (Boston, 1989), p. 53; Miri Rubin, 'Small Groups: Identity and Solidarity in the Late Middle Ages', in *Enterprise and Individuals in Fifteenth Century England*, ed. by J. Kermode (Stroud: Alan Sutton, 1991), pp. 132–50.

[74] Rusconi argues in a comparable vein about other communities of Poor Clares in fifteenth-century Italy. Roberto Rusconi, 'Women Religious in Late Medieval Italy: New Sources and Directions', in *Women and Religion in Medieval and Renaissance Italy*, pp. 305–326.

Maria doctrix: Anchoritic Women, the Mother of God, and the Transmission of Knowledge

ANNEKE B. MULDER-BAKKER

In his *Libri octo miraculorum* Caesarius of Heisterbach holds up to his readers the example of a Utrecht recluse who was on intimate terms with the mother of God. She 'used venerable images of Mary to show her love for her: often she knelt before them, venerated them, burned incense and kissed them'. At night, as she prayed in her cell, she called on Mary as well. In all this the recluse was extremely discerning and cautious. For when the devil had once appeared to her in the form of Mary and told her to kiss 'her' feet, 'some suspicion arose in her heart, for she sensed pride, and she answered: "What are you saying, my sweetest lady? You are the humblest of all and the mother of humility; how can you then ask me to kiss your feet?" When she said this the deceptive vision disappeared. And the devil who had fabricated it left behind, as evidence that it had been he, such a penetrating stench that the woman could hardly bear it.'[1]

This little miracle, simple though it seems, contains significant details. First of all it testifies to the prestige enjoyed by anchoritic women in the later Middle Ages.

---

[1] *Die Wundergeschichten des Caesarius von Heisterbach*, ed. by Alfons Hilka, 2 vols (Bonn, 1933–37), II, p. 21; compare Jaap van Moolenbroek, *Mirakels Historisch: De Exempels von Caesarius van Heisterbach over Nederland en Nederlanders* (Hilversum: Verloren, 1999), pp. 276–83. Compare L. Tewes, 'Der *Dialogus Miraculorum* des Caesarius von Heisterbach: Beobachtungen zum Gliederungs- und Werkcharacter', *Archiv für Kulturgeschichte*, 79 (1997), 13–30. After I completed this chapter two deeply relevant books were published: Rachel Fulton, *From Judgment to Passion. Devotion to Christ and the Virgin Mary, 800–1200* (New York: Columbia University Press, 2002) and Barbara Newman, *God and the Goddesses. Vision, Poetry, and Belief in the Middle Ages* (Philadelphia: University of Pennsylvania Press, 2003). I cannot enter into dialogue with these works here but will do so in my forthcoming book: *Lives of the Anchoresses. The Rise of the Urban Recluse in Medieval Europe* (Philadelphia: University of Pennsylvania Press).

Caesarius regularly uses recluses to illustrate exemplary faith. The case at hand is less an illustration of pious devotion—though that goes almost without saying—as of discernment, knowledge, and insight. His point is that only those who have the necessary knowledge can distinguish between a phantasm and a true vision. For the purposes of this study, a second detail is even more important: recluses apparently liked to be associated with Mary, the mother of God. This anchoress is evidently on confidential terms with Our Lady. She knows her through and through and addresses her in a manner that to us seems quite familiar. It is the close bond of a daughter with her mother—as, indeed, Mary is referred to as the holy mother of God and not, for example, as the Virgin Mary. This familiarity gives the daughter the confidence to behave with some irreverence and even to act in apparent disobedience.

Working on anchoresses or women recluses in the Low Countries of the Middle Ages, I became intrigued by the dominant—and highly specific role—Mary seemed to play in the spiritual and social life of these females. I therefore set about collecting source material in a more systematic way. My intention is not to study the cult of the Virgin among recluses nor to evaluate their thoughts about Marian doctrine, but to investigate, from a 'socio-historical' angle so to speak, the perceived intimate and active relationship that Mary and anchoritic women were said to maintain. It seems a mutual, almost 'human' relationship as between a mother and a daughter, or a queen and her lady-in-waiting. What was the significance of this bond for the recluse herself and—in this volume on transmission of knowledge—for her activities in the world of the common faithful?

Until recently Marian scholars, who occupied themselves with Mary's role through the centuries, showed a distinct preference for investigating the development of Marian doctrine: the process, for instance, by which Mary became the virgin mother of God, the doctrine of the Immaculate Conception, or of the bodily Assumption.[2] These issues are usually studied from a theological perspective and construed as a history from above—as speculation by theologians that might or might not have influenced lay piety below. According to Schüssler Fiorenza: 'The Mary myth has its roots [...] in a male, clerical, and ascetic culture and theology.'[3] An important consequence was that Mary has been primarily viewed as an object of devotion, not as a subject in a relationship. In this respect Marian scholarship mirrored the general picture of historical scholarship devoted to women in the Middle Ages, which tended to treat women as the silent object.[4] Apart from the

---

[2] Hilda Graef, *Mary: A History of Doctrine and Devotion*, 2 vols (London: Sheed and Ward, 1963–65) and studies mentioned below. Twenty-five years ago, in her unparalleled study *Alone of All Her Sex: The Myth and the Cult of the Virgin Mary* (London: Weidenfield and Nicholson, 1976), Marina Warner already distanced herself from this approach.

[3] Quoted by Jaroslav Pelikan, *Mary through the Centuries: Her Place in the History of Culture* (New Haven: Yale, 1996), p. 4.

[4] The series *A History of Women in the West*, ed. by Georges Duby and Michelle Perrot, 5 vols. (Cambridge, MA: Harvard University Press, 1992–94) provides a perfect example. The

theologians, literary scholars and art historians investigated the iconology of Mary and the Marian cult and the romantic love of knights and troubadours. Here, too, the focus was on Mary as an object of human devotion, and again it was mainly a devotion of men. Women were supposedly drawn more to Christ, their heavenly bridegroom. In circles of women's studies this has led to the idea that the aim of Marian doctrine was in the first place to make of Christianity a male religion, hostile towards and disdainful of women.[5]

In recent years (feminist) scholars, predominantly in Germany and France, have undertaken a broader and more systematic search for Marian devotion among the common faithful—doing history, in other words, from below. We now know that from the tenth century onwards a Marian cult dispersed widely in northern Europe, particularly in northern France and the Low Countries. It began with local miracles in cathedrals and commercial towns of northern France, followed by shrine miracles and 'relic tours' that generated money for new cathedrals. Females, semi-religious and wise old women, played a prominent part,[6] contrary to the old assumption that men, knights and monks were more attracted to the high Lady than women. By the thirteenth century Mary had become the foremost advocate of all lay people in trouble.[7] This much their research has made clear: 'if we look for medieval women in the places where they were pious believers in the presence of Mary, we find a different faith being propagated from a misogynist one.'[8] It is this scholarly path that I choose to follow.

---

second volume, devoted to the Middle Ages and entitled in English: *Silences of the Middle Ages* (1992), presents women as primarily passive objects of male patronizing.

[5] Klaus Schreiner, *Maria: Jungfrau, Mutter, Herrscherin* (Munich: Hauser, 1994), p. 501.

[6] Johannes of Coutances, *Miracula Sanctae Mariae Constantiae*, ed. by E. A. Pigeon, in *Histoire de la cathédrale de Coutances* (Coutances, 1876) pp. 367–83; quoted by Signori, see below.

[7] Gabriela Signori, *Maria zwischen Kathedrale, Kloster und Welt: Hagiographische und historiographische Annäherung an eine hochmittelalterliche Wunderpredigt* (Sigmaringen: Thorbecke, 1995) and her study in *Marie: Le Culte de la Vierge dans la société médiévale*, ed. by Dominique Iogna-Prat and others (Paris: Beauchesne, 1996); *Maria: Abbild oder Vorbild? Zur Sozialgeschichte mittelalterlicher Marienverehrung*, ed. by Hedwig Röckelein and others, (Tübingen: Diskord, 1990); *Maria in der Welt: Marienverehrung im Kontext der Sozialgeschichte (10–18 Jhr.)*, ed. by Claudia Opitz and others (Zürich: Chronos, 1993); Marzena Górecka, *Das Bild Mariens in der Deutschen Mystik des Mittelalters* (Bern: Lang, 1999); David Flory, *Marian Representations in the Miracle Tales of Thirteenth-Century Spain and France* (Washington: Catholic University of America, 2000).

[8] Schreiner, *Maria*, p. 501; compare Gabriela Signori, 'Regina coeli–regina mundi. Weiblichkeit im abendländischen Prozess der Individualisierung am Beispiel weiblicher Vergangenheit', in *Beiträge der 4. Schweizerischen Historikerinnentagung* (Zürich: Chronos, 1988), pp. 23–41.

None of these scholars, however, focus specifically on Mary as subject, on Mary's active role in the life of individuals as they perceived it; on her intimate relationship, for instance, with anchoritic women, her being the *domina*, the *doctrix* of these devout. And little attention is given to hagiographic sources. That is my intention here: to study Mary's perceived role in the spiritual life of the 'living saints' in the anchorholds of the female recluses in the lands between the Seine and the Elbe. I hope to show not only that these women lived in an intimate relationship with Mary, but that studying this relationship amounts to studying the dynamics of the transmission of knowledge—of Mary as *doctrix* towards the anchoresses and of the anchoresses towards the faithful community. I consider this an important element of the study of 'common theology' as defined in the Introduction. I will concentrate on three examples: the mother of Guibert of Nogent in the first decade of the twelfth century; Yvette of Huy, the beguine leader at the beginning of the thirteenth century; and Margaret the Lame of Magdeburg a few decades later.

The Mother of Guibert of Nogent

In his autobiography *De vita sua* Guibert of Nogent (*c.* 1054–1124) included a short biography of his mother.[9] Both mother and son, according to his story, placed their lives in the hands of the Mother of God. During Guibert's difficult birth his parents promised to dedicate the child to Mary if it proved to be born healthy and in later years, after the mother had been deprived of her husband, she turned to Mary for support. She steadfastly refused to remarry and, when Guibert had reached the age of twelve, embarked on the solitary life. She had a reclusorium built next to the abbey church of St Germer de Fly, itself built on family ground, and had two of her sons and some of her household staff enter the abbey, so that she could keep an eye on them. At the time she must have been about forty years old and had probably come to realize, like other women of her age, that a widow could have a safer and above all a more authoritative way of life as a recluse than in the world. She would experience no loss of influence; on the contrary, new possibilities for increasing her authority would offer themselves.[10] This is evident from the following anecdotes.

On one occasion, when Guibert had decided to leave the abbey—in an attempt, perhaps, to break free from his mother—she had a vision. Guibert writes that she thought she was in the abbey church, but in her vision the building and the monks

---

[9] Guibert de Nogent, *Autobiographie*, ed. and trans. by Edmond-René Labande. Classiques de l'Histoire de France au Moyen Age (Paris: Champion, 1981). I quote from the English translation, *Self and Society in Medieval France: The Memoirs of Abbot Guibert of Nogent*, ed. and introd. by John F. Benton (New York: Harper & Row, 1970).

[10] Mavis E. Mate, *Women in Medieval English Society* (Cambridge: Cambridge University Press, 1999); *Aristocratic Women in Medieval France*, ed. by Theodore Evergates (Philadelphia: University of Pennsylvania Press, 1998).

had shrunk to dwarf size:

> [S]uddenly a woman of beauty and majesty beyond measure advanced through the midst of the church right up to the altar, followed by one like a young girl whose appearance was in its deference appropriate to her whom she followed. [The Lady appeared to be the Blessed Mother of God, and the servant Guibert's mother.] Going to the altar, the lady knelt in prayer and the noble attendant who in the vision was following her did the same behind her [...]. Then Mary turned her tranquil gaze on me [Guibert] and [...] said, 'I brought him here and made him a monk. By no means will I permit him to be taken away.' After this the attendant repeated these same words in like fashion.[11]

The mother, in her role as Mary's attendant, conveyed the message to her son, and Guibert was dissuaded from his purpose.

If I understand this episode correctly, Guibert's mother, by walking in the footsteps of Mary, experienced an acquisition of power to act with authority towards others. In her perception, Mary invested her with religious authority and demanded that she become active as her servant on earth. The mother's actions would henceforth be authorized by Mary herself. Guibert relates that his mother became the confidante of people in her surroundings. They came to her for spiritual advice: 'for all who were acquainted with her, especially men and women of noble rank, took pleasure in conversing with her because of her wondrous wit and forbearance'.[12]

In his *De laude sanctae Mariae*, a tract on Marian theology, Guibert provides a theological underpinning for what he tells about his mother.[13] Mary, he maintains, was the *origo redemptionis*, the origin of our redemption. It was through her merit that Christ gained entrance to the human world; thanks to her bearing of the Christ child, the Son was able to grow into the Redeemer. After Christ's resurrection and her own Assumption she ruled with him in heaven, *regina coeli terraeque*.[14] Her ministry was compassion. It was her motherly quality, her female nature to have this compassion and to intercede with Christ for those who were devoted to her. She functioned as a mediator, a *sequester* or *mediatrix*.[15]

---

[11] *Self and Society*, pp. 84–85.

[12] *Self and Society*, p. 76.

[13] Guibert, *Liber de laude sanctae Mariae*, in PL, 156, 537–78 (537C): 'origo redemptionis'.

[14] Guibert, *De laude Mariae*, 541B: 'regina coeli terraeque'; compare 539D: 'quam nunc habeat filio in coelestibus coregnando'.

[15] Guibert, *De laude Mariae*, 557B: 'personalitas materna'; 557A: 'Ipsi plane misereri est propriam, quia quae se ad tanti immensitatem officii misericorditer a Deo perpendit assumptam, factamque inter ipsum Deum hominesque sequestram, non immerito adeo specialia ad nos habet viscera, ex quibus et propter quos est tam singulariter excellens ut misericordiam consequeremur effecta [...].' The honorary title *Mater misericordiae* only becomes prevalent from the tenth century onwards, see Graef, *Mary*, p. 195.

We can easily imagine that earthly mothers not only turned to this intercessor in times of need but also looked to her as an inspiration for their own lives. Mary's motherhood conferred honour on them by association. They could feel licensed to imitate her, as Guibert's mother had done in her vision. Noteworthy, too, in this connection is that Mary did not appear to Guibert himself but preferred to appear to his mother, who passed the message on to her son. This mother and son 'mirrored' the intimate relationship of Mary and her Son.

This is not to deny that by exalting Mary far above all human beings—she was unique and perfect, *super omnes creaturas*—Guibert in effect places her out of reach of ordinary mortals. Moreover, he immobilizes her by calling her a (passive) gate, by which the Lord entered.[16] He ascribes to her a passive intercessory role. It is through her body that she makes the incarnation of the Son possible, not so much through a personal decision or act of will. Hedwig Röckelein rightly observes that, in contrast to Mary's behaviour in the autobiography, Guibert, in his tract, backed up his bold statements about Mary's role with scarcely any actions by Mary herself.[17] We might hypothesize that Guibert tried to 'tame' his mother by taming the mother of God. But the two women seem to have taken little notice of this—and, as we shall see presently, they were not the only mothers to pay no heed to such curtailment.[18]

Guibert's Marian theology is more or less in line with that of his contemporaries, although it is intriguing to note how widely theologians diverge in their estimates of the (active) part played by Mary in the history of salvation. When Bernard of Clairvaux preached about the Annunciation, for example, he ascribed to Mary, as Guibert had done, a decisive voice in our salvation; but he, too, did not expect her to assume any active role.[19] Aelred of Rievaulx pursued a similar interpretation. In his *De institutione inclusarum*, *c.* 1160, he applied the Annunciation scene directly to the life of recluses. To his anchoritic sister he says that in her prayer life she should:

> [...] enter the room of blessed Mary and with her read [she is literate, in other words] the books which prophesy the virginal birth and the coming of Christ. [...] Greet your

---

[16] Guibert, *De laude Mariae*, 537B: 'super omnes creaturas'; and 542A: 'porta, per quam Deus ad nos ingreditur.'

[17] Hedwig Röckelein, 'Zwischen Mutter und Maria: Die Rolle der Frauen in Guibert de Nogents Autobiographie', in *Maria: Abbild oder Vorbild?*, ed. Röckelein, pp. 91–109 (p. 100).

[18] Perhaps Guibert's mother was more inspired by the less reticent devotion of Anselm of Canterbury, a regular guest at St Germer, with whom she maintained contact; see *Self and Society*, p. 133.

[19] Bernardus Claraevallensis, *Sermones in laudibus virginis matris*, in *Sancti Bernardi Opera*, ed. by Jean Leclercq and H. Rochais (Rome: Editiones Cistercienses, 1968), v, pp. 275–93. Quoted by Marinus Burcht Pranger, 'The Virgin Mary and the Complexities of Love-Language in the Works of Bernard of Clairvaux', *Cîteaux, Commentarii Cistercienses*, 40 (1989), 112–38 (pp. 121–22).

most sweet Lady together with the Angel. Cry with a loud voice: 'Hail, full of grace, the Lord is with you, blessed are you among women.'[20]

Knowing that anchoresses used their reclusorium as a base for instruction and pastoral activities, Aelred hastened to forestall any possibility that Mary's active participation in salvation history would seduce the anchoress to seek active participation in community life; he warned his sister to also remember Mary the sister of Martha:

> She did not walk about or run hither and thither [...], [she was] not busy with answering cries of the poor. She just sat at Jesus' feet and listened to what he had to say. This is your portion, dearly beloved. Dead and buried to the world, you should be deaf to all that belongs to the world and unable to speak of it.[21]

Clear language, but recluses on the continent, at least the ones I have studied, had other ideas.

In summary, Bernard and Aelred ponder the historical role of the 'historical' Mary, meditating on the Annunciation scene. They hope that Mary's piety and self-surrender will influence believers to follow her example. In this context they make no mention of other activities of Mary during her life or of a possible intercessory role after her Assumption into heaven. Guibert, on the other hand, in both his autobiography and his treatise on Mary, ascribes to her an active function as queen of heaven, although in the treatise this role is restricted to that of a humble petitioner for persons in need. Action is expected from the ruler himself, Christ the King. The Mary of Guibert's autobiography is, by contrast, an assertive and energetic companion of women on earth, not only interceding for them with God on their request but acting on her own initiative as well—and not just occasionally but through an entire lifetime. Guibert could therefore close the sketch of his mother's life: '[...] she departed to her greatly beloved and longed for Lady, about whom I have written before, to be received, we believe, with a glad welcome'.[22] This discrepancy between the treatise and the autobiography marks the point where learned theology and common theology begin to part ways.

Rupert of Deutz, born near Liège and thus in the region of beguines and *mulieres religiosae*, supplied a 'biblical' or 'historical' foundation for this divergent picture of Mary in his commentary on the Song of Songs (1125).[23] He viewed this biblical

---

[20] Aelred, *De institutione inclusarum*, ed. by C. H. Talbot, *Aelredi Rievallensis, Opera Omnia* (Turnhout: Brepols, 1971), I; I quote from the English translation in *The Works of Aelred of Rievaulx*, Cistercian Fathers series, 2, 5, (Spencer, MA: Cistercian Publications, 1971), I, pp. 41–102: *A Rule of Life for a Recluse*, p. 80.

[21] Aelred, *A Rule*, p. 75.

[22] *Self and Society*, p. 133

[23] See for the following Rupertus Tvitiensis, *Commentaria in Canticum Canticorum*, ed. by Hrabanus Haacke, CCCM, 26 (Turnhout: Brepols, 1974), quoted here with Bible verses and pages from the edition; John Van Engen, *Rupert of Deutz* (Berkeley-Los Angeles: University

book as a prophecy about the life of the Mother of God and her bond with Christ as both her Son and her beloved. The 'voices' of the two lovers in the Song of Songs are for him the voices of Mary and Christ. Rupert interprets their words by systematically relating them to verses from the gospels. The words, for example, 'Let him kiss me with the kisses of his mouth' (Song of Songs 1. 2), Rupert presents as a foreshadowing of the Annunciation as related in Luke 1. 26–28. Similarly, Song of Songs 2. 7—' I charge you [...] that ye stir not up, nor awake my love, till she please'—is linked to the period in which Mary 'kept all these sayings in her heart' before appearing in any kind of public role; for Rupert she thus becomes the prototype of the contemplative life. When her lover knocks, however, saying 'Open to me, my sister, my love', Mary runs to the door and embarks on an active life in order to spread the gospel.[24] The watchmen pull off her coat, which means that Mary now makes public, in preaching and teaching, all the words that she had kept to herself until then.[25] As informant of the evangelists she is for Rupert the true 'author' behind the people who recorded the words; she is the *magistra* of the apostles and the great prophetess of the prophets, male and female.[26] Expressing despair at the disappearance of her beloved, she laments his death (by crucifixion) but finds comfort in the institution of the Last Supper. She calls to mind the words of Christ on the cross: 'Mother, behold thy son and to the disciple: behold thy mother.'[27] In his commentary on the Gospel of John 19. 27, where these words stem from, Rupert would remark that what Christ said to John could as well have been said to each of the other disciples if they had been present there at Golgotha.[28] Christ, in other words, placed his mother at the head of all apostles.

Filled with the gifts of the Holy Spirit who had overshadowed her, she expounds the rules of the faith and proclaims the true doctrine to heretics and schismatics. Christ leads his disciples 'to the house of my mother, who teaches me', men as well

---

of California Press, 1983), pp. 291–300; Rachel Fulton, 'Mimetic Devotion, Marian Exegesis, and the Historical Sense of the Song of Songs', *Viator*, 27 (1996), 85–116 (pp. 93–94 and 101–104); see now also her *From Judgment to Passion* (see note 1).

[24] Song of Songs 5. 2, ed. by Haacke, pp. 107–108: 'Aperi mihi, scilicet os tuum, loquere, prout ad confirmandum pertinet euangelium, et in hoc optatae tibi quietis patere dispendium; ut gratum singulari pudicitiae tuae propter me rumpas silentium.'

[25] Song of Songs 5. 7, ed by Haacke, p. 116: 'tunc autem deprompsi in aperto, uidelicit necessaria multumque profutura praedicando uel conscribendo dilecti euangelio.'

[26] Song of Songs 1. 6, ed. by Haacke, p. 24: 'magistram te esse oportebat, o beata Maria, et magistram magistrorum, id est apostolorum'; 5. 9, ed. by Haacke, p. 117: 'prophetissa magna, et capax omnium prophetarum sive prophetiarum'.

[27] Song of Songs 5. 6–8, ed. by Haacke, pp. 116–17.

[28] Rupertus Tuitiensis, *In Euangelium S. Joannis Commentariorum Libri XIV*, PL, 169, 790B.

as women.[29] As we shall see presently, Rupert included himself among these disciples. They constitute Mary's household staff, so to say, or perhaps better the members of her royal household, for after her Assumption Christ himself had crowned Mary queen. [30] It may be possible, then, to interpret the words of Christ on the cross as a sort of ritual investment of Mary with the office of prophetess or *magistra* and with the leadership over her spokesmen at the moment that Christ himself had to withdraw from the scene.

Rupert's commentary draws its material partly from references to Mary as the beloved of Christ, the queen of heaven, and partly from elements of Mary's earthly role as mother. Mary is thus ascribed an active function as heavenly queen who, as *consors* of the king, co-rules the kingdom above as well as below. At the same time, what has clearly crept into this biblical commentary are ideas about the tasks of medieval matrons and housewives, who were considered responsible for the religious education of children and household staff. This lends Rupert's commentary a thrust diametrically opposed to that of many other Song of Songs treatises intended for nuns and recluses. The sisters are often compared to the 'dove in the cleft of the rock, the covert of the mountainside' (Song of Songs 2. 14) and are called upon to strive for a mysticism turned away from the world, a life lived in a *hortus conclusus*, an enclosed garden.[31]

This work of Rupert's attracted a great deal of attention in its time. Of the more than forty surviving manuscripts, ten date from the twelfth century alone. Yet, as Van Engen has pointed out, this treatise offers no new formulations of classical Marian doctrine—we read nothing about a virgin birth or an Immaculate Conception, and no doctrines are set forth about Mary as co-redeemer.[32] Its novelty and appeal lay rather in the 'historical' and magisterial role ascribed to Mary. We will find these ideas resurfacing later in the recluses I have studied as well as in other authoritative females.[33]

---

[29] Song of Songs 8. 2, ed. by Haacke, pp. 158–59: 'in domum matris meae […] cum tu mihi tua mysteria reuelaueris, habebo ego hactenus sterilis, habebo ex te filios innouatae iuuentutis, quos te faciente ordinabo mihi lectores atque lectrices, cantores atque cantatrices, sacerdotes siue pontifices propheticae atque catholicae gratiae appropinquantes […]'.

[30] Song of Songs 1. 8, ed. by Haacke, p. 28: 'amici uel familiares tui, quales primi fuerunt apostoli.' Compare 1. 17, 35 '[…] ita domestici nostri apostoli atque apostolici uiri, doctores ecclesiarum atque praelati […] et domus […] stabunt, quamdiu durabit saeculum […].' Queen of Heaven: Song of Songs 4. 8, ed. by Haacke, p. 79: 'Ita coronaberis, ut et in caelis regina sanctorum, et in terris regina sis regnorum.'

[31] See E. Ann Matter, *The Voice of my Beloved: The Song of Songs in Western Medieval Christianity* (Philadelphia: University of Pennsylvania Press, 1990) and Eloe Kingma, *De Mooiste onder de Vrouwen: Een onderzoek naar religieuze idealen in twaalfde-eeuwse commentaren op het Hooglied* (Hilversum: Verloren, 1993).

[32] Van Engen, *Rupert of Deutz*, p. 292.

[33] Ian Johnson, 'Holy Women and their Middle English Texts', in *Prophets Abroad: The*

Yvette of Huy: Mater et Magistra

Yvette of Huy (1158–1228) is my second case.[34] Mary certainly played a dominant part in her life, according to the Life written by her younger contemporary Hugh of Floreffe. Widowed at the age of eighteen and mother of three small children, Yvette had no desire to remarry, and like the mother of Guibert, managed to live on her own. As her children reached school age, she left the town to tend the lepers and took up residence in a lepers' shelter. Ten years later she had herself enclosed next to the lepers' chapel.

There she had a vision–her first—in which she had to appear before the judgment-seat of the Son of man. Beside him Mary, the queen of heaven, was sitting on her throne. Through the intercession of Mary, who defended Yvette and took her sins upon herself, Yvette's sins were forgiven, for:

> [...] what is it or what can it be that the Son is able to deny to his Mother, the bridegroom to his bride, the friend to his friend, the flesh to its blood? [...] Mary took her [Yvette's] hands and presented them to her Son, who with a kiss of his mouth reconciled himself with her and handed her back to his Mother. 'Mother, behold your daughter, [Christ spoke,] I entrust her to you as your own daughter, as your own special *ancilla* forever: guard her and protect her and guide her as your own child.'[35]

These last words were a paraphrase of those he spoke to Mary and John from the cross (John 19. 27) and an echo of the words Rupert had used in his commentary on the Song of Songs.[36] In Yvette's Life Christ seems not only to have placed his mother at the head of all apostles, but to have expanded this to include Mary's

---

Reception of Continental Holy Women in Late-Medieval England, ed. by Rosalynn Voaden (Cambridge: Brewer, 1996), pp. 177–97 (p. 179), refers to the fifteenth-century *Myrowre to Deuout Peple*, in which Mary 'is not only an exemplary role-model for meditation and devotion, she is also acknowledged as an *auctrix* behind the evangelical *auctores*, for it was she who told them the details of the Nativity and infancy of Christ'.

[34] Hugh of Floreffe, *De beata Juetta sive Jutta, vidua reclusa, Hui in Belgio* in AASS, 13 Januarii (3rd edn. Brussels, 1863), II, pp. 145–69; I quote from the English translation by Jo Ann McNamara, *The Life of Yvette of Huy* by Hugh of Floreffe (Toronto: Peregrina, 2000). See my 'Ivetta of Huy: Mater et Magistra', in *Sanctity and Motherhood: Essays on Holy Mothers in the Middle Ages*, ed. by Anneke B. Mulder-Bakker (New York: Garland, 1995), pp. 225–58; Isabelle Cochelin, 'Sainteté laïque: l'exemple de Juette de Huy', *Le Moyen Age*, 96 (1989), 396–417; Jennifer Carpenter, 'Juette of Huy, Recluse and Mother (1158–1228): Children and Mothering in the Saintly Life', in *Power of the Weak: Studies on Medieval Women* ed. by Jennifer Carpenter and others (Urbana: University of Illinois Press, 1995), pp. 57–93.

[35] *Vita Juettae*, 46: AASS, p. 154; McNamara, *Life of Yvette*, p. 85.

[36] See above. Martina Wehrli-Johns, 'Haushälterin Gottes: Zur Mariennachfolge der Beginen', in Röckelein, *Maria: Abbild oder Vorbild?*, p. 152, finds the same image in the *Life of Maria of Oignies*; she interprets it as the entrusting of the widow Mary to a substitute Son.

medieval disciples. And the ritual appears to have taken the form of an affirmation of fealty in the feudal world.

From that moment onwards Yvette had a special bond with Mary, so much so that the clergy began to wonder whether she were not neglecting the Son. But, Hugh explains, Mother and Son are of one flesh and one spirit:

> [...] the flesh he got from Mary that was conceived, begotten and suffered, that rose from the dead and went beyond the stars to the Father's right hand, honouring all human, and above all maternal nature [...]. This specific nature made them one, Mother and Son, Son and Mother, Christ and Mary. For he is bone of Mary's bone and flesh of her flesh.[37]

Here again Mary is ascribed a special role in salvation history more as a mother than as a human being; and this has implications for all earthly mothers. Not only did Mary, as Rupert of Deutz implied, acquire an extremely active and dramatic role during her earthly life through the merging of the Song of Songs and the gospel story; she also, through the union of her flesh and that of Christ, thus through her motherhood, came to share in the divine nature after her Assumption. She was then assigned the task of ruling as queen of heaven in the consortium of king and queen. Her motherhood had brought her to this exalted position and determined the tasks assigned to her. As the lady of the house Mary sent out her servants from heaven— just as Rupert had depicted her directing the apostles. In the division of labour between the king (Christ) and the queen it was especially the responsibility for women servants that Christ explicitly entrusted to her. Mary is not only *mediatrix* but *doctrix* as well, although at this point the term has not yet been used.

Thanks to her visions, Yvette appeared to have prophetic gifts, and this enabled her to act with authority. Because she also had the gift of insight and could read people's minds, she was able to admonish ordinary believers to lead a good Christian life. Priests she pilloried by denouncing their secret relations with concubines. To pious persons who considered entering a monastery or teachers in the Church who were experiencing a crisis of faith she gave pastoral advice. At this time, when Christianity was penetrating to the grassroots level, it was often religious women like Yvette, and not the official urban clergy, who acted as spiritual leaders of the common people. Their efforts were aimed at instructing their fellow citizens and disseminating new devotions.

Yvette's role therefore by far surpassed what was usually permissible for a woman, let alone for recluses as we normally imagine them, namely as devout contemplatives living in seclusion. These anchoritic women were not by definition world-forsaking mystics. Guibert's mother and Yvette evidently opted for the semi-religious life because it was only with great difficulty that they could maintain their position as lady of the house—this despite the fact that they had dedicated their lives to religious ends. As soon as their children were grown they sought refuge in a

---

[37] *Vita Juettae*, 46: AASS, p. 154; McNamara, *Life of Yvette*, p. 86.

reclusorium. They apparently had no desire to withdraw completely from society but used their reclusive existence as a step toward religious leadership in the community. Holy mother Mary proved to be an inspiring and energetic companion on their way.

Margaret the Lame of Magdeburg

My third case is Margaret the Lame of Magdeburg (about 1210–50), not a mother and widow this time, but a woman enclosed at twelve years of age.[38] Until recently she went totally unnoticed by scholars, although she must have been rather widely known in the medieval Low Countries. I found some fifteen versions of her Life, in Latin and the vernacular. The Life was written during her lifetime by her confessor, the Dominican Friar John. He faithfully noted down, it seems, every word that Margaret spoke to him.

As soon as Margaret had herself enclosed, John explains, Christ gave her his Mother as a *doctrix veritatis*: 'not blessed Peter or any other saint, but his sweetest, most beloved and most glorious Mother, who concerned herself with the poor girl and taught her to read and deigned herself to become her *doctrix* and her *magistra* of the truth'.[39] Mary provided her with elementary education and taught her *contritio*, compunction about her own deeds and feelings of remorse. Thanks to her intercession Margaret obtained a general remission of sins after two years and was subsequently endowed with a wide range of spiritual and devotional knowledge. Mary revealed to her pupil, for example, her own inner feelings and hidden thoughts. Margaret understood that Mary looked upon herself as a *solitaria* and that she had not known natural motherly feelings.[40] In this respect Margaret's thought ties in with Dominican doctrine as developed by (Pseudo) Albertus Magnus.[41] We may gather

---

[38] Johannes von Magdeburg, O.P., *Die Vita der Margareta Contracta, einer Magdeburger Rekluse des 13.Jahrhunderts*, ed. by Paul Gerhard Schmidt (Leipzig: Benno, 1992), to which I refer with page numbers. Translations are mine but see *The Vita of Margaret the Lame by Friar Johannes O.P., of Magdeburg*, trans. by Gertrud Jaron Lewis and Tilman Lewis (Toronto: Peregrina, 2001). See my 'Margaret the Lame of Magdeburg: The Social Function of a Recluse', *Journal of Medieval History*, 22 (1996), 155–69.

[39] Johannes, *Vita Margaretae*, p. 3; Lewis, *The Vita of Margaret the Lame*, p. 15.

[40] Johannes, *Vita Margaretae*, p. 25: 'quare solitaria fuit' and p. 29: 'Ipsa ita perfecta fuit, quod carnalitatem, id est mollem amorem, sicut matres solent habere, que non possunt videre lesionem filiorum, ad suum filium non habebat'; Lewis, *The Vita of Margaret the Lame*, pp. 40–46.

[41] See Albertus Magnus, *Enarrationes in primam partem Evangelii Lucae I–IX*, in *Opera Omnia*, ed. S. C. A. Borgnet (Paris, 1894–99), XXII (1894), pp. 56, 63, 87, 89 and Klaus Schreiner, 'Marienverehrung, Lesekultur, Schriftlichkeit: Bildungs- und Frömmigkeits-geschichtliche Studien zur Auslegung und Darstellung von Maria Verkündigung', *Frühmittelalterliche Studien*, 24 (1990), 325–28; see also Schreiner, *Maria, Jungfrau, Mutter*,

from this that she looked upon Mary as a kind of proto-recluse and saw herself as a second mother Mary. At one point, in fact, Mary refers to her as a (spiritual) mother, and Margaret interprets this as recognition. Elsewhere it is said that the Holy Spirit was to overshadow Margaret (like Mary in Luke 1. 35).[42] And Christ assured her that she was the vessel by which his love was transfused to other faithful.[43] Like Mary, Margaret functioned as a *mediatrix*.

Margaret, too, had visions and revelations. Most of them contain devotional material. She meditated on subjects such as the threefold pain of Christ, the five qualities of a good prayer, the seven pains of hell, and the ten virtues.[44] Her revelations resemble what Petroff has defined as devotional and didactic literature.[45] Margaret transmitted these to the faithful in her surroundings. Her Life, as we have it, gives an impression of a recluse's role in the religious community.[46] The format in which Friar John records Margaret's lessons was a favourite one with audiences lacking a formal education. As scholars of oral or newly literate cultures argue, these people enjoy lists and recitals of facts that they can easily commit to memory.[47] The Life, if understood in this sense, is less a recording of Margaret's personal saintliness than a textbook for the religious community, intended for ongoing instruction. We can construct study groups around this Life, copied in the manuscripts of Villers and Ter Cameren in Brabant, as gatherings of devout believers, who shaped their activities around this text and its interpretation. Consequently, the role of *doctrix* applied not only to Mary in relation to her beloved recluse but also to Margaret, who in her turn provided instruction for several generations of devout.[48]

---

pp. 116–23.

[42] Johannes, *Vita Margaretae*, p. 57; Lewis, *The Vita of Margaret the Lame*, p. 83.

[43] Johannes, *Vita Margaretae*, p. 56; Lewis, *The Vita of Margaret the Lame*, p. 80: 'Tu enim es vas, in quod ipsa caritas est transfusa, et cuicumque de cetero dabitur, volo, quod ex te ei detur'. Alijt Bake, who drew inspiration from Margaret the Lame, saw herself as a 'little funnel that serves between the drink and the barrel', in Wybren F. Scheepsma, 'De trechter en de spin: Metaforen voor mystiek leiderschap van Alijt Bake', *Ons Geestelijk Erf*, 69 (1995), 222–34.

[44] Threefold pain of Christ: Johannes, *Vita Margaretae*, 56; good prayer: 15–16; seven pains of hell: 47–50; ten virtues: 89–93. See my *Lives of the Anchoresses*, where I compare Margaret with her contemporary Mechtild of Magdeburg for this.

[45] Elisabeth A. Petroff, *Medieval Women's Visionary Literature* (New York: Oxford University Press, 1986), p. 3.

[46] Anneke B. Mulder-Bakker, 'The Reclusorium as an Informal Centre of Learning', in: *Centres of Learning: Learning and Location in Pre-Modern Europe and the Near East*, ed. by Jan Willem Drijvers (Leiden: Brill, 1995), pp. 246–54.

[47] Walter J. Ong, *Orality and Literacy: The Technologizing of the Word* (London: Routledge, 1982), pp. 31–77.

[48] Johannes, *Vita Margaretae*, p. 69; Lewis, *The Vita of Margaret the Lame*, p. 124:

If we try to imagine how Margaret actually acquired this knowledge, we may assume that, growing up in the episcopal town of Magdeburg, she probably had the opportunity to learn to read before she entered the anchorhold at the age of twelve. In her cell she may have gathered further knowledge by reading and listening to learned visitors and passers-by as well as by hearing mass and the hours in church. Critics scorned her for lumping together pieces of information she heard from other religious and presenting these as her own insights. They were right in the sense that Margaret certainly digested the information she obtained from conversations or sermons and assimilated it in her dreams and visions. [49]

This manner of acquiring knowledge and having it recognized in the church is a familiar one. As we saw in the Introduction, someone like Caesarius of Heisterbach placed on this knowledge the same value as on sacred knowledge gained through learning. Rupert of Deutz, too, was aware of the various ways of acquiring knowledge. At the end of his life he confessed to his patron Cuno that in the face of highly critical *magisters* and scholastic theologians[50] that he had derived the authority—and the power—of his divergent exegesis from visions and mystical illuminations. As a young adult, when faced with the difficult decision of entering the priesthood, he had a series of dreams during a period of deep despair. In one of them he walked to the church, where he saw three venerable figures—the Trinity—standing at the altar. The youngest of them, Jesus, helped shake the devils from him and the three together placed him on a large open book. He understood that this was Holy Scripture and that divine inspiration had opened its interpretation to him.[51] This went beyond what he had learned from the Church Fathers or the *magisters* in France. 'It brought him that deeper understanding of Scripture which "authorized" his own writing'.[52] Whoever was filled with the Holy Spirit—men as well as women

---

'Desideravit [...] quod Deus deberet eos illuminare ad rectam cognitionem non solum, quamdiu ipsa viveret, sed etiam post mortem. Et talem habuit cognitionem, quod totus mundus deberet adhuc per illos in posterum consolari, quia illi erant alios instructuri et plurimum illuminandi.'

[49] Johannes, *Vita Margaretae*, p. 86.

[50] Rupertus Tuitiensis, *Super quaedam capitula Regulae divi Benedicti*, in PL, 170, 482A and 490–91.

[51] Rupertus Tuitiensis, *De Gloria et Honore Filii Hominis super Mattheum*, ed. by Hrabanus Haacke, CCCM, 29 (Turnhout: Brepols, 1979), p. 373 containing 'aureas [...] sanctarum memorias'. He understood: 'quod uere Deus librum suum, id est Scripturam sanctam mihi aperuit, et multis sanctorum sententiis, quorum in sancta ecclesia digne celebris est memoria et uelut aurum rutilat, aliquanta meliora dixerim'.

[52] Van Engen, *Rupert of Deutz*, p. 351. Compare Rupertus Tuitiensis, *In Euangelium S. Joannis Commentariorum Libri XIV*, in PL, 170, 480, 482; Song of Songs 5. 4, ed. by Haacke, pp. 110–11. In connection with this gender research one cannot fail to notice that when talking about himself Rupert feels more inspired by Jesus, with whom he also has a relationship based on love.

and Mary first of all—spoke with divine authority. And could not keep silent.[53]

We have come full circle. The history of Maria *doctrix* in the Middle Ages is a history of authorization. It is the story of Mary's rise to power and authority and of her empowering of saintly females, recluses in particular. The result was that the women felt entitled to transmit the living word spoken to them from above. Thanks to the merciful compassion of the *Mater misericordiae,* merciful mothers on earth were authorized to play a Marian role in society. The intriguing question remains as to how ordinary believers in the West came to embrace this peculiar common theology. And why recluses especially appealed to it. The answer to this question goes beyond the scope of this study but I will offer a few remarks here.

Maria doctrix

The apocryphal gospels from the second century supplemented the summary information about Mary in the New Testament with lifelike details. Mary, they tell us, was brought by her parents to the temple at the age of three, like small girls in the Middle Ages who were destined for life in a convent. In great solitude she had dedicated herself to the service of God. Nuns could therefore easily recognize in her a proto-nun, and recluses a proto-recluse. Frau Ava, for example, a recluse from the twelfth century and the first one known to be a poet, described Mary in the temple as:

> She was the most splendid of all maidens because from the first
> she had fully kept her promise
> that she would be God's maiden and avoid all things human
> for the benefit of the whole world. She was pure inside and out.
> Gabriel the angel appeared in the house.[54]

After Mary, mother of our Lord and Saviour, had become the *theotokos* in the East,[55]

---

[53] Rupertus Tuitiensis, *De gloria et honore Filii*, p. 384 on Matthew 12: 'ego autem extunc os meum aperui (Psalms 118 and 131) et cessare quin scriberem nequaquam potui, et usque nunc, etiam si uelim, tacere non possum. Sit hoc mihi facere illud, quod supra memoraui de Canticis, scilicet inueniri dilectum foris, et deosculari, ut iam me nemo despiciat, apprehendere eum et inducere in domum matris meae, et in cubiculum genitricis meae, ut aliquis filiorum eius ex hoc proficiat, meque doceri a spiritu ueritatis et dare illi poculum ex uino condito, id est sermonem ueritatis et rectum et bene sonantem ex Spiritu sancto […].'

[54] *Die Dichtungen der Frau Ava*, ed. by Friedrich Maurer (Tübingen: Niemeyer, 1996), p. 11: 'Si war aller magede herist von diu daz si allererist/ Dar an vol wonete daz si geheizen habete,/ Daz si gotes maget ware und allez manchunde verbare/ Zaller werlde wunnen, si was reine uzen unde innen./Gabriel der angelus der erscein in dem hus.'

[55] Averil Cameron, 'The Theotokos in Sixth-century Constantinople', in Cameron, *Continuity and Change in Sixth-century Byzantium* (London: Variorum, 1981), pp. 79–108; I.

she sailed in all her majesty to the West. There she acquired her own cycle of church festivals that could rival the feast days centred on Christ. The high point here was the festival of the Assumption of Mary with her crowning as queen of heaven. In the *Legenda Aurea* (thirteenth century) this event is expanded with a highly detailed account of Mary's life.[56] Marzena Górecka could therefore rightly conclude: 'The principle of Mary veneration in all its forms was the transferral of characteristics of Christ to his mother'.[57]

Mary is seen as *Maria regina* or *Regina coeli terraeque,* queen of heaven and earth. Her queenship resonated with ideas of terrestrial king- and queenship in the West, with ideas about the *consortium regni* and the roles of queens in the princely household on earth. As we learn from recent studies,[58] earthly queens in the High Middle Ages had their share in lordship and power, but the nature of their power differed from that of men. Michael Clanchy shows, for example, that in contrast to the strict and just king, queens exerted powers of 'agreement and love: [t]he king is law, the queen is mercy'.[59] In these centuries, when rulers usually lacked the means to rule 'by law and judgment' and had to rely on agreement and love, this queenly power was not an incidental quality, it was power of a crucial nature.[60] We could even say that queenly intervention and mercy 'kept society going'. The same holds true for Mary's power. In the tenth century a new honorary title was forged for her, that of *Mater misericordiae.*

Kalavrezou, 'Images of the Mother: When the Virgin Mary Became Meter Theou', *Dumbarton Oaks Papers,* 44 (1990), 165–73.

[56] P. Verdier, 'Les textes de Jacques de Voragine et l'iconographie du couronnement de la Vierge', in *Legenda Aurea: Sept siècles de diffusion,* ed. by B. Dunn-Lardeau (Paris: Vrin, 1986), p. 95f.

[57] Górecka, *Das Bild Mariens,* p. 84; see *Arnoldt Angenendt, Heilige und Reliquien: Die Geschichte ihres Kultes vom frühen Christentum bis zur Gegenwart* (Munich: Beck, 1994), pp. 217–25.

[58] Margaret Howell, *Eleanor of Provence: Queenship in Thirteenth-century England* (Oxford: Blackwell, 1998); Pauline Stafford, *Queen Emma and Queen Edith. Queenship and Women's Power in Eleventh-Century England* (Oxford: Blackwell, 1997), p. 55–56.

[59] Michael Clanchy, 'Law and Love in the Middle Ages', in *Disputes and Settlements: Law and Human Relations in the West,* ed. by John Bossy (Cambridge: Cambridge University Press, 1983), pp. 47–68 (p. 47).

[60] See Simon Roberts, 'The Study of Dispute: Anthropological Perspectives', in *Disputes and Settlements,* pp. 1–24 and other studies in this volume; Stephen D. White, 'Proposing the Ordeal and Avoiding it: Strategy and Power in Western French Litigation, 1050–1110', in *Cultures of Power: Lordship, Status, and Process in Twelfth-century Europe,* ed. by Thomas N. Bisson (Philadelphia: University of Pennsylvania Press, 1995), pp. 89–124 and other studies in this volume; Wim P. Blockmans, 'Beheersen en overtuigen: Reflecties bij nieuwe visies op staatsvorming', *Tijdschrift voor Sociale Geschiedenis,* 16 (1990), 18–30, and other studies in this issue.

A second characteristic of queenly power in the medieval West was the oral sphere in which it functioned. Medieval society had, traditionally, its oral and written segments, each with its own set of standards and its own ways of remembering. Alongside the up-and-coming councils and institutions with written charters, old bonds and consultative bodies lived on, vivid and influential, with their own customs and their own (often orally transmitted) memory. Family and friends, with the queen as *consors regni* at the fore, had a sphere of their own. Women acted there, as housewives and mothers have always done, as embodiments of wisdom, benevolent maternal figures, having the privilege of interceding with husband and son.[61]

Mary, *regina coeli terraeque*, as we get to know her from the hagiographical sources, lent herself neatly to this queenly role. We see her interceding with her Son, as a queen was wont to do. Unlike Christ the King, who was believed to rule by judgement and law, she asks for mercy and love. She is the *Mater misericordiae* and acts in the sphere of age-old customs and orality. As with earthly queens, her prerogatives are not defined by doctrine or Canon Law, and her decisions are not recorded in charters. Instead they are told in legends and collections of exempla— which goes a long way in explaining why historians have so often overlooked the 'common law' power of the queen, just as they overlooked the 'common theology' position of Mary.

Mary ruled her royal household, her kingdom in heaven and on earth, in a way similar to that of terrestrial queens. She had her own personnel, saints in heaven and religious females on earth. Like the earthly queen, she was a cultivated and well-educated lady: she read books and the Hours; she instructed her children (her own or her adopted daughters). As Schreiner puts it: 'Mary, viewed with the eyes of the Middle Ages, was the embodiment of the educated woman with a great love of books and reading.'[62]

This queenly role was theologically defended and explained by conceiving of Mary along Guibert's lines as the pivot in salvation history and by arguing, as Yvette's hagiographer did, her bodily Assumption and equalization with Christ. Her motherhood of God had made all this possible and her maternal qualities provided concrete detail. The teaching was supported, or visualized, by theological and visual imagery such as the *sedes sapientiae* metaphor.[63] In Liège and elsewhere in the Low Countries cathedrals and parish churches had statues of the enthroned Mary with the

---

[61] See Lois L. Huneycut, 'Intercession and the High-Medieval Queen: The Esther topos', in: *Power of the Weak*, pp. 126–47 (p. 126). The queen studied here, Matilda wife of Henry I of England, is a good twelfth-century parallel of Jeanne of Valois, whom I studied in 'Jeanne of Valois. The Power of a Consort', in *Capetian Women*, ed. by Kathleen Nolan (New York: Palgrave, 2003), pp. 253–69.

[62] Schreiner, *Maria* p. 115; in her case we should think of Books of Hours and devotional books, of course, and not of learned Latin treatises.

[63] See Laura Spitzer, 'The Cult of the Virgin and Gothic Sculpture: Evaluating Opposition in the Chartres West Façade Capital Frieze', *Gesta*, 33 (1994), 132–50.

Christ-child on her lap. These images 'amplify' Old Testament ideas of Sophia, the daughter of God, helpmeet in creation and revelation.[64] Meister Eckhart testified to this development when he maintained that Wisdom is the name of a Mother.[65]

Theologically, the queenly role could be further rooted in the biblical prophetic tradition in which both Mary and her earthly adepts were given a place. Mary was regarded as the New Testament fulfilment of Old Testament types such as the prophetess Miriam or Deborah or Hulda. The living saints of the Middle Ages, with Hildegard of Bingen leading the way, came to claim their own place in this august line. In the Acts of the Apostles it is stated: 'And on my servants (*douloi*) and on my handmaidens (*doulai*) I will pour out my Spirit and they shall prophesy.' Here we have what could be termed a biblical proof text for a male line of apostolic *servi* led by the *servus servorum Dei* and a female line of s*ervae Domini* headed by Mary, a line of prophetesses.[66] Medieval anchoresses liked to think of themselves as belonging to this second line.

Mothers of the Community

Recluses, of whom there must have been hundreds in northern Europe were held in high esteem. They were surrounded by an aura of sanctity and ascribed special powers. They were regarded as God's chosen messengers, as intermediaries between God and man, *mediatrices* in a twofold sense: like Mary they gave birth to Christ in their heart; but they also dispensed God's grace to the faithful. They educated and taught, disseminating sacred knowledge and explaining the Scriptures. They guided the faithful. They were mothers of mercy. They identified with their role model, Mary.

Like Mary and the earthly queens, they were maternal figures and they functioned in the oral segment of society. As they were not ordained, they had no 'written' institutional power. Yet, as they operated as teachers and preachers, the faithful regarded them as prophetesses in the tradition of Miriam, Deborah, Hulda, and Mary the Mother of God herself. Just as they believed that Mary had 'authorized' the teaching of the apostles and the inspired knowledge of medieval writers like Rupert, they came to believe that Mary legitimated the thoughts and actions of these female disciples. Anchoresses, too, walked in Mary's footsteps in the sense that they first set their sights on a reclusorium and subsequently, from that base, went public with their

---

[64] Compare Pelikan, *Mary*, p. 25.

[65] Eckhart, *Sermon* 40, in Bernard McGinn and Frank Tobin, *Meister Eckhart: Teacher and Preacher* (New York: Paulist, 1986), p. 302.

[66] Pelikan, *Mary*, p. 84; usually *doulai* is translated as *ancillae*, which has acquired the connotation of a passive servant; for this reason the feminine form of *servus* should be given preference.

inspired wisdom. Mary lent them an authority that was even accepted as such by the Church hierarchy.

In the community of the faithful, therefore, recluses presented themselves as the helpmeets of the Queen of Heaven and acted in her name. They were accepted in these new roles—this we can infer from the life story of both Guibert's mother and Yvette—because they had in many cases belonged to the circle of (aristocratic) pious lay women before they had themselves enclosed in an anchorhold. These women were often well-educated, self-confident, independently acting females; they were persons to be reckoned with in the community.[67] In a way they now became the lady of the communal household as they had previously been the lady of an aristocratic household. Just as priests acted as 'fathers' of the community, these women acted as their counterpart as 'mothers'.[68] And they passed on the knowledge Mary had entrusted to them.

This was not the *scientia* of the schools, not sacred knowledge written down in books, not learned theology. It was common theology, living wisdom, incarnated knowledge, the Word acquiring shape through maternal nature: holy mother Mary the *doctrix* in heaven and the holy mother anchoresses as her disciples on earth.

Translated by Myra Scholz

---

[67] Evergates, *Aristocratic Women in Medieval France*, p. 5.

[68] Compare S. Tanz and Ernst Werner, *Spätmittelalterliche Laienmentalitäten im Spiegel von Visionen, Offenbarungen und Prophezeiungen* (Frankfurt a.M.: Lang, 1993), p. 65: 'Dahinter stand ein Konzeption weiblicher Begnadung, die eine Analogie zum männlichen Priesteramt bildete'. [Behind this was a conception of female prerogative analogous to the male office of priest.]

Index

Medieval Women: Texts and Contexts

Titles in series

Jutta and Hildegard : The Biographical Sources, ed. by Anna Silvas (1998).

New Trends in Feminine Spirituality: The Holy Women of Liège and their Impact, ed. by Juliette Dor, Lesley Johnson and Jocelyn Wogan-Browne (1999).

Medieval Women: Texts and Contexts in Late Medieval Britain: Essays for Felicity Riddy, ed. by Jocelyn Wogan-Browne, Rosalynn Voaden, Arlyn Diamond, Ann Hutchinson, Carol Meale, and Lesley Johnson (2000).

The Knowing of Woman's Kind in Childing: A Middle English Version of Material Derived from the Trotula and other Sources, ed. by Alexandra Barratt (2001).

Send Me God: The Lives of Ida the Compassionate of Nivelles, Nun of La Ramée, Arnulf, Lay Brother of Villers, and Abundus, Monk of Villers, by Goswin of Bossut, trans. by and with an introduction by Martinus Cawley OCSO and with a preface by Barbara Newman (2003).

St Katherine of Alexandria: Texts and Contexts in Western Medieval Europe, ed. by Jacqueline Jenkins and Katherine J. Lewis (2003).

Writing the Wilton Women: Goscelin's Liber confortatorius and Legend of Edith, ed. by Stephanie Hollis (forthcoming, 2004).